9/2000

Laws of the United States
Divorce

D1565229

BRANCH

Quick Reference Law Series

Laws of the
United States

Divorce

Daniel Sitarz
Attorney-at-Law

Nova Publishing Company
Small Business and Consumer Legal Books and Software
Carbondale Illinois

Editorial and research assistance by Janet Harris Sitarz, Julie Morgan, and Carol Kelly. Design by Rose Weisburd and Linda Jorgensen-Buhman.

Manufactured in the United States.

Laws of the United States: Divorce ISBN 0-935755-68-3

Nova Publishing Company is dedicated to providing up-to-date and accurate legal information to the public. All Nova publications are periodically revised to contain the latest available legal information.

1st Edition; 1st Printing: March, 1999

This publication is designed to provide accurate and authoritative information in regard to the subject matter covered. It is sold with the understanding that the publisher and author are not engaged in rendering legal, accounting, or other professional services. If legal advice or other expert assistance is required, the services of a competent professional person should be sought.

From a Declaration of Principles jointly adopted by a Committee of the American Bar Association and a Committee of Publishers

DISCLAIMER
Because of possible unanticipated changes in governing statutes and case law relating to the application of any information contained in this book, the author, publisher, and any and all persons or entities involved in any way in the preparation, publication, sale, or distribution of this book disclaim all responsibility for the effects or consequences of any document prepared or action taken in reliance upon information contained in this book. No representations, either express or implied, are made or given regarding the consequences of the use of any information contained in this book. Purchasers and persons intending to use this book for the preparation of any documents are advised to check specifically on the current applicable laws in any jurisdiction in which they intend the documents to be effective. This book is not printed, published, sold, circulated, or distributed with the intention that it be used to procure or aid in the procurement of any effect or consequence in any jurisdiction in which such procurement or aid may be restricted by statute.

Nova Publishing Company
Small Business Legal Books and Software
1103 West College Street
Carbondale, IL 62901
Editorial: (800) 748-1175

Distributed to the trade by:
National Book Network
4720 Boston Way
Lanham, MD 20706
Orders: (800) 462-6420

TABLE OF CONTENTS

INTRODUCTION

This book is part of Nova Publishing Company's Quick Reference Law series. The purpose of this series is to provide concise, comprehensive and authoritative guides to the law of all states in specific legal areas. This book contains a summary of the divorce laws of all states and the District of Columbia. It has been compiled directly from the most recently-available statute books and legislation for each state and has been abridged for clarity and succinctness. Every effort has been made to assure that the information contained in this guide is accurate and complete. However, laws are subject to constant change. Therefore, prior to reliance on any legal points which are particularly important in certain situations, the current status of a specific law should be checked directly in the appropriate law book. After each section of information, the exact name of the law book and the chapter or section number where the information can be found is noted. The correct terminology for each state is used in these listings. However, some states use certain language interchangeably. In those states, the most commonly-used language is stated. The following information is listed for each state:

RESIDENCY REQUIREMENTS AND WHERE TO FILE: The specific time limits that spouses must have lived in a state (and possibly county) are explained. Which particular county (or parish) that is the correct venue for filing is also listed.

LEGAL GROUNDS FOR DIVORCE: The specific language of the grounds for divorce in each state are listed. All states have no-fault grounds with some states having more than one no-fault ground. If this is the case, they are specified by numbering each particular ground. Some states have also retained some fault-based divorce grounds. These are referred to as "General" grounds.

NAME OF COURT IN WHICH TO FILE FOR DIVORCE: The information under this heading shows the name of the correct court for filing for divorce.

DOCUMENT CAPTION INFORMATION: The correct language for the caption for a court action for divorce is listed. This is generally either a Petition for Dissolution of Marriage or a Complaint for Divorce. The language used to describe the case is also noted. For example: "In the Matter of the Marriage of

_____, Plaintiff and _____, Defendant." Generally, this will either be Plaintiff and Defendant or Petitioner and Respondent, although some states allow joint Co-Petitioners. The title of the document that will be used to declare the divorce final is also noted.

LEGAL SEPARATION: This information explains the situation in each state relating to legal court-ordered separation. The grounds and residency requirements for court-ordered separations are included.

SIMPLIFIED OR SPECIAL DIVORCE PROCEDURES: Many states now have instituted procedures which allow for simplified procedures to be used in obtaining a divorce. In addition, some states have mandatory forms which are required to be used. All of the details of any specific method to shorten or streamline the divorce process are contained under this heading.

MEDIATION OR COUNSELING REQUIREMENTS: Most states have now instituted voluntary mediation or conciliation services that are available to spouses on request or on the order of the judge. The details are listed here.

PROPERTY DISTRIBUTION: A description of which property is subject to division upon divorce and what factors are considered in the distribution are contained in this section. Community, separate, non-marital, and marital property are defined for each state.

ALIMONY/MAINTENANCE/SPOUSAL SUPPORT: The laws and factors for consideration relating to the awarding of alimony are discussed under this heading.

SPOUSE'S NAME: Each state's laws regarding the restoration of a spouse's name are included in this listing.

CHILD CUSTODY: The details of how child custody decisions are made are contained under this heading. Each state's particular factors for consideration are explained. Specific state provisions for joint custody are also detailed.

CHILD SUPPORT: The various laws relating to child support are outlined. In recent years, this area has become the most complex aspect of divorce. Virtually all states now have detailed child support guidelines that are to be applied in child support situations. The availability of specific state child support guidelines and general state requirements to guarantee child support payments are noted.

PRE-MARITAL AGREEMENTS: Any state provisions relating to pre-marital (prenuptial) agreements are contained in this listing.

ALABAMA

RESIDENCY REQUIREMENTS AND WHERE TO FILE: When one of the spouses is a nonresident of the state, the spouse filing for divorce must have been a resident of the state for at least 6 months before filing for divorce. The divorce may be filed in any of the following: (1) the county where the defendant resides; (2) the county where the spouses both resided at the time of their separation; or (3) the county where the plaintiff resides if the defendant is a non-resident of Alabama. [Code of Alabama; Title 30, Chapters 2-4 and 2-5].

LEGAL GROUNDS FOR DIVORCE: No-Fault: (1) Irretrievable breakdown of the marriage; (2) complete incompatibility of temperament such that the parties can no longer live together; (3) voluntary separation for over 1 year. [Code of Alabama; Title 30, Chapter 2-1].

General: (1) Physically and incurably incapacitation; (2) Adultery; (3) voluntary abandonment for 1 year preceding filing of complaint; (4) imprisonment (for over 2 years if the total sentence is over 7 years); (5) unnatural sexual behavior before or after the marriage; (6) alcoholism; (7) drug abuse; (8) wife pregnant by another at the time of the marriage without the husband's knowledge; (9) physical abuse or reasonable fear of physical abuse; (10) living separate and apart without cohabitation for over 2 years without the husband supporting the wife (divorce must be filed by wife). [Code of Alabama; Title 30, Chapters 2-1 and 2-2].

NAME OF COURT IN WHICH TO FILE FOR DIVORCE: Circuit Court. "In the Circuit Court for _____ County, Alabama." [Code of Alabama; Title 30, Chapter 2-1].

DOCUMENT CAPTION INFORMATION: Complaint for Divorce. "In Re: the Marriage of:_____, Plaintiff and _____, Defendant." Final document title: Judgement of Divorce.

LEGAL SEPARATION: A divorce "from bed and board" may be granted for cruelty or for any of the same causes for which a standard divorce may be granted if the spouse filing desires that the divorce be limited to a divorce "from bed and board." [Code of Alabama: Title 30, Chapter 2-30].

9

SIMPLIFIED OR SPECIAL DIVORCE PROCEDURES: There is no legal provision in Alabama for summary divorce. In addition, specific evidence must be presented at a court hearing to support a default judgement in a divorce case. However, acceptance and waiver of service is allowed if signed by the defendant and a credible witness. Effective January 1, 1997, there is a 30-day waiting period after the filing of the summons and complaint before a judge may issue a final judgement of divorce. Testimony in uncontested divorces may be taken before a court clerk, by sworn statements, or by transcripts of oral depositions. A standardized Child Support Guidelines form and Child Support Income Statement/Affidavit must be filed in every case in which child support is requested. [Code of Alabama: Title 30, Chapter 2-8.1; Alabama Rules of Civil Procedure; Rules 4, 43(a), 53, and 55 and Alabama Rules of Judicial Administration: Rule 32].

MEDIATION OR COUNSELING REQUIREMENTS: There is no legal provision in Alabama for mediation.

PROPERTY DISTRIBUTION: There is no statutory provision in Alabama for property division. Under Alabama case law, Alabama is an "equitable distribution" state and the judge has full discretion to divide any jointly-owned real estate or personal property, but does not have the authority to award the wife's separate property to the husband (regardless of whether the wife's separate property was obtained before or after the marriage). Gifts and inheritances are considered separate property and are not subject to division unless they have been used for the common benefit of both spouses. The property division need not necessarily be exactly equal, but it must be equitable. Marital fault may be considered in the division of property. (Alabama Case Law).

ALIMONY/MAINTENANCE/SPOUSAL SUPPORT: The judge has full discretion to award an allowance for maintenance to either spouse, if such spouse has insufficient property to provide for his or her own maintenance. This award may be made out of the property belonging to the other spouse, unless it is separate property (acquired by gift or inheritance, or acquired prior to the marriage) and was never used for the common benefit of the marriage. The factors to be considered are: (1) the value of the estate of both spouses; and (2) the condition of the spouse's family. Up to 50% of a spouse's retirement benefits may be used for alimony if the retirement was accumulated during a marriage of 10 years or more. Misconduct of either spouse may be considered in the determination as to whether to award maintenance and may totally bar the right to any maintenance. Any award of maintenance will be terminated if the recipient is living openly with a member of the opposite sex or has remarried. [Code of Alabama: Title 30, Chapters 2-51, 2-52, and 2-55].

SPOUSE'S NAME: An ex-wife may be prevented from using the last name of the ex-husband. Under general common law principles, a wife may be resume the use of her maiden or former name upon divorce. [Code of Alabama: Title 30, Chapter 2-11].

CHILD CUSTODY: Custody of any children of the marriage may be granted to either parent. Factors to be considered are: (1) the age and sex of the child; (2) the safety and well-being of the child; (3) and the moral character of the parents. The wishes of the child are also a factor to be considered. There is a legal presumption against giving custody to any person who has inflicted any violence against either a spouse or a child. In abuse cases, the judge is required to consider any history of domestic abuse and may not consider the fact that a parent or spouse has relocated to avoid abuse. As of January 1, 1997, Alabama officially favors joint custody (but not equal physical custody) if in the best interests of the child and the parents agree. Factors to be considered are (1) parental custody agreement; (2) parental cooperation; (3) parental ability to encourage love and sharing; (4) any history of abuse; (5) geographic proximity of parents. Joint custody may be awarded. However, if the wife abandons the husband and the children are over 7 years old, the husband is granted custody if he is suitable. Grandparents may be given visitation rights. [Code of Alabama: Title 30, Chapters 1-131, 150, 152; and 3-1, 3-4 and Alabama Case Law].

CHILD SUPPORT: The court may order either parent to provide child support. There are official Child Support Guidelines contained in the Alabama Rules of Judicial Administration: Rule 32. These guidelines are presumed to be correct unless there is a showing that the amount would be unjust or inappropriate under the particular circumstances of a case. A written agreement between the parents for a different amount with a reasonable explanation for the deviation from the guidelines will also be allowed. A standardized Child Support Guidelines form and Child Support Income Statement/Affidavit must be filed in every case in which child support is requested. There is also a procedure for expedited processing in child support cases. Alabama driver's licenses may be suspended for failure to pay child support. [Code of Alabama: Title 30, Chapter 3-171 and Alabama Rules of Judicial Administration: Rules 32 and 35].

PREMARITAL AGREEMENTS: Alabama has no specific statutes pertaining to premarital agreements.

ALASKA

RESIDENCY REQUIREMENTS AND WHERE TO FILE: If the marriage has been solemnized, and the Plaintiff is a resident of the state, he or she can bring the action at any time. However, if the marriage was not solemnized in Alaska, the Plaintiff can rely on the residence of the other spouse in Alaska to file for divorce/dissolution. [Alaska Statutes; Title 25, Chapters 22-10.030, 24.080 and 24.090].

LEGAL GROUNDS FOR DIVORCE/DISSOLUTION OF MARRIAGE: No-Fault: Incompatibility of temperament which has caused the irremediable breakdown of the marriage. [Alaska Statutes; Title 25, Chapter 24.200].

General: (1) Adultery; (2) incurable mental illness and confinement for 18 months; (3) drug abuse; (4) failure to consummate marriage; (5) conviction of a felony; (6) willful desertion of over 1 year; (7) cruel and/or inhuman treatment; (8) personal indignities; (9) incompatibility of temperament; and (10) habitual drunkenness. [Alaska Statutes; Title 25, Chapter 24.050].

NAME OF COURT IN WHICH TO FILE FOR DIVORCE/DISSOLUTION OF MARRIAGE: Superior Court. "Superior Court for the State of Alaska; #_____ Judicial District." [Alaska Rules of Court Procedure and Administration.]

DOCUMENT CAPTION INFORMATION: Petition for Dissolution of Marriage (if filed on no-fault grounds: See below under "Simplified or Special Dissolution of Marriage Procedures"); "In the Matter of the Dissolution of the Marriage of _____, Petitioner and _____, Respondent." Final document title: Decree of Dissolution of Marriage.

Complaint for Divorce (if filed on fault-based grounds), "In Re: the Marriage of _____, Plaintiff and _____, Defendant." Final document title: Judgement of Divorce. [Alaska Statutes; Title 25, Chapter 24.210 and 24.230].

LEGAL SEPARATION: There is no specific legal provision in Alaska for legal separation.

SIMPLIFIED OR SPECIAL DISSOLUTION OF MARRIAGE PROCEDURES: The spouses may jointly petition the court for a dissolution of their marriage on the grounds of incompatibility of temperament which has caused the irremediable breakdown of the marriage, under the following conditions: (1) If there are minor children or the wife is pregnant, the spouses have agreed on the custody, visitation, and support of the child or children. They must also have agreed on whether the child support payments should be made through the state child support enforcement agency, and on the tax consequences of the agreement regarding the child or children; (2) the spouses have agreed to the distribution of all jointly-owned property (including retirement benefits) and the payment of spousal support, if any, and the tax consequences of these payments, if any (the amount of the property distributed to each spouse must be fair and just); (3) the spouses have agreed as to the payment of all unpaid obligations incurred by either or both of them, and to the payment of obligations incurred jointly in the future.

The petition for dissolution of marriage may be made by one spouse individually if: (1) the grounds for the dissolution of marriage is the incompatibility of temperament, evidenced by extended separation of the spouses, which has caused the irremediable breakdown of the marriage; (2) the petitioning spouse has been unable to ascertain the other spouse's position regarding the dissolution of their marriage, the division of their property, and the division of their obligations, custody, support and visitation of any child or children, because the whereabouts of the other spouse is unknown to the petitioning spouse, after reasonable efforts to locate the absent spouse; (3) the other spouse can not be personally served with process inside or outside the state. Filing for a dissolution of marriage does not preclude filing for a divorce.

Official state forms for obtaining a dissolution of marriage under these provisions may be obtained from the Clerk of any Superior Court, or from the Division of Social Services of the Alaska Department of Health and Social Services. [Alaska Statutes; Title 25, Chapters 24-200 to 24-260].

MEDIATION OR COUNSELING REQUIREMENTS: Either spouse may request mediation in an attempt to reach a settlement. If no request is made, the judge may order the spouses to submit to mediation if it is felt that a more satisfactory settlement may be achieved. The court will appoint a mediator. [Alaska Statutes; Title 25, Chapter 24.060].

PROPERTY DISTRIBUTION: Alaska is an "equitable distribution" state. Both joint and separate property which has been acquired during the marriage will be divided in a "just" manner. Any fault of the spouses shall not be taken into account. If necessary to achieve a fair result in a "fault-based" divorce action, property acquired before the marriage may be divided also. In a "no-fault" dissolution of marriage action, property acquired prior to the marriage will not be divided unless the spouses agree or it is in the best interests of any

13

children to do so. Gifts and inheritances are also subject to division by the court. Factors considered are: (1) length of marriage, (2) the age and health of the parties, (3) the earning capacity of each spouse, (4) educational backgrounds, training, employment skills, work experiences, length of absence from the job market, and custodial responsibilities for children during the marriage, (5) the financial condition of each spouse, (6) the parties conduct regarding their assets, (7) the desirability of awarding the family home to the spouse with primary physical custody of children, (8) the time and manner of acquisition of their property, (9) the income producing capacity of the property and its value, and (10) all other relevant factors. Non-monetary contributions to the marriage (for example: home-making) are also considered. [Alaska Statutes; Title 25, Chapters 24.160 and 24.230].

ALIMONY/MAINTENANCE/SPOUSAL SUPPORT: Maintenance may be awarded to either spouse for support. The award may be made as a lump-sum or may be ordered paid in installments. Any fault of the spouses may not be taken into account. Factors considered are: (1) length of marriage, (2) position in life of the parties during marriage, (3) the age and health of the parties, (4) the earning capacity of each spouse, (5) the financial condition of each spouse, (6) the parties conduct regarding their assets, (7) the division of the spouse's property, and (8) all other relevant factors. Non-monetary contributions to the marriage (for example: home-making) are also considered. [Alaska Statutes; Title 25, Chapter 24.160].

SPOUSE'S NAME: The name of either spouse may be changed in the Judgement for Divorce or in the Decree for Dissolution of Marriage. [Alaska Statutes; Title 25, Chapters 24.165 and 24.230].

CHILD CUSTODY: Custody is determined with the best interests of the child in mind. Factors to be considered are: (1) the capability and desire of each parent to meet the child's needs; (2) the physical, emotional, mental, religious, and social needs of the child; (3) the preference of the child (if the child is of sufficient age and capacity); (4) the love and affection between the child and each parent; (5) the length of time the child has lived in a stable, satisfactory environment and the desirability of maintaining continuity; (6) the desire and ability of each parent to allow an open and loving frequent relationship between the child and the other parent; (7) any evidence of domestic violence, child abuse or neglect, or spousal abuse; (8) any evidence of substance abuse that affects the emotional or physical well-being of the child, (9) any other factors the court considers relevant. Neither parent is considered to be entitled to custody. [Alaska Statutes; Title 25, Chapter 24.150].

Joint/shared custody may be awarded. For shared custody to be awarded, the court considers the following factors: (1) the child's needs and education; (2) any special needs of the child that may be better met by one parent; (3) any findings of a neutral mediator; (4) the optimal time for the child to be with each parent; (5) the physical proximity of the parents as it relates to where the child will reside and where the child will attend school; (6) the advantage of keeping the child in the community where he presently resides; (7) whether shared custody will promote more frequent or continuing contact between the child and the parents; (8) the length of time the child has lived in a stable, satisfactory environment and the desirability of maintaining continuity; (9) the fitness and suitability of each of the parents (including any evidence of substance abuse); (10) any history of violence by either parent; (11) the preference of the child (if the child is of sufficient age and capacity); (12) the stability of the home of each parent; (13) any substance abuse; and (14) any other relevant factors. [Alaska Statutes; Title 25, Chapter 20.090].

CHILD SUPPORT: Either or both parents may be ordered to provide child support. Child support payments may be ordered paid to a court-appointed trustee or through the state child support enforcement agency. There are official Child Support Guidelines contained in Alaska Rules of Civil Procedure; Rule 90.3. These Guidelines are presumed to be correct unless there is a showing that the amount would be manifestly unjust under the particular circumstances in a case. Factors for deviation from the guidelines are: (1) especially large family size; (2) significant income of the child; (3) health or other extraordinary expenses; (4) unusually low expenses; and (5) the parent with the child support obligation has an income below Federal poverty level. For parents with income over $72,000, the above 6 factors do not apply. In those instances, the factors are: (1) that an increased award is just and proper; (2) the needs of the children; (3) the standard of living of the children; (4) the extent to which the standard of living of the children should be reflective of the parent's ability to pay. Each parent must file a verified statement of income. There is a Child Support Guidelines Worksheet contained in Alaska Rules of Civil Procedure; Rule 90.3. [Alaska Statutes; Title 25, Chapter 24.160, 27.010—27-900 and Alaska Rules of Civil Procedure; Rule 90.3].

PREMARITAL AGREEMENTS: Alaska has no specific statutes pertaining to premarital agreements.

ARIZONA

RESIDENCY REQUIREMENTS AND WHERE TO FILE: One of the spouses must have lived in the state at least 90 days before filing for dissolution of marriage. The divorce should be filed in the county in which the petitioner resides at the time of filing. There is also a 60 day waiting period after the service of process on the Respondent (or after the Respondent's acceptance of service. [Arizona Revised Statutes Annotated; Title 12, Chapter 401; and Title 25, Chapters 312 and 329].

LEGAL GROUNDS FOR DISSOLUTION OF MARRIAGE: No-Fault: Irretrievable breakdown of the marriage and desire to live separate and apart. [Arizona Revised Statutes Annotated; Title 25, Chapter 312-314].

General: Irretrievable breakdown of the marriage and desire to live separate and apart. [Arizona Revised Statutes Annotated; Title 25, Chapter 312-314].

NAME OF COURT IN WHICH TO FILE FOR DISSOLUTION OF MARRIAGE: Superior Court. "In the Superior Court in and for the County of _____, Arizona." [Arizona Revised Statutes Annotated; Title 25, Chapter 311].

DOCUMENT CAPTION INFORMATION: Petition for Dissolution of Marriage. "In Re: the Marriage of _____, Petitioner and _____, Respondent." Final document title: Decree of Dissolution of Marriage.

LEGAL SEPARATION: Irretrievable breakdown of the marriage or that one spouse desires to live separate and apart are the grounds for legal separation in Arizona. One of the spouses must live in the state of Arizona when the action for legal separation is filed. No residency time limit is specified. If one spouse objects to a legal separation, the case will be amended to be an action for dissolution of the marriage. [Arizona Revised Statutes Annotated; Titles 25, Chapter 313].

SIMPLIFIED OR SPECIAL DISSOLUTION OF MARRIAGE PROCEDURES: Acceptance and waiver of service is allowed. In addition, Arizona law expressly encourages separation agreements. Also, dissolution of marriage petitions may be heard before a court commissioner if an appearance and waiver is filed.

[Arizona Revised Statutes Annotated; Title 25, Chapter 317; and Arizona Rules of Civil Procedure; Rule 4(f); and Arizona Rules of the Supreme Court; Rule 91].

MEDIATION OR COUNSELING REQUIREMENTS: Prior to filing for dissolution of marriage, either spouse may ask the court to order mediation for the purpose of a reconciliation to save the marriage or to obtain an amicable settlement and avoid further litigation. After a dissolution of marriage has been filed, either spouse may request that the dissolution of marriage proceedings be transferred to the Conciliation Court for mediation. Official forms for requesting this transfer are available from the clerk of any Superior Court. In addition, if one spouse denies that the marriage is irretrievably broken, the court may delay the case for up to 60 days and order the spouses to attend a conciliation conference. [Arizona Revised Statutes Annotated; Title 25, Chapters 312, 316 and 381.09+].

PROPERTY DISTRIBUTION: Arizona is a "community property" state. Separate property is retained by the owner of the property. Any property acquired by either spouse outside of Arizona shall be deemed to be community property if the property would have been community property if acquired within Arizona. Community or marital property (property acquired during the marriage) is divided and awarded equitably. Marital misconduct is not considered in the division. The court may consider excessive or abnormal expenditures of community property; and any destruction, concealment, or fraudulent disposition of community property in making the division. The court may place a lien upon a spouse's separate property in order to secure payment of child support or spousal support. [Arizona Revised Statutes Annotated; Title 25, Chapter 318]

ALIMONY/MAINTENANCE/SPOUSAL SUPPORT: Maintenance can be awarded to either spouse, if the spouse seeking maintenance: (1) lacks sufficient property to provide for his or her reasonable needs; or (2) is unable to support him or herself through appropriate employment; or (3) is the custodian of a child whose age and condition is such that the custodian should not be required to seek employment outside the home; or (4) lacks earning ability in the labor market to adequately support him or herself; or (5) contributed to the educational opportunities of the other spouse; or (6) had a marriage of long duration and is of an age which may preclude the possibility of gaining employment adequate to support him or herself. Marital misconduct is not a factor to be considered for maintenance order. The factors to be considered are: (1) the time for the spouse to acquire education and training for suitable employment; (2) the spouse's future earning capacity; (3) the spouse's standard of living during the marriage; (4) the duration of the marriage; (5) the ability of the spouse providing maintenance to meet his or her needs while providing the maintenance to the other; (6) the financial resources of the spouse seeking maintenance (including marital property awarded and the spouse's ability to meet his or her needs independently); (7) any destruction, concealment, fraudulent disposition, or excessive expenditures of jointly-held property; (8) the comparative financial resources of the spouses including their comparative earning capacities; (9) the age of the spouses; (10) the physical and emotional condition of the spouses; (11) the usual occupations of the spouses during the marriage; and (12) the vocational skills of the spouse seeking maintenance. [Arizona Revised Statutes Annotated; Title 25, Chapters 319].

SPOUSE'S NAME: A spouse's former or maiden name may be restored upon request. [Arizona Revised Statutes Annotated; Title 25, Chapter 325]

CHILD CUSTODY: In awarding custody, the court considers the best interests of the child and the following factors: (1) the preference of the child; (2) the desire and ability of each parent to allow an open, loving, and frequent relationship between the child and the other parent; (3) the wishes of the parents; (4) the child's adjustment to his or her home, school, and community; (5) the mental and physical health of the child and the parents; (6) the relationship between the child and the parents and any siblings; (7) any evidence of significant spouse or child abuse (8) any coercion or duress in obtaining a custody agreement; (9) which parent(s) have provided primary care of the child; and (10) any evidence of or conviction for drug abuse. No preference is to be given on the basis of the parent's sex. If custody is contested, all other issues in the case are decided first. Joint custody may be awarded if the parents submit a written agreement providing for joint or shared custody and it is found to be in the best interests of the child. After a consideration of the general child custody factors (above) and the following additional factor: (1) that the joint custody agreement is logistically possible. The court can order joint custody over the objection of one parent. Grandparents and great-grandparents may be awarded visitation rights. [Arizona Revised Statutes Annotated; Title 25, Chapters 401+ and Arizona Case Law].

CHILD SUPPORT: Either parent may be ordered to pay child support, without regard to marital misconduct, based on the following factors: (1) the financial resources of the child; (2) the standard of living the child would have enjoyed had the marriage not dissolved; (3) the physical, emotional, and educational needs of the child; (4) the financial resources and obligations of both parents; (5) any destruction, concealment, fraudulent disposition, or excessive expenditure of jointly-held property; and (6) the duration of child visitation and any related expenses. Awards of child support are to be paid through the court unless the spouses agree otherwise. In addition, there are specific Arizona Supreme Court guidelines for child support payments available from the Clerk of any Superior Court. The amount of support established by using the official guidelines will be the required amount of child support, unless the court finds such an amount would be inappropriate or unjust. Every child support order must assign one or both of the parents responsibility for providing medical insurance coverage for the child and for payment of any medical expenses not covered by insurance. Unless there is contrary evidence presented in court, the court will assume that the non-custodial parent is capable of full-time work at the Federal minimum wage (unless the parent is under 18 years of age and attending high-school). [Arizona Revised Statutes Annotated; Title 25, Chapters 320].

PREMARITAL AGREEMENTS: The agreement must be in writing and signed by both parties and is enforceable without consideration. The agreement will not be enforceable if the party can prove either that he or she did not execute the agreement voluntarily, the agreement was unconscionable when executed, and before execution of the agreement the spouse was not provided a fair and reasonable disclosure of the property or financial obligations of the other spouse, did not voluntarily waive any right to the disclosure of this information, and did not have adequate knowledge of these obligations. If a provision of the agreement modifies or terminates spousal support which causes that spouse to be eligible for public assistance, the court may order the other spouse to pay support. If the marriage is determined to be void, the agreement is enforceable only to the extent to avoid an inequitable result. [Arizona Revised Statutes Annotated; Title 25, Chapter 202].

ARKANSAS

RESIDENCY REQUIREMENTS AND WHERE TO FILE: The divorce should be filed in the county of the plaintiff. However, if the plaintiff is a non-resident of Arkansas, the divorce may be filed for in the county where the defendant resides. The venue requirements may be waived in Arkansas. The parties must wait 30 days before the degree can be entered. [Arkansas Code of 1987 Annotated; Title 9, Chapters 12-3101 and 12-303].

LEGAL GROUNDS FOR DIVORCE: No-Fault: Voluntarily living separate without cohabitation for 18 months. [Arkansas Code of 1987 Annotated; Title 9, Chapter 12-301].

General: (1) impotence; (2) adultery; (3) confinement for incurable insanity or separation caused by mental illness for a period of 3 years; (4) conviction of a felony; (5) cruel and inhuman treatment which endangers the life of the spouse; (6) personal indignities; (7) habitual intemperance (drunkenness) for 1 year; (8) commission and/or conviction of an infamous crime; and (9) nonsupport whereby the spouse is able to provide support but willfully fails to provide suitable maintenance for the complaining spouse. [Arkansas Code of 1987 Annotated; Title 9, Chapter 12-301].

NAME OF COURT IN WHICH TO FILE FOR DIVORCE: Chancery Court. "In the Chancery Court of _____ Arkansas." [Arkansas Code of 1987 Annotated; Title 9, Chapter 12-301].

DOCUMENT CAPTION INFORMATION: Complaint for Divorce. "In Re: the Marriage of _____, Plaintiff and _____, Defendant." Final document title: Decree of Divorce.

LEGAL SEPARATION: Legal separation may be granted for the following reasons: (1) impotence; (2) adultery; (3) confinement for incurable insanity or separation caused by mental illness for a period of 3 years; (4) conviction of a felony; (5) willful desertion for 1 year; (6) cruel and inhuman treatment which endangers the life of the spouse; (7) personal indignities; (8) habitual intemperance (drunkenness) for 1 year; (9) commission and/or conviction of an infamous crime; (10) voluntary separation for 18 months; and (11) nonsupport whereby the spouse is able to provide support but willfully fails to provide

20

suitable maintenance for the complaining spouse. [Arkansas Code of 1987 Annotated; Title 9, Chapter 12-301].

SIMPLIFIED OR SPECIAL DIVORCE PROCEDURES: In an uncontested divorce, proof of a spouse's residency, proof of separation, and proof of no cohabitation may be provided by a signed affidavit from a third party. In addition, in an uncontested divorce, proof of the grounds for divorce need not be corroborated by a third party. [Arkansas Code of 1987 Annotated; Title 9, Chapters 12-306, 12-313, and 12-316].

MEDIATION OR COUNSELING REQUIREMENTS: There is no legal provision in Arkansas for mediation.

PROPERTY DISTRIBUTION: Arkansas is an "equitable distribution" state. All of the marital property acquired during the marriage is divided equally between the spouses. However, if the court finds the division to be unfair, it may redistribute the property, after consideration of the following factors: (1) the contribution of each spouse to the acquisition of the marital property, including the contribution of each spouse as homemaker; (2) the length of the marriage; (3) the age and health of the spouses; (4) the occupation of the spouses; (5) the amount and sources of income of the spouses; (6) the vocational skills of the spouses; (7) the employability of the spouses; (8) the estate, liabilities, and needs of each spouse and the opportunity of each for further acquisition of capital assets and income; (9) and the federal income tax consequences of the court's division of the property. The separate property of each spouse, consisting of property acquired prior to the marriage, and any gifts or inheritances, is retained by the spouse owning it, unless the court finds it necessary to divide the separate property in order to achieve an equitable distribution. [Arkansas Code of 1987 Annotated; Title 9, Chapter 12-315].

ALIMONY/MAINTENANCE/SPOUSAL SUPPORT: Alimony may be granted to either spouse in fixed installments for a specific period of time and subject to contingencies such as death of either spouse or remarriage of the receiving spouse. Where the grounds for divorce are voluntary separation for 3 years, fault may be considered in dividing the property. The factors for consideration specified in the statute are that the amount be reasonable based on the circumstances of the parties and the nature of the case. Alimony payments may be ordered to be paid through the registry of the court. [Arkansas Code of 1987 Annotated; Title 9, Chapter 12-312].

SPOUSE'S NAME: The court may restore the wife's pre-marriage name. [Arkansas Code of 1987 Annotated; Title 9, Chapter 12-318].

CHILD CUSTODY: Child custody is awarded based on the welfare and best interests of the child, after a consideration of the following factors: (1) the circumstances of the parents and child; (2) the nature of the case; (3) which parent is most likely to allow frequent and continuing contact with the other parent; and (4) any acts of domestic violence. Joint or shared custody may been awarded if it is found to be in the best interests of the child. The sex of the parent is not a factor for decisions relating to child custody. [Arkansas Code of 1987 Annotated; Title 9, Chapter 13-101 and Arkansas Case Law].

CHILD SUPPORT: In awarding a reasonable amount of child support, the court is to consider the following factors: (1) the circumstances of the parents and child; and (2) the nature of the case. Child support payments may be ordered to be paid through the registry of the court and the court may require that a bond securing payment be required. There is an official Arkansas Family Support guidelines chart which is presumed to be correct, unless the court finds that the amount would be inappropriate or unjust, considering the following factors: (1) any necessary medical, dental, or psychological care or insurance; (2) the creation or maintenance of trust fund for the child; (3) day care expenses; (4) extraordinary time spent with the non-custodial parent; and (5) any additional support provided by the parent obligated to pay support. This chart should be available from the Clerk of any Chancery Court. In addition, an official Affidavit of Financial Means must be filed with divorce cases which involves issues relating to child support. [Arkansas Code of 1987 Annotated; Title 9, Chapters 12-312 and 14-105].

PREMARITAL AGREEMENT: The agreement must be in writing, signed, and acknowledged by both parties and is enforceable without consideration. The agreement is not enforceable if the person can prove 1) the person did not execute the agreement voluntarily; or 2) the agreement was unconscionable when executed and before execution of the agreement the person was not provided a fair and reasonable disclosure of the property or financial obligations of the other party; the party did not voluntarily waive any right to the disclosure of these obligations and that he or she did not have adequate knowledge of the obligations of the other party. If a provision of the agreement modifies or eliminates spousal support and that causes the party to be eligible for public assistance, a court may require the other party to provide support necessary to avoid that eligibility. If a marriage is determined to be void, the agreement is enforceable only to the extent necessary to avoid an inequitable result. [Arkansas Code of 1987 Annotated; Title 9, Chapters 11-402, 11-406, 11-407.

CALIFORNIA

RESIDENCY REQUIREMENTS AND WHERE TO FILE: A spouse filing for dissolution of marriage must have been a resident of the state for 6 months and a resident of the county where the dissolution of marriage is filed for 3 months. In addition, there is a waiting period of 6 months after the service of process or the appearance by the respondent before the dissolution of marriage becomes final. [Annotated California Code; Sections 2320 and 2339].

LEGAL GROUNDS FOR DISSOLUTION OF MARRIAGE: No-Fault: Irreconcilable differences which have caused the irremediable breakdown of the marriage. [Annotated California Code; Section 2310].
General: Incurable insanity. [Annotated California Code; Section 2310].

NAME OF COURT IN WHICH TO FILE FOR DISSOLUTION OF MARRIAGE: Superior Court. "Superior Court of California, County of _____." [Annotated California Code; Section 2330].

DOCUMENT CAPTION INFORMATION: Petition for Dissolution of Marriage. "In Re: the Marriage of _____, Petitioner and _____, Respondent." (Official mandatory and optional forms for filing a Dissolution of Marriage are available from the County Clerk of any county). [Annotated California Code; Section 2330 and Judicial Council Forms]. Final document title: Final Judgement of Dissolution of Marriage.

LEGAL SEPARATION: The grounds for obtaining a legal separation in California are: (1) irreconcilable differences; and (2) incurable insanity. A spouse filing for legal separation must have been a resident of the state for 6 months and a resident of the county where the action for legal separation is filed for 3 months. [Annotated California Code; Sections 2310 and 2320].

SIMPLIFIED OR SPECIAL DISSOLUTION OF MARRIAGE PROCEDURES: A marriage of 5 years or less may be dissolved by summary action. A Joint Petition for Summary Dissolution of Marriage may be filed if: (1) either spouse has met the residency requirement for a standard dissolution of marriage; (2) there is an irremediable breakdown of the marriage due to irreconcilable differences; (3) there are no children born of or adopted during the marriage;

23

(4) the wife is not pregnant; (5) neither spouse owns any real estate; (6) there are no unpaid debts exceeding $4,000 incurred during the marriage; (7) the total value of the community property (including any deferred compensation or retirement plans but excluding cars and loans) is less than $25,000; (8) neither spouse has separate property (excluding cars and loans) exceeding $25,000 in value [On January 1 of every odd-numbered year, the dollar amounts in this section may be revised]; (9) the spouses have signed an agreement regarding the division of their assets and their liabilities and have signed any documents or given proof of any transfers necessary to effectuate the agreement; (10) the spouses waive any rights to spousal support [maintenance]; (11) the spouses waive their right to appeal the dissolution of marriage and their right to a new trial upon entry of the final Dissolution of Marriage judgement; (12) the spouses have read and understand the summary dissolution of marriage brochure available from the county clerk; and (13) both spouses desire that the marriage be dissolved. Official mandatory and optional forms for filing for a Summary Dissolution of Marriage are available from the County Clerk of any county. [Annotated California Code; Sections 2400 and 2401, and Judicial Council Forms].

MEDIATION OR COUNSELING REQUIREMENTS: When spouses seek a no-fault dissolution of marriage (on the grounds of irremediable breakdown of the marriage) and it appears to the court that there is a reasonable possibility of reconciliation, the court will stay the dissolution of marriage proceedings for 30 days. If there is no reconciliation at the end of this 30-day period, either spouse may move for a dissolution of marriage or legal separation. In addition, a confidential counseling statement must be filed in any county which has a Conciliation Court. Official forms to this effect are available from the County Clerk of any county which has a Conciliation Court. In addition, if child custody is contested, a mediation conference will be ordered at which the mediator may choose to exclude any attorneys of the parents. [Annotated California Code; Sections 2334(a)(c), 3170, 3182(a), and California Family Law Court Rule 1224].

PROPERTY DISTRIBUTION: California is a "community property" state. Any jointly-held property is presumed to be "community" property, unless it is clearly stated in a deed or written agreement that the property is "separate" property. Unless the spouses agree otherwise, all community and quasi-community property is divided equally between the spouses. If economic circumstances warrant, however, the court may award any asset to one spouse on such conditions as it feels proper to provide for a substantially equal distribution of property. In addition, if one of the spouse's has deliberately misappropriated community property, the court may make an unequal division of the community property. Marital contributions to the education and training of the other spouse that substantially increases or enhances the other spouse's earning capacity are reimbursable to the community property. Each spouse shall be responsible for the following debts: (1) those incurred prior to marriage, (2) any separate debts during the marriage that were not incurred to benefit the community (marriage), (3) their equitable share of any community debts made during the marriage, and (4) any debts incurred after separation and before dissolution of marriage if the debts were for non-necessities and an equitable share of debts incurred during this period if the debts were for necessities. [Annotated California Code; Sections 2581, 2601, 2602, 2620, 2621, 2623, 2625, and 2641].

ALIMONY/MAINTENANCE/SPOUSAL SUPPORT: The court may award support to either spouse in any amount and for any period of time that the court deems just and reasonable, based on the standard of living achieved during the marriage. The factors considered are: (1) whether the spouse seeking support is the custodian of a child whose circumstances make it appropriate for that spouse not to seek outside employment; (2) time necessary to acquire sufficient education and training to enable the spouse to find appropriate employment, and that spouse's future earning capacity; (3) standard of living established during the marriage; (4) duration of the marriage; (5) comparative financial resources of the spouses, including their comparative earning abilities in the labor market; (6) needs and obligations of each spouse; (7) contribution of each spouse to the marriage, including homemaking, child care, education, and career building of the other spouse; (8) age and health of the spouses; (9) physical and emotional conditions of the spouses; (10) tax consequences to each spouse; (11) ability of the supporting spouse to pay, taking into account that spouse's earning capacity, earned and unearned income, assets, and standard of living; (12) balance of hardships to each party; and (13) any other just and equitable factor. Marital misconduct is not a factor (except attempted murder). The goal is specifically to make the supported spouse self-supporting in a reasonable period of time (generally considered to be half the length of the marriage). [Annotated California Code; Section 4320, 4324, and 4330].

SPOUSE'S NAME: On a party's request, the court shall restore a spouse's former or birth name, regardless of the last name of any custodial child. [Annotated California Code; Section 2080 and 2081].

CHILD CUSTODY: Joint or sole custody may be awarded based on the best interests of the child and the following factors: (1) preference of the child, if the child is of sufficient age and capacity; (2) desire and ability of each parent to allow an open and loving frequent relationship between the child and the other parent; (3) child's health, safety, and welfare; (4) history of child or spouse abuse by anyone seeking custody or who has had any caretaking relationship with the child, including anyone dating the parent; (5) nature and amount of contact with both parents, and (6) continued use of alcohol or controlled substances. Marital misconduct may also be considered. Custody is awarded in the following order of preference: (1) to both parents jointly; (2) to either parent; (3) to the person in whose home the child has been living; or (4) to any other person deemed by the court suitable to provide adequate and proper care and guidance for the child. However, it is not presumed that joint custody is necessarily the preferred choice, unless there is an agreement between the parents regarding joint custody. No preference in awarding custody is to be given because of parent's sex. The court may order a parent to give the other parent 30-days notice of any plans to change the residence of a child. [Annotated California Code; Sections 3011, 3024, 3040, 3042].

CHILD SUPPORT: Either parent may be ordered to pay an amount necessary for the support, maintenance, and education of the child. Child support payments may be awarded on a temporary basis during custody or child support proceeding. There is a mandatory minimum amount of child support which is determined by official forms which are available from the County Clerk of any county. These minimum payment amounts will apply unless there is a reasonable agreement between the parents providing otherwise that states that (1) the parents state that they are fully informed of their rights regarding child support under California law, (2) the child support amount is being agreed to without coercion or duress, (3) both parents declare that their children's needs will be adequately met, (4) the right to child support has not been assigned to the county and that no public assistance is pending, and (5) the agreement is in the best interests of the child involved. A parent may be required to provide medical insurance coverage for a child if such coverage is available at a reasonable cost. The parent required to pay may be required to give reasonable security for the support payments. In addition, there are detailed and extensive statutory provisions in California relating to the securing of child support payments. [Annotated California Code; Sections 3024, 3600, 3751, 3900, 4001, 4012, 4055, 4065 and Judicial Council Forms; and California Rules of Court].

PREMARITAL AGREEMENT: Agreement must be in writing and signed by both parties and is enforceable without consideration. The agreement will not be enforceable if the party can prove either 1) that the agreement was not executed voluntarily; 2) the agreement was unconscionable when executed because the party was not provided a fair and reasonable disclosure of the property or financial obligations of the other party, the party did not voluntarily waive any right to this disclosure, and that the party did not have adequate knowledge of these obligations. If the marriage is determined to be void, the agreement is enforceable only to the extent necessary to avoid an inequitable result. [Annotated California Code; Sections 1611, 1615, and 1616].

COLORADO

RESIDENCY REQUIREMENTS AND WHERE TO FILE: One spouse must have been a resident of Colorado for 90 days prior to filing for dissolution of marriage. The dissolution of marriage may be filed for in: (1) the county where the respondent resides; or (2) the county in which the petitioner resides if the respondent has been served in the same county or is a non-resident of Colorado. [Colorado Revised Statutes; Article 10, Section 14-10-106; and Colorado Rules of Civil Procedure, Rule 98].

LEGAL GROUNDS FOR DISSOLUTION OF MARRIAGE: No-Fault: Irretrievable breakdown of the marriage. [Colorado Revised Statutes; Article 10, Section 14-10-106].

General: Irretrievable breakdown of the marriage is the only grounds for dissolution of marriage in Colorado. [Colorado Revised Statutes; Article 10, Section 14-10-106].

NAME OF COURT IN WHICH TO FILE FOR DISSOLUTION OF MARRIAGE: District Court. "In the District Court in and for the County of _____ and State of Colorado." [Colorado Revised Statutes; Article 10, Section 14-10-106].

DOCUMENT CAPTION INFORMATION: Petition for Dissolution of Marriage. "In Re: the Marriage of _____, Petitioner and _____, Respondent." Final document title: Decree of Dissolution of Marriage.

LEGAL SEPARATION: If there has been an irretrievable breakdown of the marriage, the spouses may file for a legal separation. One spouse must have been a resident of Colorado for 90 days prior to filing for legal separation. [Colorado Revised Statutes; Article 10, Section 14-10-106].

SIMPLIFIED OR SPECIAL DISSOLUTION OF MARRIAGE PROCEDURES: A dissolution of marriage may be obtained by affidavit of either or both of the spouses if: (1) there are no minor children and the wife is not pregnant; or both spouses are represented by counsel and have entered into a separation agreement granting custody and child support; (2) there are no disputes; (3) there is no marital property; or the spouses have agreed on the division of

27

marital property; and (4) the adverse party (non-filing spouse) has been served with the dissolution of marriage papers. A signed affidavit stating the facts in the case must be filed with the petition. [Colorado Revised Statutes; Article 10, Section 14-10-120.3].

MEDIATION OR COUNSELING REQUIREMENTS: At the request of either spouse or their attorney, or at the discretion of the court, the court may appoint a marriage counselor in any dissolution of marriage or legal separation proceeding and delay the proceedings for 30 to 60 days to allow for counseling. In addition, the court may order a parent of a child to attend a program concerning the impact of separation and dissolution on children. Finally, a court may appoint an arbitrator to resolve disputes between parents concerning child support and custody [Colorado Revised Statutes; Article 10, Sections 14-12-106, 14-10-110, 14-10-123.7, 14-10-128.5].

PROPERTY DISTRIBUTION: Colorado is an "equitable distribution" state. The separate property of each spouse which was owned prior to the marriage or obtained by gift or inheritance is retained by that spouse. All other property acquired during the marriage will be divided, without regard to any fault, based on the following: (1) the contribution of each spouse to the acquisition of the marital property, including the contribution of each spouse as homemaker; (2) the value of each spouse's separate property; (3) the economic circumstances of each spouse at the time the division of property is to become effective, including the desirability of awarding the family home or right to live in it to the spouse having custody of any children; (4) and any increase or decrease in the value of the separate property of the spouse during the marriage or the depletion of the separate property for marital purposes. [Colorado Revised Statutes; Article 10, Section 14-10-113].

ALIMONY/MAINTENANCE/SPOUSAL SUPPORT: Either spouse may be awarded support for a just period of time, without regard to any marital fault, if the spouse seeking maintenance: (1) lacks sufficient property, including his or her share of any marital property, to provide for his or her needs, and (2) is unable to support his or herself through appropriate employment, or has custody of a child and the circumstances are such that the spouse should not be required to seek employment outside the home.

The award of maintenance is based upon a consideration of the following factors: (1) the time necessary to acquire sufficient education and training to enable the spouse to find appropriate employment, and that spouse's future earning capacity; (2) the standard of living established during the marriage; (3) the duration of the marriage; (4) the ability of the spouse from whom support is sought to meet his or her needs while meeting those of the spouse seeking support; (5) the financial resources of the spouse seeking maintenance, including marital property apportioned to such spouse and such spouse's ability to meet his or her needs independently; (6) the age of the spouses; (7) the physical and emotional conditions of the spouses; and (8) any custodial and child support responsibilities. Maintenance payments may be ordered to be paid directly to the court for distribution to the spouse. [Colorado Revised Statutes; Article 10, Sections 14-10-114 and 14-10-117].

SPOUSE'S NAME: There is no legal provision in Colorado for restoration of the spouse's name upon divorce. However, there is a general statute which allows for the change of a person's name upon petition to the court. [Colorado Revised Statutes; Article 10, Section 13-15-101].

CHILD CUSTODY: Joint or sole custody will be determined with regard to the best interests of the child, without regard to the sex of the parent, and after considering the following factors: (1) the preference of the child; (2) the desire and ability of each parent to allow an open and loving frequent relationship between the child and the other parent; (3) the wishes of the parents; (4) the child's adjustment to his or her home, school, and community; (5) the mental and physical health of all individuals involved; (6) the relationship of the child with parents, siblings, and other significant family members; (7) any child abuse or spouse abuse by either parent; (8) credible evidence of the ability of the parties to cooperate and to make decisions jointly; (9) whether the past pattern of involvement of the parties with the child reflects a system of values, time commitment, and mutual support which would indicate an ability as joint custodians to provide a positive and nourishing relationship with the child; (10) the physical proximity of the parties to each other; (11) whether an award of joint custody will promote more frequent or continuing contact between the child and each of the parties. Visitation may be restricted if there is a danger to the child.

Joint custody may be awarded on the petition of both parents if they submit a reasonable plan for custody. The plan submitted to the court for joint custody should address the following issues: (1) the location of each parent; (2) the periods of time during which each parent will have physical custody of the child; (3) the legal residence of the child; (4) the child's education; (5) the child's religious training, if any; (6) the child's health care; (7) finances to provide for the child's needs; (8) holidays and vacations; and (9) any other factors affecting the physical or emotional health or well-being of the child.

The actual joint custody award is based on all of the factors involved in standard custody decisions and on the following additional factors: (1) the ability of the parents to cooperate and make decisions jointly; (2) the ability of the parents to encourage the sharing of love, affection, and contact between the child and the other parent; (3) whether the past pattern of involvement of the parents with the child reflects a system of values and mutual support which indicates the parent's ability as joint custodians to provide a positive and nourishing relationship; (4) the physical proximity of the parents to each other as this relates to the practical considerations of where the child will reside; (5) the ability of each parent to maintain adequate housing for the child; and (6) whether an award of joint custody will promote more frequent or continuing contact between the child and each of the parents. [Colorado Revised Statutes; Article 10, Sections 14-123.5, 14-124, and 14-129].

CHILD SUPPORT: The court may order reasonable and necessary child support to be paid by either or both parents, without regard to marital fault, after considering the following factors: (1) the financial resources of the child; (2) the financial resources of the custodial parents; (3) the standard of living the child would have enjoyed if the marriage had not been dissolved; (4) the physical and emotional conditions and educational needs of the child; and (5) the financial resources and needs of the noncustodial parent. Provisions for medical insurance and medical care for any children may be ordered to be provided. There are specific child support guidelines specified in the statute. In addition, standardized child support guideline forms are available from the Clerk of any District Court. Child support payments may be ordered to be paid through the Clerk of the Court. After July 1, 1997, child support must continue through high school graduation, unless certain factors are met. [Colorado Revised Statutes; Article 10, Sections 14-10-115 and 14-10-117].

PREMARITAL AGREEMENT: The agreement must be in writing and signed by both parties and is enforceable without consideration. After the agreement becomes effective, it may be amended or revoked only by a written agreement signed by both parties. The amended agreement is enforceable without consideration. The agreement is not enforceable if it is proven that (1) the agreement was not executed voluntarily or (2) before execution of the agreement the party was not provided a fair and reasonable disclosure of the property or financial obligations of the other party. If the marriage is determined to be void, the agreement is enforceable only to the extent to avoid an inequitable result. [Colorado Revised Statutes; Sections 14-2-303, 14-2-306, 14-2-307, and 14-2-308].

CONNECTICUT

RESIDENCY REQUIREMENTS AND WHERE TO FILE: The dissolution of marriage may be filed by either spouse if a resident. However, the dissolution of marriage will not be finalized until one spouse has been a resident for one (1) year; unless one of the spouses was a resident of Connecticut at the time of the marriage and returned with the intention of permanent residence; or if the grounds for the dissolution of marriage arose in Connecticut. In cases which involve support, the dissolution of marriage is to be filed in the county in which the plaintiff resides. In all other cases, the dissolution of marriage may be filed in any county which is most convenient to both spouses. [Connecticut General Statutes Annotated; Title 46b, Chapter 44; and Title 51, Chapter 349].

LEGAL GROUNDS FOR DISSOLUTION OF MARRIAGE: No-Fault: (1) Irretrievable breakdown of the marriage; (2) incompatibility and voluntary separation for 18 months with no reasonable prospect for reconciliation. [Connecticut General Statutes Annotated; Title 46b, Chapter 40].
　　　General: (1) Adultery; (2) life imprisonment; (3) confinement for incurable insanity for a total of 5 years; (4) willful desertion and nonsupport for 1 year; (5) 7 years absence; (6) cruel and inhuman treatment; (7) fraud; (8) habitual intemperance (drunkenness); (9) commission and/or conviction of an infamous crime involving a violation of conjugal duty and imprisonment for at least 1 year. [Connecticut General Statutes Annotated; Title 46b, Chapter 40].

NAME OF COURT IN WHICH TO FILE FOR DISSOLUTION OF MARRIAGE: Superior Court. [Connecticut General Statutes Annotated; Title 46b, Chapter 42].

DOCUMENT CAPTION INFORMATION: Complaint for Dissolution of Marriage. "In Re: the Marriage of: _____, Plaintiff and _____, Defendant." Final document title: Decree of Dissolution of Marriage.

LEGAL SEPARATION: A legal separation may be granted on the following grounds: (1) irretrievable breakdown of the marriage; (2) incompatibility and voluntary separation; (3) adultery; (4) life imprisonment; (5) confinement for incurable insanity for a total of 5 years; (6) willful desertion and nonsupport for 1 year; (7) cruel and inhuman treatment; (8) fraud; (9) habitual intemperance (drunkenness); (10) commission and/or conviction of an infamous crime involving a violation of conjugal duty and imprisonment for at least 1 year. There is no residency requirement noted in the statute. [Connecticut General Statutes Annotated; Title 46b, Chapter 40].

SIMPLIFIED OR SPECIAL DISSOLUTION OF MARRIAGE PROCEDURES: Proof of the breakdown of the marriage can be made by: (1) the spouses signing an agreement or statement that their marriage is irretrievably broken; or (2) both spouses stating in court that their marriage is irretrievably broken and submitting an agreement concerning the care, custody, visitation, maintenance, support, and education after custody of their children, if any, and concerning alimony and the disposition of any property. [Connecticut General Statutes Annotated; Title 46b, Chapter 51].

MEDIATION OR COUNSELING REQUIREMENTS: Within 90 days after the dissolution of marriage has been filed, either spouse or the attorney for any minor children may submit a request for conciliation to the clerk of the court. Two mandatory counseling sessions will be ordered. Mediation services may also be available from the court for property, financial, custody and visitation issues. [Connecticut General Statutes Annotated; Title 46b, Chapter 53 and 53(a)].

PROPERTY DISTRIBUTION: Connecticut is an "equitable distribution" state. The court may assign to either spouse all or part of the property of the other spouse, including any gifts and inheritances, based on the following factors: (1) contribution of each spouse to the acquisition of the marital property, including any contribution as homemaker; (2) length of the marriage; (3) age and health of the spouses; (4) occupations of the spouses; (5) amount and sources of income of the spouses; (6) vocational skills of the spouses; (7) employability of the spouses; (8) estate, liabilities, and needs of each spouse and the opportunity of each for further acquisition of capital assets and income; (9) circumstances that contributed to the estrangement of the spouses; and (10) causes of the dissolution of marriage. [Connecticut General Statutes Annotated; Title 46b, Chapter 81].

ALIMONY/MAINTENANCE/SPOUSAL SUPPORT: Alimony may be awarded to either spouse, based on the following factors: (1) causes for the dissolution of marriage, including any marital fault; (2) distribution of the marital property; (3) whether the spouse seeking support is the custodian of a child whose condition or circumstances make it appropriate for that spouse not to seek outside employment; (4) duration of the marriage; (5) age of the spouses; (6) physical and emotional conditions of the spouses; (7) usual occupations of the spouses during the marriage; (8) needs of each spouse; and (9) vocational skills and employability of the spouse seeking support and alimony. [Connecticut General Statutes Annotated; Title 46b, Chapters 82 and 86].

SPOUSE'S NAME: Either spouse's birth name shall be restored upon request. [Connecticut General Statutes Annotated; Title 46b, Chapter 63].

CHILD CUSTODY: Joint or sole custody is awarded based upon the best interests of the child and the following factors: (1) causes for the dissolution of marriage if relevant to the best interests of the child; (2) wishes of the child if the child is of sufficient age and is capable of forming an intelligent choice; and (3) whether the party satisfactorily completed participation in a parenting education program. There are no other specific state guidelines for consideration. There is a presumption that joint custody is in the best interests of the child if both parents have agreed to joint custody. [Connecticut General Statutes Annotated; Title 46b, Chapters 56, 56a, and 84].

CHILD SUPPORT: Either parent may be ordered to contribute child support, based on the following factors: (1) financial resources of the child; (2) age, health, and station of the parents; (3) occupation of each parent; (4) earning capacity of each parent; (5) amount and sources of income of each parent; (6) vocational skills and employability of each parent; (7) age and health of the child; (8) child's occupation; (9) vocational skills of the child; (10) employability of the child; (11) estate and needs of the child; and (12) relative financial means of the parents. Either parent may be ordered to provide health insurance for the child. There are official Child Support Guidelines. These Guidelines are presumed to be correct unless there is a showing that the amount would be inequitable or inappropriate under the particular circumstances in a case. [Connecticut General Statutes Annotated; Title 46b, Chapters 84, 215b, 816].

PREMARITAL AGREEMENT: The agreement must be in writing and signed by both parties and is enforceable without consideration. After marriage, the agreement may be amended or revoked only by a written agreement signed by the parties. The amendment is enforceable without consideration. The agreement is not enforceable if it is proven that (1) the agreement was not executed voluntarily; (2) the agreement was unconscionable when executed or when enforcement is sought; (3) before the execution of the agreement, the party was not provided a fair and reasonable disclosure of the amount, character and value of property, financial obligations and income of the other party; or (4) such party was not afforded a reasonable opportunity to consult with independent counsel. If a provision of the agreement modifies or terminates spousal support allowing the spouse to be eligible for public assistance, the court may require that the other party provide spousal support. If the marriage is determined to be void, the agreement is enforceable only to the extent necessary to avoid an inequitable result. [Connecticut General Statutes Annotated; Title 46b, Chapters 36c, 36f, 36g, and 36h].

DELAWARE

RESIDENCY REQUIREMENTS AND WHERE TO FILE: One spouse must have been a resident for 6 months immediately prior to filing for divorce. The divorce may be filed for in a county where either spouse resides. [Delaware Code Annotated; Title 13, Chapter 15, Sections 1504 and 1507].

LEGAL GROUNDS FOR DIVORCE: No-Fault: (1) Irretrievable breakdown of the marriage and reconciliation is improbable (a marriage is considered "irretrievably broken" when it is characterized by one of the following: (a) voluntary separation; (b) separation caused by the other spouse's misconduct or mental illness; or (c) separation caused by incompatibility. [Delaware Code Annotated; Title 13, Chapter 15, Section 1505].

General: Separation caused by mental illness. [Delaware Code Annotated; Title 13, Chapter 15, Section 1505].

NAME OF COURT IN WHICH TO FILE FOR DIVORCE: Family Court. "In the Family Court for the State of Delaware, In and For _____ County." [Delaware Code Annotated; Title 13, Chapter 15, Sections 1504 and 1507].

DOCUMENT CAPTION INFORMATION: Petition for Divorce. "In Re: the Marriage of: _____, Petitioner and _____, Respondent." Final document title: Decree of Divorce.

LEGAL SEPARATION: There is no legal provision in Delaware for legal separation.

SIMPLIFIED OR SPECIAL DIVORCE PROCEDURES: The respondent may file an appearance which will fulfill the requirement of service of process. In addition, a sample Petition for Divorce is contained in Delaware Code Annotated; Title 13, Chapter 15, Section 1507. [Delaware Code Annotated; Title 13, Chapter 15, Section 1508].

MEDIATION OR COUNSELING REQUIREMENTS: In a contested divorce, the court may delay the proceedings for 60 days to allow the spouses to seek counseling or order a mediation conference. In addition, there are mediation/arbitration units attached to the Delaware Family Court. Finally, the court may require parents seeking divorce to participate in a certified "parenting education course." If the parent has a history of domestic violence, they may be required to attend additional, more intensive courses. [Delaware Code Annotated; Title 13, Chapter 15, Section 1517].

PROPERTY DISTRIBUTION: Delaware is an "equitable distribution" state. A spouse's separate property is that (1) obtained prior to the marriage; (2) obtained by inheritance; (3) specified as separate property by an agreement between the spouses; or (4) property acquired in exchange for separate property or an increase in value of separate property. All separate property is retained by the spouse who owns such property. Marital property acquired during the marriage, including any property acquired by gift, is to be divided equitably, without regard to fault, based on the following factors: (1) the contribution of each spouse to the acquisition of the marital property, including the contribution of each spouse as homemaker; (2) the value of each spouse's personal property; (3) the economic circumstances of each spouse at the time the division of property is to become effective; (4) the length of the marriage; (5) the age and health of the spouses; (6) the occupation of the spouses; (7) the amount and sources of income of the spouses; (8) the vocational skills of the spouses; (9) the employability of the spouses; (10) the estate, liabilities, and needs of each spouse and the opportunity of each for further acquisition of capital assets and income; (11) the federal income tax consequences of the court's division of the property; (12) liabilities of the spouses; (13) any prior marriage of each spouse; (14) whether the property award is instead of or in addition to maintenance. [Delaware Code Annotated; Title 13, Chapter 15, Section 1513].

ALIMONY/MAINTENANCE/SPOUSAL SUPPORT: Either spouse may be awarded alimony if: (1) he or she is dependent on the other spouse; (2) lacks sufficient property, including any award or marital property, to provide for his or her reasonable needs; and (3) is unable to support him or herself through appropriate employment or is the custodian of a child whose condition or circumstances make it appropriate that he or she not be required to seek employment. Either spouse may be awarded alimony for no longer than a period of time equal to 50% of the length of the marriage. There is, however, no time limit if the marriage lasted for over 20 years.

Marital misconduct is not a factor to be considered in an award or alimony. The factors to be considered are: (1) the time necessary to acquire sufficient education and training to enable the spouse to find appropriate employment, and that spouse's future earning capacity; (2) the standard of living established during the marriage; (3) the duration of the marriage; (4) the ability of the spouse from whom support is sought to meet his or her needs while meeting those of the spouse seeking support; (5) the financial resources of the spouse seeking alimony, including marital property apportioned to such spouse and such spouse's ability to meet his or her needs independently; (6)

the tax consequences; (7) the age of the spouses; (8) the physical and emotional conditions of the spouses; (9) whether either spouse has foregone or postponed economic, education or other employment opportunities during the course of the marriage; and (10) any other factor that the court finds just and appropriate.

Any party awarded alimony has a duty to make an effort to seek vocational training and employment unless the court finds that it would be inequitable to require this because of (1) a severe physical or mental disability, (2) his or her age, or (3) the needs of any children living with the spouse receiving alimony. Unless the spouses agree otherwise, alimony is terminated upon death, remarriage, or cohabitation with another person. [Delaware Code Annotated; Title 13, Chapter 15, Section 1512].

SPOUSE'S NAME: Upon request, the wife may resume her former or maiden name. [Delaware Code Annotated; Title 13, Chapter 15, Section 1514].

CHILD CUSTODY: Joint or sole child custody is awarded based on the best interests of the child and after considering the following factors: (1) preference of the child; (2) the wishes of the parents; (3) the child's adjustment to his or her home, school, and community; (4) the mental and physical health of all individuals involved; (5) the relationship of the child with parents, siblings, and other significant family members; (6) the past and present compliance by both parents with the duty to support the child; and (7) evidence of domestic violence. No preference to be given because of parent's sex.

In addition, in any case involving minor children, the petitioning parent must submit with the petition a signed affidavit that states that the parent has been advised of or has read the following list of children's rights. The list of rights must be included in the affidavit. The children's rights are: (1) the right to a continuing relationship with both parents; (2) the right to be treated as an important human being, with unique feelings, ideas, and desires; (3) the right to continuing care and guidance from both parents; (4) the right to know and appreciate what is good in each parent without one parent degrading the other; (5) the right to express love, affection, and respect for each parent without having to stifle that love because of disapproval by the other parent; (6) the right to know that the parents' decision to divorce was not the responsibility of the child; (7) the right not to be a source of argument between the parents; (8) the right to honest answers to questions about the changing family relationships; (9) the right to be able to experience regular and consistent contact with both parents and the right to know the reason for any cancellation of time or change of plans; and (10) the right to have a relaxed, secure relationship with both parents without being placed in a position to manipulate one parent against the other. [Delaware Code Annotated; Title 13, Chapter 7, Section 722 and 1507].

CHILD SUPPORT: Each parent has an equal duty to support any children. The following factors are considered in awards of child support: (1) the financial resources of the child; (2) the standard of living the child would have enjoyed if there had been no divorce; (3) the age and health of the parents; (4) the earning capacity of each parent; (5) the amount and sources of income of each parent; (6) the age, health, or station of the child; (7) the estate and needs of the child; and (8) the relative financial means of the parents. [Delaware Code Annotated; Title 13, Chapter 5, Sections 501, 514, and 701].

PREMARITAL AGREEMENT: The agreement must be in writing and signed by both parties and is enforceable without consideration. After marriage, the agreement may be amended or revoked only by a written agreement signed by the parties and this agreement is enforceable without consideration. The agreement is not enforceable if proven that (1) the agreement was not executed voluntarily; (2) the agreement was unconscionable when executed since the party was not provided a fair and reasonable disclosure of the financial or property obligations of the other party, did not voluntarily waive the right to the disclosure of this information and did not have adequate knowledge of these obligations. If the marriage is determined to be void, the agreement is enforceable only to the extent necessary to avoid an inequitable result. [Delaware Code Annotated; Title 13, Sections 322, 325, 326, and 327].

DISTRICT OF COLUMBIA (WASHINGTON D.C.)

RESIDENCY REQUIREMENTS AND WHERE TO FILE: One of the spouses must have been a resident of Washington D.C. for 6 months immediately prior to filing for divorce. Military personnel are considered residents if they have been stationed in Washington D.C. for 6 months. [District of Columbia Code Annotated; Title 16, Chapter 9, Section 902].

LEGAL GROUNDS FOR DIVORCE: No-Fault: (1) Mutual voluntary separation without cohabitation for 6 months; (2) living separate and apart without cohabitation for 1 year. [District of Columbia Code Annotated; Title 16, Chapter 9, Sections 904, 905, and 906].

General: (1) Mutual voluntary separation without cohabitation for 6 months; (2) living separate and apart without cohabitation for 1 year; (3) adultery; and (4) cruelty. [District of Columbia Code Annotated; Title 16, Chapter 9, Sections 904, 905, and 906].

NAME OF COURT IN WHICH TO FILE FOR DIVORCE: Superior Court— Family Division. "In the Superior Court of the District of Columbia—Family Division." [District of Columbia Court Rules; Volume 2, Appendix I].

DOCUMENT CAPTION INFORMATION: Complaint for Divorce. "In Re: the Marriage of: _____, Plaintiff and _____, Defendant." Final document title: Final Decree of Divorce.

LEGAL SEPARATION: Legal separation (from bed and board) may be granted on the following grounds: (1) adultery; (2) cruel and inhuman treatment; (3) voluntary separation; and (4) living separate and apart without cohabitation. One of the spouses must have been a resident for 6 months prior to filing for legal separation. Military personnel are considered residents if they have been stationed in Washington D.C. for 6 months. [District of Columbia Code Annotated; Title 16, Chapter 9, Sections 902 and 904-906].

SIMPLIFIED OR SPECIAL DIVORCE PROCEDURES: There are no legal provisions in Washington D.C. for simplified divorce.

MEDIATION OR COUNSELING REQUIREMENTS: The court may order either or both spouses to attend parenting classes in those cases in which child custody is an issue. [District of Columbia Code Annotated; Title 16, Chapter 9, Sections 911(2)d].

PROPERTY DISTRIBUTION: Washington D.C. is an "equitable distribution" jurisdiction. If there is no valid property distribution agreement, each spouse retains his or her separate property (acquired before the marriage or acquired during the marriage by gift or inheritance) and any increase in such separate property and any property acquired in exchange for such separate property. All other property, regardless of how title is held, shall be divided equitably and reasonably, based on relevant factors, including: (1) the contribution of each spouse to the acquisition of the marital property, including the contribution of each spouse as homemaker; (2) the length of the marriage; (3) the occupation of the spouses; (4) the vocational skills of the spouses; (5) the employability of the spouses; (6) the estate, liabilities, and needs of each spouse and the opportunity of each for further acquisition of capital assets and income; (7) the assets and debts of the spouses; (8) any prior marriage of each spouse; (9) whether the property award is instead of or in addition to alimony; (10) any custodial provisions for the children; (11) the age and health of the spouses; and (12) the amount and sources of income of the spouses. The conduct of the spouses during the marriage is not a factor for consideration. [District of Columbia Code Annotated; Title 16, Chapter 9, Section 910].

ALIMONY/MAINTENANCE/SPOUSAL SUPPORT: Either spouse may be awarded alimony, during the divorce proceeding or after, if it is just or proper. There are no specific factors listed in the statute. However, martial fault may be considered. [District of Columbia Code Annotated; Title 16, Chapter 9, Sections 911, 912 and 913].

SPOUSE'S NAME: Upon request, the birth name or previous name may be restored. [District of Columbia Code Annotated; Title 16, Chapter 9, Section 915].

CHILD CUSTODY: Sole or joint custody may be granted during and after a divorce proceeding based on the best interests of the child, without regard to spouse's sex or sexual orientation, race, color, national origin, or political affiliations. The following factors shall also be considered: (1) the preference of the child, if the child is of sufficient age and capacity; (2) the wishes of the parents; (3) the child's adjustment to his or her home, school, and community; (4) the mental and physical health of all individuals involved; (5) the relationship of the child with parents, siblings, and other significant family members; (6) the willingness of the parents to share custody and make shared decisions; (7) the prior involvement of the parent in the child's life; (8) the geographical proximity of the parents; (9) the sincerity of the parent's request;

(10) the age and number of children; (11) the demands of parental employment; (12) the impact on any welfare benefits; (13) any evidence of spousal or child abuse; (14) financial capability of providing custody; and (15) the benefit to the parties. There is a rebuttable presumption that joint interest is in the best interests of the child; unless child abuse, neglect, parental kidnapping or other intrafamily violence has occurred. The court may order the parents to submit a written parenting plan for custody. [District of Columbia Code Annotated; Title 16, Chapter 9, Sections 911 and 914].

CHILD SUPPORT: Either parent may be ordered to pay reasonable child support during and after a divorce proceeding. Detailed specific child support guidelines are contained in Title 16, Chapter 9, Section 916.1 and 916.2. Variations from the official child support guidelines are allowed based on the following factors: (1) the child's needs are exceptional; (2) the non-custodial parent's income is substantially less than the custodial parent's income; (3) a property settlement between the parents provides resources for the child above the minimum support requirements; (4) the non-custodial parent provides support for other dependents and the guideline amounts would cause hardship; (5) the non-custodial parent needs a temporary reduction (of no longer than 12 months) in support payments to repay a substantial debt; (6) the custodial parent provides medical insurance coverage; (7) the custodial parent receives child support payments for other children and the custodial parents household income is substantially greater than that of the non-custodial parent; and (8) any other extraordinary factors. Child support may be ordered to be paid through the Clerk of the Superior Court. [District of Columbia Code Annotated; Title 16, Chapter 9, Sections 911 and 916].

PREMARITAL AGREEMENT: The agreement must be in writing and signed by both parties and is enforceable without consideration. An agreement is not enforceable if the party can prove that (1) the agreement was not voluntarily executed; (2) the agreement was unconscionable when executed and before the execution the party was not provided a fair and reasonable disclosure of the property or financial obligations of the other party, the party did not voluntarily waive any right to the disclosure of these obligations, and the party did not have adequate knowledge regarding these obligations. If a provision of the agreement modifies or eliminates spousal support and that causes the party to be eligible for public assistance, the court may require the party to provide support to the extent to avoid that eligibility. If the marriage is determined to be void, the agreement is enforceable only to the extent necessary to avoid an inequitable result, unless the agreement expressly provides that it shall be enforceable in the event the marriage is determined to be void. [District of Columbia Code Annotated, Title 16, Chapter 30, Sections 142, 146, and 147.

FLORIDA

RESIDENCY REQUIREMENTS AND WHERE TO FILE: One of the spouses must have been a resident for 6 months prior to filing for dissolution of marriage. The dissolution of marriage should be filed in either: (1) the county where the defendant resides; or (2) the county where the spouses last lived together prior to separating. [Florida Case Law and Florida Statutes Annotated; Chapter 61.021].

LEGAL GROUNDS FOR DISSOLUTION OF MARRIAGE: No-Fault: Irretrievable breakdown of the marriage. [Florida Statutes Annotated; Chapter 61.052].
    General: Mental incapacity for at least 3 years. [Florida Statutes Annotated; Chapter 61.052].

NAME OF COURT IN WHICH TO FILE FOR DISSOLUTION OF MARRIAGE: Circuit Court. "In the Circuit Court in and for the County of _____, Florida." [Florida Rules of Civil Procedure].

DOCUMENT CAPTION INFORMATION: Petition for Dissolution of Marriage. "In Re: the Marriage of: _____, Petitioner and _____, Respondent." Final document title: Final Judgement of Dissolution of Marriage. [Florida Statutes Annotated; Chapter 61.043].

LEGAL SEPARATION: A spouse may file for separate maintenance and child support. [Florida Statutes Annotated; Chapter 61.09].

SIMPLIFIED OR SPECIAL DISSOLUTION OF MARRIAGE PROCEDURES: Florida has a procedure for a Simplified Dissolution of Marriage. In order to qualify to use this procedure, the spouses must certify that: (1) there are no minor or dependent children of the spouses and the wife is not pregnant; (2) the spouses have made a satisfactory division of their property and have agreed as to payment of their joint obligations; (3) that one of the spouses has been a resident of Florida for 6 months immediately prior to filing for dissolution of marriage; (4) and that their marriage is irretrievably broken. The spouses must appear in court to testify as to these items and file a Certificate of a Corroborating Witness as to the residency requirement. Each must also attach a financial affidavit to the Simplified Dissolution Petition. Specific forms and an

41

instruction brochure are available from the Clerk of any Circuit Court. In addition, sample forms for various aspects of a standard dissolution of marriage are available in the Florida Family Law Rules of Procedure. Financial disclosures are now mandatory in Florida. [Florida Family Law Rules of Procedure; Rules 12.105, 12.285, and Family Law Forms 12.900+].

MEDIATION OR COUNSELING REQUIREMENTS: If there are minor children involved, or if one of the spouses denies that the marriage is irretrievably broken, the court may delay the proceedings for up to 3 months and order the spouses to seek counseling, may order the spouses to attempt reconciliation, or may order the spouses to attend mediation sessions. [Florida Statutes Annotated; Chapters 61.052 and 61.183].

PROPERTY DISTRIBUTION: Florida is an "equitable distribution" state. The spouse's non-marital property will be retained by each spouse. Non-marital property is all property acquired prior to the marriage, property acquired by gift or inheritance, and any property considered to be non-marital according to a written agreement between the spouses. The court is required to begin with the premise that all marital property should be equally divided. All of the spouse's marital property may be divided on an equitable basis, based on the following factors: (1) the contribution to the marriage by each spouse including the contribution of each spouse as homemaker; (2) the length of the marriage; (3) the age and health of the spouses; (4) the amount and sources of income of the spouses; (5) the estate, liabilities, and needs of each spouse and the opportunity of each for further acquisition of capital assets and income; (6) the standard of living established during the marriage; (7) the time necessary for a spouse to acquire sufficient education to enable the spouse to find appropriate employment; (8) any other factor necessary to do equity and justice between the spouses. Marital misconduct is not specified as a factor in any division of property. There are also specific rules which govern whether a party is entitled to setoffs or credits upon the sale of the marital home. Furthermore, any retirement plans will be distributed upon divorce. [Florida Statutes Annotated: Chapter 61.075, 61.076 and 61.077].

ALIMONY/MAINTENANCE/SPOUSAL SUPPORT: The court may grant rehabilitative or permanent alimony to either spouse in either lump-sum or periodic payments or both. Adultery is a factor in the award. Other factors which are considered are: (1) the time necessary to acquire sufficient education and training to enable the spouse to find appropriate employment, and that spouse's future earning capacity; (2) the standard of living established during the marriage; (3) the duration of the marriage; (4) the sources of income available to either party; (5) the contribution of each spouse to the marriage, including services rendered in homemaking, child care, education, and career building of the other spouse; (6) the age of the spouses; (7) the physical and emotional conditions of the spouses; each spouse's share of marital assets and liabilities; and (8) any other factor the court deems just and equitable. Alimony payments may be ordered to be paid through a state depository, but this is not required if there are no minor children. [Florida Statutes Annotated; Chapter 61.08].

SPOUSE'S NAME: There is no legal provision in Florida for restoration of a spouse's name upon divorce. However, there is a general statutory provision that allows for a person to change his or her name by petition filed with the court. [Florida Statutes Annotated; Chapter 68.07].

CHILD CUSTODY: Joint or sole custody may be granted. Joint custody is referred to as "shared parental responsibility." Both parents are given equal consideration in any award of custody. Custody is granted according to the best interests of the child, based on the following factors: (1) the moral character and prudence of the parents; (2) the capability and desire of each parent to meet the child's needs; (3) preference of the child, if the child is of sufficient age and capacity; (4) the love and affection existing between the child and each parent; (5) the length of time the child has lived in a stable, satisfactory environment and the desirability of maintaining continuity; (6) the desire and ability of each parent to allow an open and loving frequent relationship between the child and the other parent; (7) the child's adjustment to his or her home, school, and community; (8) the mental and physical health of the parents; (9) the material needs of the child; (10) the stability of the home environment likely to be offered by each parent; (11) any evidence of spouse abuse; and (12) any other relevant factors. No preference is to be given because of parent's sex. Custody and visitation may not be denied based on the fact that a parent or grandparent may be infected with human immunodeficiency virus. The court may order rotating custody if it is in the best interests of the child. There is a parenting course requirement. [Florida Statutes Annotated; Chapters 61.13, 61.21 and 61.121].

CHILD SUPPORT: The court may order either parent to pay child support during and after a dissolution of marriage proceeding in an equitable amount, based on the nature and circumstances of the case. There are specific child support guidelines set out in Florida Statutes Annotated; Chapter 61.30. In addition, there are specific factors for consideration upon which the child support guidelines may be adjusted: (1) extraordinary medical, psychological, educational, or dental expenses; (2) independent income of the child; (3) the custodial parent receiving both child support and spousal support; (4) seasonal variations in a parent's income or expenses; (5) the age of the child, taking into consideration the greater needs of older children; (6) any special needs of the family; (7) the terms of any shared parental arrangement; (8) the total assets of the parents and the child; (9) the impact of the IRS dependency exemption and waiver of that exemption; (10) when the application of the child support guidelines requires a person to pay another person more than

55% of his or her gross income for child support; and (11) any other adjustment which is needed to achieve an equitable result which may include but is not limited to a reasonable and necessary existing expense or debt. Health insurance for the child and life insurance covering the life of the parent ordered to pay support may be required by the court. Child support payments may be ordered to be paid through a state depository. [Florida Statutes Annotated; Chapters 61.13 and 61.30].

PREMARITAL AGREEMENTS: Florida has no specific statutes pertaining to premarital agreements.

GEORGIA

RESIDENCY REQUIREMENTS AND WHERE TO FILE: The spouse filing must have been a resident of Georgia for 6 months and file for divorce in the county of residence. However, a non-resident may file for divorce against a spouse who has been a resident of Georgia for 6 months. In such cases, the divorce must be filed for in the county in which the respondent resides. [Code of Georgia Annotated; 19-5-2].

LEGAL GROUNDS FOR DIVORCE: No-Fault: Irretrievable breakdown of the marriage. [Code of Georgia Annotated; 19-5-3].
General: (1) impotence; (2) adultery; (3) conviction of and imprisonment of over 2 years for an offense involving moral turpitude; (4) habitual intoxication and/or drug addiction; (5) confinement for incurable insanity; (6) separation caused by mental illness; (7) willful desertion for 1 year; (8) cruel and inhuman treatment which endangers the life of the spouse; (9) consent to marriage was obtained by fraud, duress, or force; (10) spouse lacked mental capacity to consent (including temporary incapacity resulting from drug or alcohol use); (11) the wife was pregnant by another at the time of the marriage unknown to the husband; and (12) incest. [Code of Georgia Annotated; 19-5-3].

NAME OF COURT IN WHICH TO FILE FOR DIVORCE: Superior Court. "In the Superior Court of _____ County, Georgia." [Georgia Civil Practice Act and Code of Georgia Annotated; 19-5-1].

DOCUMENT CAPTION INFORMATION: Petition for Divorce. "In Re: the Marriage of: _____, Petitioner and _____, Respondent." Final document title: Final Judgment and Decree of Divorce. A sample judgment and decree is available at the Code of Georgia Annotated; 19-5-12.

LEGAL SEPARATION: There are legal provisions in Georgia for separate maintenance. [Code of Georgia Annotated; 19-6-10].

SIMPLIFIED OR SPECIAL DIVORCE PROCEDURES: There are no legal provisions in Georgia for simplified divorce.

MEDIATION OR COUNSELING REQUIREMENTS: There are no legal provisions in Georgia for divorce mediation.

PROPERTY DISTRIBUTION: Georgia is an "equitable distribution" state. The courts will distribute the marital property, including any gifts and inheritances, equitably. There are no factors to be considered specified in the statute. [Code of Georgia Annotated; 19-5-13 and Georgia Case Law].

ALIMONY/MAINTENANCE/SPOUSAL SUPPORT: Permanent or temporary alimony may be awarded to either spouse, unless the separation was caused by that spouse's desertion or adultery. The following factors are to be considered: (1) the contribution of each spouse to the acquisition of the marital property, including the contribution of each spouse as homemaker, in child care, education and career building of the other spouse; (2) the duration of the marriage; (3) the financial resources of each spouse; (4) the age and physical and emotional condition of both spouses; (5) the value of each spouse's separate property; (6) the earning capacity of each spouse; (7) any fixed liabilities of either spouse; (8) the standard of living established during the marriage; (9) the time necessary for a spouse to acquire sufficient education to enable the spouse to find appropriate employment; (10) the needs of the party seeking alimony; (11) the ability of the other party to pay; (12) the conduct of each party towards the other; and (13) other relevant factors the court deems equitable and proper. All obligations for alimony terminate upon remarriage of the party to which the alimony was owed. Voluntary cohabitation of spouses when there has been a total divorce shall terminate alimony. [Code of Georgia Annotated; 19-6-5, 19-6-12].

SPOUSE'S NAME: If requested, a spouse's name may be restored. [Code of Georgia Annotated; 19-5-12 and 19-5-16].

CHILD CUSTODY: Joint or sole custody is granted, based upon the best interests of the child and a consideration of the following factors: (1) the wishes of the child (considering the child's age and maturity); (2) the safety of the child; and (3) any history of domestic abuse. There is a presumption against awarding joint custody in Georgia when there is a history of domestic abuse. [Code of Georgia Annotated; 19-9-1 to 19-9-64].

CHILD SUPPORT: Both parents are liable for the support of minor children. The court may award child support from either parent, based on their customary needs and the parents ability to pay. There are no specific factors for consideration set out in the statute. However, there are official child support guidelines set out in the statute that are to be followed in all cases in which the parents are not able to reach an agreement. In such cases there are factors which will be followed in special circumstances. The special circumstances include: (1) the age of the children; (2) a child's medical costs or extraordinary needs; (3) educational costs; (4) day care costs; (5) shared physical custody arrangements; (6) a parent's support obligations to another household; (7) hidden income of a parent; (8) the income of the parent with custody; (9) contributions of the parents; (10) extreme economic circumstances; (11) a parent's own extraordinary needs; (12) historic spending levels of the family; (13) the cost of health and accident insurance coverage for the child; (14) any extraordinary visitation travel expenses; (15) in kind income for the self-employed; (16) other support a party is providing or will be providing; (17) considerations of the economic cost of living factors; and (18) any other factor which the judge deems to be required by the ends of justice. [Code of Georgia Annotated; 19-6-14 and 19-6-15.]

PREMARITAL AGREEMENTS: Georgia has no specific statutes pertaining to premarital agreements.

HAWAII

RESIDENCY REQUIREMENTS AND WHERE TO FILE: The spouse filing for divorce must have been present in Hawaii for 3 months. However, a final divorce will not be granted unless one spouse has been a resident for 6 months. The divorce should be filed in either: (1) the judicial district where the plaintiff resides; or (2) the judicial district where the spouses last lived together. [Hawaii Revised Statutes; Title 580, Chapter 1].

LEGAL GROUNDS FOR DIVORCE: No-Fault: (1) irretrievable breakdown of the marriage; and (2) living separate and apart without cohabitation for 2 years and it would not be harsh or oppressive to the defendant spouse to grant the divorce. [Hawaii Revised Statutes; Title 580, Chapter 41].

General: Legal separation and there has been no reconciliation. [Hawaii Revised Statutes; Title 580, Chapter 41].

NAME OF COURT IN WHICH TO FILE FOR DIVORCE: Family Court. [Hawaii Revised Statutes, Title 580, Section 1].

DOCUMENT CAPTION INFORMATION: Complaint for Divorce. "In Re: the Marriage of: _____, Plaintiff and _____, Defendant." Final document title: Decree of Divorce.

LEGAL SEPARATION: The spouse filing for separation must have been a resident for 3 months. The grounds for legal separation are the same as the grounds for a divorce. [Hawaii Revised Statutes; Titles 580, Chapter 1, 580, Chapter 71].

SIMPLIFIED OR SPECIAL DIVORCE PROCEDURES: The "irretrievable breakdown of the marriage" may be shown by both spouses stating so in an affidavit or by one spouse stating so in an affidavit and the other spouse not denying it. The court, in such cases, may waive a hearing in uncontested divorces and grant the divorce based on the affidavit. [Hawaii Revised Statutes; Title 580, Section 42].

MEDIATION OR COUNSELING REQUIREMENTS: If one of the spouses denies that there has been an irretrievable breakdown of the marriage, the court may delay the proceedings for 60 days and advise the spouses to seek counseling. [Hawaii Revised Statutes; Title 580, Chapter 42].

PROPERTY DISTRIBUTION: Hawaii is an "equitable distribution" state. The court will distribute all of the spouse's property, including the community, joint, and separate property, in a just and equitable manner, based on the following factors: (1) the burdens imposed upon either spouse for the benefit of the children; (2) the position each spouse will be left in after the divorce; (3) the relative abilities of the spouses; (4) the respective merits of the spouses; and (5) all other circumstances. [Hawaii Revised Statutes; Title 580, Chapter 47].

ALIMONY/MAINTENANCE/SPOUSAL SUPPORT: The court may award either spouse maintenance, for either an indefinite period or a specific period to allow the receiving spouse to become self-supporting. Marital misconduct is not a factor to be considered. The factors to be considered are: (1) the standard of living established during the marriage; (2) the duration of the marriage; (3) the ability of the spouse from whom support is sought to meet his or her needs while meeting those of the spouse seeking support; (4) the ability of the spouse seeking maintenance to meet his or her needs independently; (5) the comparative financial resources of the spouses; (6) the needs and obligations of each spouse; (7) the age of the spouses; (8) the physical and emotional conditions of the spouses; (9) the usual occupation of the spouses during the marriage; (10) the vocational skills and employability of the spouse seeking support and maintenance; (11) the probable duration of the need of the spouse seeking support and maintenance; (12) any custodial and child support responsibilities; and (13) other factors which measure the financial condition in which the spouses will be left as a result of the divorce. [Hawaii Revised Statutes; Title 580, Chapter 47].

SPOUSE'S NAME: If requested, the wife may resume the use of her maiden name. [Hawaii Revised Statutes; Title 574, Chapter 5].

CHILD CUSTODY: Joint or sole child custody may be awarded to either or both of the parents based on the best interests of the child and upon the wishes of the child, if the child is of sufficient age and capacity to form an intelligent choice. Joint custody will be allowed if it can be arranged to assure the child of continuing contact with both parents. There are no other specific factors for consideration set out in the statute. [Hawaii Revised Statutes; Title 571, Chapter 46].

CHILD SUPPORT: The court may order either or both parents to provide child support in a just and equitable manner. Factors to be considered are: (1) the relative merits of the parties; (2) the relative abilities of the parties; (3) the condition of the parties after the divorce; (4) the burdens imposed on the parties for the benefit of the child; and (5) all other circumstances of the case. There are official Child Support Guidelines set out in the statute. [Hawaii Revised Statutes; Title 576D, Chapter 7, and Title 580, Chapter 47].

PREMARITAL AGREEMENTS: The premarital agreement must be in writing and signed by both parties and is enforceable without consideration. An agreement will not be enforceable if the party proves that the agreement was not executed voluntarily, the agreement was unconscionable when executed and before the agreement's execution, the party was not provided a fair and reasonable disclosure of the property or financial obligations of the other party and the party did not voluntarily waive any right to the disclosure of the property or financial obligations and did not have adequate knowledge of these obligations. If a provision modifies or terminates spousal support and that causes the spouse to be eligible for public assistance, the court may require the other party to provide support necessary to avoid eligibility for public assistance. If the marriage is determined to be void, the agreement is enforceable only to the extent necessary to avoid an inequitable result. [Hawaii Revised Statutes; Title 5720, Chapters 2, 6, and 7].

IDAHO

RESIDENCY REQUIREMENTS AND WHERE TO FILE: The spouse filing for divorce must have been a resident of Idaho for 6 full weeks immediately prior to filing for divorce. The divorce should be filed in: (1) the county where the defendant resides; or (2) if the defendant is not a resident of Idaho, the county where the plaintiff resides or designates in the complaint. [Idaho Code; Title 5, Chapter 404; and Title 32, Chapter 701].

LEGAL GROUNDS FOR DIVORCE: No-Fault: (1) irreconcilable differences; and (2) living separate and apart without cohabitation for a period of 5 years. [Idaho Code; Title 32, Chapters 603, and 610].

General: (1) adultery; (2) permanent insanity; (3) conviction of a felony; (4) willful desertion; (5) cruelty; (6) willful neglect; and (7) habitual intemperance (drunkenness). [Idaho Code; Title 32, Chapters 603].

NAME OF COURT IN WHICH TO FILE FOR DIVORCE: District Court. "In the District Court of the _____ Judicial District for the State of Idaho, In and For the County of _____."

DOCUMENT CAPTION INFORMATION: Complaint for Divorce. "In Re: the Marriage of: _____, Plaintiff and _____, Defendant." Final document title: Decree of Divorce.

LEGAL SEPARATION: There is no legal provision in Idaho for legal court-ordered separation. However, the spouses may live separate and apart. [Idaho Code; Title 32, Chapter 610].

SIMPLIFIED OR SPECIAL DIVORCE PROCEDURES: Divorces may be granted upon the default of the defendant. In addition, marital settlement agreements regarding property are specifically authorized. They must be in writing and notarized in the same manner as deeds. If the marital settlement agreement has any provisions which concern real estate, it must be recorded in the county recorder's office. [Idaho Code; Title 32, Chapters 917 and 918].

MEDIATION OR COUNSELING REQUIREMENTS: There is a mandatory 20-day delay in the granting of all divorces, unless there is an agreement by the

51

spouses. During this period, either spouse may request that there be a meeting held to determine if there is any practical chance for reconciliation. If there is determined to be a chance for reconciliation and there are minor children of the marriage, the court may delay the proceedings for up to 90 days for an attempt at reconciliation. [Idaho Code; Title 32, Chapter 716].

PROPERTY DISTRIBUTION: Idaho is a "community property" state. Each spouse's separate property consists of (1) all property acquired prior to the marriage; (2) property acquired by gift either before or during the marriage; and (3) property acquired by individual gift before or during the marriage. The court will divide all other property (the community property) of the spouses in a substantially equal manner, unless there are compelling reasons to provide otherwise. The court will consider the following factors: (1) marital misconduct, (2) length of the marriage; (3) age and health of spouses; (4) occupation of the spouses; (5) amount and sources of income of spouses; (6) vocational skills of spouses; (7) employability of spouses; (8) any premarital agreement; (9) present and potential earning capability of each spouse; (10) any retirement benefits, including social security, civil service, military and railroad retirement benefits; (11) the liabilities of the spouses; (12) the needs of the spouses; and (13) whether the property award is instead of or in addition to maintenance. [Idaho Code; Title 32, Chapters 712 and 903].

ALIMONY/MAINTENANCE/SPOUSAL SUPPORT: The court may award maintenance to a spouse, if that spouse (1) lacks sufficient property to provide for his or her reasonable needs; and (2) is unable to support his or herself through employment. The award of maintenance is based on the following factors: (1) time necessary to acquire sufficient education and training to enable the spouse to find appropriate employment, and that spouse's future earning capacity; (2) duration of the marriage; (3) ability of the spouse from whom support is sought to meet his or her needs while meeting those of the other spouse; (4) financial resources of the spouse seeking maintenance, including any marital property apportioned and such spouse's ability to meet his or her needs independently; (5) the tax consequences to each spouse; (6) the age and physical and emotional conditions of the spouse seeking maintenance; (7) the fault of either party. [Idaho Code; Title 32, Chapter 705].

SPOUSE'S NAME: There is no legal provision in Idaho for restoration of a spouse's name upon divorce. However, there is a general statutory provision that allows a person to apply for a name change by petition to the court. [Idaho Code; Title 7, Chapter 7-802].

CHILD CUSTODY: Joint or sole child custody may be awarded according to the best interests of the child, and based on the following factors: (1) the preference of the child; (2) the wishes of the parents; (3) the mental and physical health of all individuals involved; (4) the relationship of the child with parents, siblings, and other significant family members; (5) the child's adjustment to his or her home, school, and community; (6) a need to promote continuity and stability in the life of the child; and (7) domestic violence, whether or not in the presence of the child. Joint custody is allowed if it can be arranged to assure the child with frequent and continuing contact with both parents. Unless shown otherwise, it is presumed that joint custody is in the best interests of the child. If the child is residing with a grandparent, the court may recognize the grandparent as having the same standing as a parent. [Idaho Code; Title 32, Chapters 717 and 717B].

CHILD SUPPORT: The court may order either or both parents to provide child support until the child is 18, without regard to marital misconduct, and based upon the following factors: (1) the financial resources of the child; (2) the standard of living the child enjoyed during the marriage; (3) the physical and emotional conditions and educational needs of the child; (4) the financial resources, needs, and obligations of both the noncustodial and the custodial parent (normally, not including the parent's community property share of the financial resources or obligations with a new spouse); (5) the availability of reasonable medical insurance coverage for the child; (6) and the actual tax benefits achieved by the parent claiming the federal dependency exemption for income tax purposes. There are provisions in Idaho for child support payments to be paid to the clerk of the court unless otherwise ordered by the court. There are specific child support guidelines adopted by the Idaho Supreme Court which are presumed to be correct unless evidence is presented that shows that the award would be inappropriate or unjust. Finally, all child support orders issued in Idaho must contain provisions allowing enforcement of the order by income withholding if the payments become over 1 month late. [Idaho Code; Title 32, Chapters 706, 706A, and 1205].

PREMARITAL AGREEMENTS: The agreement must be in writing and signed by both parties and is enforceable without consideration. After marriage, the agreement may be amended or revoked by a written agreement signed by both parties and this amendment is enforceable without consideration. The agreement is not enforceable if proven that (1) the party did not execute the agreement voluntarily; (2) the agreement was unconscionable when executed in that the party was not provided a fair and reasonable disclosure of the property or financial obligations of the other party, did not voluntarily waive the right to the disclosure of this information and did not have adequate knowledge of these obligations. If an agreement term modifies or terminates spousal support causing the party to be eligible for public assistance, the court may require the party to pay spousal support. If the marriage is determined to be void, the agreement is enforceable only to the extent necessary to avoid an inequitable result. [Idaho Code; Title 32, Chapters 922, 924, 925, and 926].

ILLINOIS

RESIDENCY REQUIREMENTS AND WHERE TO FILE: The spouse filing for dissolution must have been a resident of Illinois for 90 days immediately prior to filing for dissolution of marriage. The dissolution of marriage may be filed in a county where either spouse resides. [750 Illinois Compiled Statutes; Chapter 5, Sections 104 and 401].

LEGAL GROUNDS FOR DISSOLUTION OF MARRIAGE: No-Fault: Irreconcilable differences has caused the irretrievable breakdown of the marriage and reconciliation has failed or further attempts at reconciliation are impractical and the spouses have been living separate and apart without cohabitation for 2 years. (If both spouses consent, the time period becomes 6 months). [750 Illinois Compiled Statutes; Chapter 5, Section 401].

General: (1) impotence; (2) adultery; (3) habitual drunkenness for 2 years and/or drug addiction; (4) conviction of a felony; (5) willful desertion for 1 year; (6) cruel and inhuman treatment; (7) attempted poisoning or otherwise endangering the life of the spouse; (8) infection of the other spouse with a communicable disease; and (9) bigamy. [750 Illinois Compiled Statutes; Chapter 5, Section 401].

NAME OF COURT IN WHICH TO FILE FOR DISSOLUTION OF MARRIAGE: Circuit Court. "In the Circuit Court of the _____ Judicial District, _____ County, Illinois." [Illinois Civil Practice Act].

DOCUMENT CAPTION INFORMATION: Petition for Dissolution of Marriage. "In Re: the Marriage of: _____, Petitioner and _____, Respondent." Final document title: Judgment for Dissolution of Marriage. [750 Illinois Compiled Statutes; Chapter 5, Section 105].

LEGAL SEPARATION: The residency requirement specified in the statute is that an action for legal separation must be brought where the Respondent resides or in the county where the parties last resided together as man and wife. Any person living separate and apart from his or her spouse, without fault, may obtain a legal separation with provisions for reasonable support and maintenance. [750 Illinois Compiled Statutes; Chapter 5, Section 402].

SIMPLIFIED OR SPECIAL DISSOLUTION OF MARRIAGE PROCEDURES: Marital settlement agreements are specifically allowed and encouraged [750 Illinois Compiled Statutes; Chapter 5, Section 502]. In addition, Illinois has an approved "Joint Simplified Dissolution" procedure and petition found in 750 Illinois Compiled Statutes; Chapter 5, Section 452. To use this simplified procedure, (1) the spouses must not have been married over 5 years, (2) the spouses must neither have had nor adopted any children, (3) the wife cannot now be pregnant by the husband; (4) Neither spouse can own any real estate; (5) Both spouses must certify that neither is dependent on the other for support (or must waive any type of alimony); (6) the market value of all marital property must be less than $5,000.00; (7) the combined gross annual income of both spouses must be less than $25,000.00; (8) that the residency requirements are met; (9) the parties have disclosed to each other all assets and tax returns for all years of marriage; and (10) the parties have executed a written agreement regarding all assets over $100.00 and allocated responsibility for debts and liabilities. Forms are available at any Office of the Clerk of a Circuit Court.

MEDIATION OR COUNSELING REQUIREMENTS: At the request of either spouse, or on the court's own initiative, the court may order a conciliation conference if it is felt that there is a prospect of reconciliation. [750 Illinois Compiled Statutes; Chapter 5, Section 404].

PROPERTY DISTRIBUTION: Illinois is an "equitable distribution" state. Each spouse retains the non-marital (separate) property that he or she owned prior to the marriage and any property acquired by gift or inheritance during the marriage. The court will distribute all other marital property, without regard to fault, considering the following factors: (1) the contribution of each spouse to the acquisition or dissipation of the marital property, including the contribution of each spouse as homemaker or to the family unit; (2) the value of each spouse's non-marital property; (3) the economic circumstances of each spouse at the time the division of property is to become effective, including the desirability of awarding the family home to the spouse having custody of the children; (4) the length of the marriage; (5) the age and health of the spouses; (6) the occupation of the spouses; (7) the amount and sources of income of the spouses; (8) the vocational skills of the spouses; (9) the employability of the spouses; (10) the estate, liabilities, and needs of each spouse and the opportunity of each for further acquisition of capital assets and income; (11) the federal income tax consequences of the court's division of the property; (12) any premarital agreement; (13) liabilities of the spouses; (14) whether the property award is instead of or in addition to maintenance; and (15) any custodial provisions for the children. [750 Illinois Compiled Statutes; Chapter 5, Section 503].

ALIMONY/MAINTENANCE/SPOUSAL SUPPORT: The court may award maintenance to either spouse for a period of time it considers just, if the court concludes that the spouse seeking maintenance is (1) unable to support him or herself through appropriate employment or is the custodian of a child whose condition or circumstances make it appropriate that he or she not be required to seek employment outside the home; and (2) lacks sufficient resources, including any marital property, to provide for his or her reasonable needs; or (3) is otherwise without sufficient income. Marital fault is not a factor. The factors to be considered are: (1) the time necessary to acquire sufficient education and training to enable the spouse to find appropriate employment; (2) the standard of living established during the marriage; (3) the duration of the marriage; (4) the age of the spouses; (5) the physical and emotional conditions of the spouses (6) the ability of the spouse from whom support is sought to meet his or her needs while meeting those of the spouse seeking support; (7) the financial resources of the spouse seeking maintenance, including marital property apportioned to such spouse and such spouse's ability to meet his or her needs independently; (8) the tax consequences to each spouse; and (9) any custodial and child support responsibilities. [750 Illinois Compiled Statutes; Chapter 5, Section 504].

SPOUSE'S NAME: Upon the wife's request, her maiden or former name will be restored. [750 Illinois Compiled Statutes; Chapter 5, Section 413]

CHILD CUSTODY: Sole or joint custody may be awarded, based upon the best interests of the child and upon the following factors: (1) preference of the child; (2) the wishes of the parents; (3) the child's adjustment to his or her home, school, and community; (4) the mental and physical health of all individuals involved; (5) the relationship of the child with parents, siblings, and other significant family members; (6) any history of violence by a parent, whether directed against the child or against another person; and (7) the willingness and ability of each parent to encourage a close and continuing relationship between the child and the other parent. Marital misconduct that does not directly affect the parent's relationship with the child is not to be considered. There is a presumption that the maximum involvement and cooperation of the parent's is in the best interests of the child. However, this is not to be considered a presumption that joint custody is always in the best interests of the child.

For an award of joint custody, the court will also consider the following factors: (1) the ability of the parents to cooperate effectively and consistently; (2) the residential circumstances of each parent; and (3) any other relevant factor. The parents shall prepare a Joint Parenting Agreement (which may be part of a Marital Settlement Agreement) which will specify each parent's rights and responsibilities for (1) personal care of the child; (2) major educational, health care, and religious training decisions. The Joint Parenting Agreement will also include provisions specifying mediation of problems and periodic review of the terms of the Agreement. Joint parenting does not necessarily mean equal parenting time. The physical residence for the child is to be determined by either (1) an agreement between the parents; or (2) a court order based on the factors listed above. [750 Illinois Compiled Statutes; Chapter 5, Sections 602, 602.1, and 610].

CHILD SUPPORT: Either or both parents may be ordered to pay reasonable and necessary child support, without regard to marital fault or misconduct. The following factors are considered: (1) the financial resources of the child; (2) the standard of living the child would have enjoyed if the marriage had not been dissolved; (3) the physical and emotional conditions and educational needs of the child; and (4) the financial resources, needs, and obligations of both the noncustodial and the custodial parent. The court may require support to include payment of a child's health insurance premium. Support payments may be ordered to be paid directly to the clerk of the court. There are official guidelines for the amount of support contained in the statute. Illinois Driver's licenses may be revoked if child support obligations are not met. [625 Illinois Compiled Statutes; Chapter 5, Sections 7-703; 750 Illinois Compiled Statutes; Chapter 5, Sections 505, 505.2 and 507].

PREMARITAL AGREEMENTS: A premarital agreement must be in writing and signed by both parties and is enforceable without consideration. The agreement is not enforceable if the party proves that (1) the party did not execute the agreement voluntarily; (2) the agreement was executed unconscionably in that the party was not provided a fair and reasonable disclosure of the property and financial obligations of the other party and did not waive the right to the disclosure of this information and did not have adequate knowledge of these obligations. If a provision of the agreement modifies or terminates spousal support which causes hardship, the court may require the party to provide support. If the marriage is determined to be void, the agreement is enforceable only to the extent necessary to avoid an inequitable result. [750 Illinois Compiled Statutes; Chapter 10, Sections 3, 7, and 8].

INDIANA

RESIDENCY REQUIREMENTS AND WHERE TO FILE: One of the spouses must have been a resident of the state for 6 months and the county in which the petition is filed for 3 months immediately prior to filing for dissolution of marriage. [Annotated Indiana Code; 31-1-11.5-6].

LEGAL GROUNDS FOR DISSOLUTION OF MARRIAGE: No-Fault: Irretrievable breakdown of the marriage. [Annotated Indiana Code; 31-1-11.5-3].

General: (1) impotence at time of marriage; (2) conviction of a felony subsequent to the marriage; and (3) incurable mental illness for 2 years. [Annotated Indiana Code; 31-1-11.5.3].

NAME OF COURT IN WHICH TO FILE FOR DISSOLUTION OF MARRIAGE: Superior Court, Circuit Court, or Domestic Relations Court. "_____ Court of _____ County, Indiana." [Annotated Indiana Code; 31-1-23-10].

DOCUMENT CAPTION INFORMATION: Petition for Dissolution of Marriage. "In Re: the Marriage of: _____, Petitioner and _____, Respondent." Final document title: Final Dissolution of Marriage Decree.

LEGAL SEPARATION: One of the spouses must have been a resident of the state for 6 months and the county for 3 months immediately prior to filing for legal separation. A legal separation may be granted on the grounds that it is currently intolerable for the spouses to live together. [Annotated Indiana Code; 31-1-11.5-3 and 11.5-5.6].

SIMPLIFIED OR SPECIAL DISSOLUTION OF MARRIAGE PROCEDURES: The court may enter a summary dissolution decree without holding a court hearing in all cases in which the following requirements have been met: (1) 60 days have elapsed since the filing of a petition for dissolution; (2) the petition was verified and signed by both spouses; (3) the petition contained a written waiver of a final hearing; (4) the petition contained either (a) a statement that there are no contested issues, or (b) that the spouses have made a written agreement in settlement of any contested issues. If there are some remaining contested issues, the court may hold a final hearing on those remaining contested issues. In addition, marital settlement agreements are specifically authorized in Indiana. [Annotated Indiana Code; 31-1-11.5-8 and 11.5-10].

MEDIATION OR COUNSELING REQUIREMENTS: Upon the request of either spouse or if the court believes that there is a reasonable possibility of reconciliation, the dissolution of marriage proceedings may be delayed for up to 45 days and the spouses may be ordered to seek counseling. [Annotated Indiana Code; 31-1-11.5-8].

PROPERTY DISTRIBUTION: Indiana is an "equitable distribution" state. The court will divide all of the spouse's property in a just manner, whether jointly or separately owned and whether acquired before or after the marriage, including any gifts or inheritances. There is a presumption that an equal division is just and reasonable. Marital fault is not a factor. The following factors are considered: (1) the contribution of each spouse to the acquisition of the marital property, regardless whether the contribution was income-producing; (2) the economic circumstances of each spouse at the time the division of property is to become effective, including the desirability of awarding the family residence to the spouse having custody of the children; (3) the actual earnings and the present and potential earning capability of each spouse; (4) the extent to which the property was acquired by each spouse prior to marriage or through gift or inheritance; (5) the conduct of the spouses during the marriage as it relates to the disposition of their property; and (6) tax consequences of property disposition. If there is insufficient marital property, the court may award money to either spouse as reimbursement for the financial contribution by one spouse toward the higher education of the other. [Annotated Indiana Code; 31-1-11.5-11.1].

ALIMONY/MAINTENANCE/SPOUSAL SUPPORT: Maintenance will be awarded to a spouse who: (1) is physically or mentally incapacitated to the extent that they are unable to support themselves; or (2) lacks sufficient property to provide support for his or herself and any incapacitated child and must forgo employment to care for the physically or mentally incapacitated child. Marital fault is not a factor. In addition, rehabilitative maintenance may be granted to a spouse for up to 3 years, based on the following factors: (1) the time and expense necessary to acquire sufficient education and training to enable the spouse to find appropriate employment; (2) the educational level of each spouse at the time of the marriage and at the time the action is commenced; (3) whether an interruption in the education, training, or employment of a spouse who is seeking maintenance occurred during the marriage as a result of homemaking or child care responsibilities, or both; (4) the earning capacity of each spouse, including educational background, training, employment skills, work experience, and length of presence or absence from the job market. [Annotated Indiana Code; 31-1-11.5-11].

SPOUSE'S NAME: Upon request, the wife's former name may be restored. [Annotated Indiana Code; 31-1-11.5-18].

CHILD CUSTODY: Joint or sole custody is granted based on the best interests of the child, and based upon the following factors: (1) the age and sex of the child; (2) the preference of the child; (3) the wishes of the parents; (4) the child's adjustment to his or her home, school, and community; (5) the mental and physical health of all individuals involved; and (6) the relationship of the child with parents, siblings, and other significant family members.

Joint custody may be awarded if it is in the best interest of the child and based upon the following factors: (1) the physical proximity of the parents to each other as this relates to the practical considerations of where the child will reside; (2) the fitness and suitability of the parents; (3) the nature of the physical and emotional environment in the home of each of the persons awarded joint custody; (4) the willingness and ability of the persons awarded joint custody to communicate and cooperate in advancing the child's welfare; (5) the wishes of the child; and (6) whether the child has established a close and beneficial relationship with both of the persons awarded joint custody. [Annotated Indiana Code; 31-1-11.5-21].

CHILD SUPPORT: Either parent may be ordered to pay reasonable child support, without regard to marital fault, based on the following factors: (1) the standard of living the child would have enjoyed if the marriage had not been dissolved; (2) the physical and emotional conditions and educational needs of the child; and (3) the financial resources, needs, and obligations of both the noncustodial and the custodial parent. Support may be ordered to include medical, hospital, dental and educational support. Support payments may be required to be paid through the clerk of the court. Specific Indiana Child Support Guidelines are contained in the Appendix to Title 31, Article 1, Chapter 11.5-12 of the Annotated Indiana Code. These guidelines, however, are not mandatory. [Annotated Indiana Code; 31-1-11.5-12].

PREMARITAL AGREEMENTS: The agreement must be in writing and signed by both parties and is enforceable without consideration. After marriage, the agreement may be amended or revoked only by a written agreement signed by the parties and the amendment is enforceable without consideration. The agreement is not enforceable if a party proves that (1) the agreement was not executed voluntarily; (2) the agreement was unconscionable when executed. If the agreement modifies or terminates spousal support and causes hardship, the court may require the party to provide spousal support. If the marriage is determined to be void, the agreement is enforceable only to the extent necessary to avoid an inequitable result. [Annotated Indiana Code; Title 31, Chapters 11-3-4, 11-3-7, 11-3-8 and 11-3-9].

IOWA

RESIDENCY REQUIREMENTS AND WHERE TO FILE: If the defendant spouse is a resident of Iowa and was personally served the dissolution of marriage papers, there is no residency requirement for the spouse filing the dissolution of marriage. Otherwise, there is a 1 year residency requirement. In addition, there is a 90-day waiting period prior to the dissolution of marriage becoming final. The dissolution of marriage may be filed in a county where either spouse resides. [Iowa Code Annotated; Sections 598.2, 598.6, and 598.19].

LEGAL GROUNDS FOR DISSOLUTION OF MARRIAGE: No-Fault: Breakdown of the marriage relationship to the extent that the legitimate objects of matrimony have been destroyed and there remains no reasonable likelihood that the marriage can be preserved. [Iowa Code Annotated; Sections 598.5 and 598.17].

General: The only grounds for dissolution of marriage in Iowa are that there has been a breakdown of the marriage relationship to the extent that the legitimate objects of matrimony have been destroyed and there remains no reasonable likelihood that the marriage can be preserved. [Iowa Code Annotated; Sections 598.5 and 598.17].

NAME OF COURT IN WHICH TO FILE FOR DISSOLUTION OF MARRIAGE: District Court. "In the District Court for the County of _____, Iowa." [Iowa Code Annotated; Section 598.4].

DOCUMENT CAPTION INFORMATION: Petition for Dissolution of Marriage. "In Re: the Marriage of: _____, Petitioner and _____, Respondent." Final document title: Decree of Dissolution of Marriage.

LEGAL SEPARATION: If the defendant spouse is a resident of Iowa and was personally served legal papers, there is no residency requirement for the spouse filing the legal separation. Otherwise, there is a one-year residency requirement. The grounds for legal separation in Iowa are that there has been a breakdown of the marriage relationship to the extent that the legitimate objects of matrimony have been destroyed and there remains no reasonable likelihood that the marriage can be preserved. [Iowa Code Annotated; Sections 598.5, 598.6, 598.17, and 598.28].

SIMPLIFIED OR SPECIAL DISSOLUTION OF MARRIAGE PROCEDURES: There are no legal provisions in Iowa for simplified dissolution of marriage. However, sample petition captions and contents are contained in Iowa Code Annotated; Sections 598.4 and 598.5. In addition, both spouses are required to file Financial Affidavits on official forms which are available from the clerk of every district court. [Iowa Code Annotated; Sections 598.13, 598.4, and 598.5].

MEDIATION OR COUNSELING REQUIREMENTS: If either spouse requests, or on the court's own initiative, the spouses may be ordered to participate in conciliation procedures for a period of 60 days. A course on children's needs is required for all parents when custody is at issue. [Iowa Code Annotated; Section 598.16 and 598.19A].

PROPERTY DISTRIBUTION: Iowa is an "equitable distribution" state. The court will divide all of the spouse's property whether it was acquired before or after the marriage, except any gifts and inheritances received prior to or during the marriage. A portion of the property may be set aside in a fund for the support, maintenance, and education of any minor children. The following factors are considered in any division of property: (1) the contribution of each spouse to the acquisition of the marital property, including the contribution of each spouse as homemaker or in child care; (2) any property brought to the marriage by each party; (3) the contribution by one party to the education, training, or increased earning capacity of the other; (4) the length of the marriage; (5) the age and physical and emotional health of the spouses; (6) the federal income tax consequences of the court's division of the property; (7) the time and expense necessary for a spouse to acquire sufficient education to enable the spouse to find appropriate employment; (8) any premarital or marital settlement agreement; (9) the present and potential earning capability of each spouse, including educational background, training, employment skills, work experience, and length of absence from the job market; (10) whether the property award is instead of or in addition to alimony and the amount and duration of any such alimony award; (11) the total economic circumstances of the spouses, including any pension benefits; (12) the desirability of awarding the family home to the spouse with custody of any children; (13) any custodial provisions for the children; (14) the amount and duration of any maintenance payments; and (15) any other factors the court considers relevant. [Iowa Code Annotated; Section 598.21].

ALIMONY/MAINTENANCE/SPOUSAL SUPPORT: Maintenance may be granted to either spouse for a limited or indefinite time, based on the following factors: (1) the time necessary to acquire sufficient education and training to enable the spouse to find appropriate employment and become self-supporting; (2) the standard of living established during the marriage; (3) the duration of the marriage; (4) the financial resources of the spouse seeking alimony, including marital property apportioned to such spouse and such spouse's ability to meet his or her needs independently; (5) the tax consequences to each spouse; (6) the age of the spouses; (7) the physical and emotional conditions of the spouses; (8) the work experience and length of absence from the job market of the spouse seeking alimony; (9) the vocational skills and employability of the spouse seeking support and alimony; (10) custodial and child support responsibilities; (11) the educational level of each spouse at the time of the marriage and at the time the action for support is commenced; (12) any premarital or other agreements; (13) the earning capacity of the spouse seeking maintenance, including the educational background, employment skills, and work experience; and (14) any other factor the court deems just and equitable. Marital misconduct is not a factor. Maintenance payments may be ordered to be paid through the court. [Iowa Code Annotated; Sections 598.21, 598.22, and 598.32].

SPOUSE'S NAME: Upon dissolution of marriage, either spouse may request to change his or her name to a former or maiden name. [Iowa Code Annotated; Section 598.37].

CHILD CUSTODY: Joint or sole custody may be awarded in the best interests of the child and in a manner which will encourage the parents to share the rights and responsibilities of raising the child. Joint custody may be awarded if either parent requests and if it is in the best interests of the child and based on the following factors: (1) the ability of the parents to cooperate and make decisions jointly; (2) the ability of the parents to encourage the sharing of love, affection, and contact between the child and the other parent; (3) the physical proximity of the parents to each other as this relates to the practical considerations of where the child will reside; (4) the fitness and suitability of the parents; (5) the reasonable preference of the child, if the court deems the child to be of sufficient intelligence, understanding, and experience to express a preference; (6) whether both parents have actively cared for the child before and since the separation; (7) whether the psychological and emotional needs and development of the child will suffer because of lack of contact with both parents; (8) whether the safety of the child will be jeopardized by an award of joint custody or unsupervised visitation; and (9) whether one or both parents agree to, or are opposed to, joint custody. However, the court may grant joint custody even when both parents do not agree to joint custody. [Iowa Code Annotated; Section 598.41].

CHILD SUPPORT: Either or both parents may be ordered to pay a reasonable and necessary amount of child support, based on a consideration of the following factors: (1) the child's need for close contact with both parents; (2) the recognition of joint parental responsibilities for the welfare of the child; and (3) consideration of each case's individual facts. Child support payments may be ordered to be paid directly to the court. The amount of child support determined by use of the Guideline Charts is presumed to be correct, but may be adjusted for fairness or special needs of the child. [Iowa Code Annotated; Section 598.21].

PREMARITAL AGREEMENTS: The agreement must be in writing and signed by both parties and is enforceable without consideration. The agreement can be revoked by a written agreement signed by both parties. To revoke without consent of the other spouse, must prove (1) the agreement was not voluntarily executed; (2) the agreement was unconscionable when executed; (3) before the execution of the agreement the person was not provided with a fair and reasonable disclosure of the property or financial obligations of the other spouse and person did not have adequate knowledge of these obligations. If the marriage is determined to be void, the agreement is enforceable only to the extent necessary to avoid an inequitable result. [Iowa Code Annotated; Sections 596.4, 596.7, 596.10].

KANSAS

RESIDENCY REQUIREMENTS AND WHERE TO FILE: Either spouse must have been a resident of Kansas for 60 days immediately before filing for divorce. The divorce may be filed for in a county where either spouse resides. [Kansas Statutes Annotated; Chapter 60, Article 6, Subjects 607 Article 16, Subject 1603].

LEGAL GROUNDS FOR DIVORCE: No-Fault: Incompatibility. [Kansas Statutes Annotated; Chapter 60, Article 16, Subject 1601].
General: (1) failure to perform a material marital duty or obligation; and (2) incompatibility due to mental illness. [Kansas Statutes Annotated; Chapter 60, Article 16, Subject 1601].

NAME OF COURT IN WHICH TO FILE FOR DIVORCE: District Court. "In the District Court in and for the County of _____, Kansas." [Kansas Statutes Annotated; Chapter 60, Article 16, Subject 1601].

DOCUMENT CAPTION INFORMATION: Petition for Divorce. "In the Matter of the Marriage of _____, Petitioner and _____, Respondent." Final document title: Decree of Divorce. [Kansas Statutes Annotated; Chapter 60, Article 16, Subject 1604].

LEGAL SEPARATION: Either spouse must have been a resident of Kansas for 60 days immediately before filing for legal separation. The grounds for legal separation are: (1) incompatibility; (2) failure to perform a marital duty or obligation; and (3) incompatibility due to mental illness. [Kansas Statutes Annotated; Chapter 60, Article 16, Subjects 1601 and 1603].

SIMPLIFIED OR SPECIAL DIVORCE PROCEDURES: Only one spouse need testify as to the facts in the divorce. In addition, marital settlement agreements are specifically authorized. Also child custody and child residency agreements are specifically authorized and are presumed to be in the best interests of the child. [Kansas Statutes Annotated; Chapter 60, Article 16, Subjects 1609 and 1610].

MEDIATION OR COUNSELING REQUIREMENTS: On either spouse's request, or on its own initiative, the court may require that the spouses seek marriage counseling if marriage counseling services are available in the judicial district where the divorce is sought. Unless in emergency situations, there is a mandatory 60-day delay from the time the petition is filed until a final Decree of Divorce may be granted. [Kansas Statutes Annotated; Chapter 60, Article 16, Subjects 1608 and 1617].

PROPERTY DISTRIBUTION: Kansas is an "equitable distribution" state. The court may divide all of the spouse's property, including: (1) any gifts and inheritances, (2) any property owned before the marriage, (3) any property acquired in a spouse's own right during the marriage, and (4) any property acquired by the spouse's joint efforts. Property distribution may include actual division of the property, an award of all or part of the property to one spouse with a just and reasonable payment to the other, or a sale of the property and a division of the proceeds. The court considers the following factors: (1) the length of the marriage; (2) the age and health of the spouses; (3) how and by whom the property was acquired; (4) the conduct of the spouses during the marriage as it relates to the disposition of their property; (5) the present and future earning capacity of the spouses; (6) family ties and obligations; (7) any dissipation of assets by a spouse; (8) the tax consequences of property distribution; (9) any other factor necessary to do equity and justice between the spouses; (10) the property owned by the parties; and (11) the allowance of maintenance or not. [Kansas Statutes Annotated; Chapter 60, Article 16, Subject 1610].

ALIMONY/MAINTENANCE/SPOUSAL SUPPORT: Either spouse may be awarded maintenance for a period of up to 121 months. After 121 months, the recipient may apply for an extension of one more 121-month period. The amount awarded is whatever is judged to be fair, just, and equitable. There are no specific statutory factors for consideration. Payments are to be made through the clerk of the court or through the court trustee. [Kansas Statutes Annotated; Chapter 60, Article 16, Subject 1610].

SPOUSE'S NAME: Upon a spouse's request, a wife's maiden name will be restored. [Kansas Statutes Annotated; Chapter 60, Article 16, Subject 1610].

CHILD CUSTODY: If the parents have entered into a written agreement regarding child custody, the court will approve it if it is in the best interests of the child. Where there is no agreement, the court may award joint or sole custody based on the best interests of the child and upon the following factors: (1) the length of time and circumstances under which the child may have been under the care of someone other than a parent; (2) preference of the child; (3) the wishes of the parents; (4) the child's adjustment to his or her home, school, and community; (5) the relationship of the child with parents, siblings, and other significant family members; (6) the willingness of each parent to respect and appreciate the bond between the child and the other parent; and (7) any evidence of spousal abuse. There is to be no preference given based on the sex of the parent, regardless of the age of the child. Joint custody may be awarded if the court finds both parents suitable. The court may order that a joint custody plan be submitted to the court by the parents. [Kansas Statutes Annotated; Chapter 60, Article 16, Subject 1610].

CHILD SUPPORT: Either or both parents may be ordered to pay child support, without regard to any marital misconduct, based on the following factors: (1) the financial resources of the child; (2) the physical and emotional conditions and educational needs of the child; and (3) the financial resources, needs, and obligations of both the noncustodial and the custodial parent. Child support payments are to be paid through the clerk of the court or through the court trustee, unless the court orders otherwise. There are specific Supreme Court Child Support Guidelines contained in Kansas Statutes Annotated Chapter 20, Subject 165. [Kansas Statutes Annotated; Chapter 20, Subject 165 and Chapter 60, Article 16, Subject 1610].

PREMARITAL AGREEMENTS: The agreement shall be in writing and signed by both parties and is enforceable without consideration. After marriage, the agreement may be amended or revoked only by a written agreement signed by the parties and this amendment is enforceable without consideration. The agreement is not enforceable if the party proves (1) the agreement was not voluntarily executed; (2) the agreement was unconscionable when executed because the party was not provided a fair and reasonable disclosure of the property or financial obligations of the other party, the party did not voluntarily waive the right to the disclosure of this information, the party did not have adequate knowledge of these obligations. If a provision of the agreement modifies or terminates spousal support causing the party to be eligible for public assistance, the court may require spousal support to be paid to the party. If the marriage is determined to be void, the agreement is enforceable only to the extent necessary to avoid an inequitable result. [Kansas Statutes Annotated; Chapter 23, Article 8, Subjects 803, 806, 807, and 808].

KENTUCKY

RESIDENCY REQUIREMENTS AND WHERE TO FILE: Either spouse must have been a resident (or a member of the armed services stationed in Kentucky) for 180 days prior to filing. The dissolution of marriage must be filed in a county where either spouse usually resides. [Kentucky Revised Statutes; Title 35, Chapters 403.140 and 452.470].

LEGAL GROUNDS FOR DISSOLUTION OF MARRIAGE: No-Fault: Irretrievable breakdown of the marriage. A final dissolution of marriage will not be granted until the spouses have lived apart for 60 days. ("Living apart" includes living in the same house but not sharing sex). [Kentucky Revised Statutes; Title 35, Chapter 403.170].

General: Irretrievable breakdown of the marriage is the only grounds for dissolution of marriage in Kentucky. [Kentucky Revised Statutes; Title 35, Chapter 403.140].

NAME OF COURT IN WHICH TO FILE FOR DISSOLUTION OF MARRIAGE: Circuit Court. "_____ Circuit Court, Kentucky." [Kentucky Rules of Civil Procedure].

DOCUMENT CAPTION INFORMATION: Petition for Dissolution of Marriage. "In Re: the Marriage of: _____, Petitioner and _____, Respondent." Final document title: Decree of Dissolution of Marriage.

LEGAL SEPARATION: Irretrievable breakdown of the marriage is the only grounds for legal separation (or divorce from bed and board) in Kentucky. The spouse filing for legal separation must have been a resident (or a member of the armed services stationed in Kentucky) for 180 days prior to filing. [Kentucky Revised Statutes; Title 35, Chapters 403.050 and 403.140].

SIMPLIFIED OR SPECIAL DISSOLUTION OF MARRIAGE PROCEDURES: Marital settlement agreements and separation agreements are specifically authorized. The terms of the separation agreement are binding on the court unless if finds it unconscionable. [Kentucky Revised Statutes; Title 35, Chapter 403.180]

MEDIATION OR COUNSELING REQUIREMENTS: If one spouse disagrees that the marriage is irretrievably broken, the court may delay the dissolution of marriage proceeding for 60 days and suggest the spouses seek counseling. In addition, at a spouse's request or on the courts own initiative, a concilia-tion conference may be ordered by the court. [Kentucky Revised Statutes; Title 35, Chapter 403.170].

PROPERTY DISTRIBUTION: Kentucky is an "equitable distribution" state. The spouses are allowed to keep their separate property (property acquired before the marriage and any gifts or inheritances). All other property (their marital property) is divided, without regard to any marital misconduct, in just pro-portions, based on the following factors: (1) the contribution of each spouse to the acquisition of the marital property, including the contribution of each spouse as homemaker; (2) the value of each spouse's separate property; (3) the economic circumstances of each spouse at the time the division of prop-erty is to become effective, including the desirability of awarding the family home to the spouse awarded custody of any children; and (4) the length of the marriage. [Kentucky Revised Statutes; Title 35, Chapter 403.190].

ALIMONY/MAINTENANCE/SPOUSAL SUPPORT: Either spouse may be awarded maintenance if: (1) that spouse lacks the property to provide for his or her own needs; and (2) that spouse is unable to find appropriate employment, or is unable to work because of obligations to care for children or others in his or her custody. Marital fault is not a factor to be considered. The award is then based on the following factors: (1) the time necessary to acquire suffi-cient education and training to enable the spouse to find appropriate employ-ment, and that spouse's future earning capacity; (2) the standard of living established during the marriage; (3) the duration of the marriage; (4) the abil-ity of the spouse from whom support is sought to meet his or her needs while meeting those of the spouse seeking support; (5) the financial resources of the spouse seeking maintenance, including marital property apportioned to such spouse and such spouse's ability to meet his or her needs independently and any share of a child support award intended for the custodian; and (6) the age, physical and emotional conditions of the spouse seeking maintenance. [Ken-tucky Revised Statutes; Title 35, Chapter 403.200].

SPOUSE'S NAME: If there are no children, and at the wife's request, the wife's maiden name may be restored. [Kentucky Revised Statutes; Title 35, Chapter 403.230].

CHILD CUSTODY: The court may award sole or joint custody, giving equal consideration to either spouse. Custody is awarded based on the best interests of the child and on the following factors: (1) preference of the child; (2) the wishes of the parents; (3) the child's adjustment to his or her home, school, and community; (4) the mental and physical health of all individuals involved;

(5) the relationship of the child with parents, siblings, and other significant family members; (6) information, records and evidence of domestic abuse. Any conduct of a parent which does not affect the relationship with the child is not to be considered. Abandonment of the family home by a parent is not to be considered if the parent fled due to physical harm or threats of physical harm by the other spouse. [Kentucky Revised Statutes; Title 35, Chapter 403.270].

CHILD SUPPORT: Either or both parents may be ordered to provide a reasonable amount of child support, without regard to any marital misconduct, and based on the following factors: (1) the financial resources of the child; (2) the standard of living the child would have enjoyed if the marriage had not been dissolved; (3) the physical and emotional conditions and educational needs of the child; and (4) the financial resources, needs, and obligations of both the noncustodial and the custodial parent. Kentucky has adopted official Child Support Guidelines which are contained in the statute. These guidelines are presumed to be correct, but may be adjusted based on the following considerations: (1) a child's extraordinary medical or dental needs; (2) a child's extraordinary educational, job training, or special needs; (3) either parent's extraordinary needs, such as medical expenses; (4) the independent financial resources of the child; (5) the combined parental income in excess of the Kentucky child support guidelines amounts; (6) an agreement between the parents on child support, provided that no public assistance is being provided; and (7) any other extraordinary circumstance. In addition, the court may order a parent to provide health care insurance coverage for the child. [Kentucky Revised Statutes; Title 35, Chapters 403.211, and 403.212].

PREMARITAL AGREEMENTS: Kentucky has no specific statutes pertaining to premarital agreements.

LOUISIANA

RESIDENCY REQUIREMENTS AND WHERE TO FILE: A divorce can be brought where either party is domiciled or in the parish of the last matrimonial domicile. [Louisiana Code of Civil Procedure, Article 9; Chapter 308].

LEGAL GROUNDS FOR DIVORCE: No-Fault: That a spouse desires a divorce is grounds for divorce in Louisiana. There are no requirements to show marital breakdown, fault, living separate and apart, or any other basis for a divorce. After the filing of the petition, the divorce will be granted after a period of 180 days has elapsed from the filing date and if the spouses have lived separate and apart since the filing of the divorce petition. Reconciliation is essentially the only defense to a divorce sought on these grounds. [Louisiana Civil Code Annotated, Title V, Article 102, 104].

General: (1) That the spouses have been living separate and apart for a period of 6 months or more on the date of filing the petition; (2) that the other spouse has committed adultery; and (3) that the other spouse has committed a felony and has been sentenced to death or imprisonment with hard labor. [Louisiana Civil Code Annotated, Title V, Article 103].

NAME OF COURT IN WHICH TO FILE FOR DIVORCE: District Court. "_____ Judicial District Court, Parish of _____, Louisiana." [Louisiana Code of Civil Procedure].

DOCUMENT CAPTION INFORMATION: Petition for Divorce. "In Re: the Marriage of: _____, Petitioner/Plaintiff and _____, Respondent/Defendant." Final document title: Final Judgment of Divorce.

LEGAL SEPARATION: The grounds for legal separation (separation from bed and board) in Louisiana were repealed effective January 1, 1991. However, a spouse may petition the court for spousal and/or child support and restitution of separate property during a marriage. This is intended to provide for those spouses who desire to live apart, but not divorce. [Louisiana Statutes Annotated, Article 9; Chapter 291].

SIMPLIFIED OR SPECIAL DIVORCE PROCEDURES: The new no-fault divorce grounds in Louisiana are very simplified. No answer need be made by a respondent to a Petition for Divorce filed in Louisiana. In order to obtain a final Judgement of Divorce, a motion entitled "Rule to Show Cause" must be filed with the court. However, each judicial district in Louisiana may have specific individual rules pertaining to divorce actions. Please refer to the Louisiana Rules of Court for the rules in a particular judicial district. Sample forms for use in various divorce case situations (including a sample Petition for Divorce) are contained in Louisiana Forms; Forms 370+. [Louisiana Civil Code Annotated, Article 102 and Louisiana Forms; Forms 370+; Louisiana Code of Civil Procedure; Articles 3951-3956].

MEDIATION OR COUNSELING REQUIREMENTS: If child custody is an issue, the court may require that the parents submit to mediation. [Louisiana Revised Statutes Annotated, Article 9, Section 332].

PROPERTY DISTRIBUTION: Louisiana is a "community property" state. A spouse's separate property, consisting of property acquired prior to the marriage and property acquired by gift or inheritance, is awarded to that spouse. The community property is divided equally between the spouses. Personal property necessary for the safety and well-being of the spouse filing for divorce and any children in his or her custody (including food, eating utensils, clothing, and any other items necessary for their safety and well-being) will be awarded to the spouse filing. Either spouse may ask the court for use and occupancy of the family residence pending the final division of the community property. The court bases the temporary award of the family residence on the following factors: (1) the value of each spouse's personal property; (2) the economic circumstances of each spouse at the time the division of property is to become effective; and (3) needs of the children. In addition, a spouse may be awarded a sum of money for his or her financial contributions made during a marriage to the education or training of a spouse that increased the other spouse's earning capacity. [Louisiana Civil Code Annotated, Title V; Chapter 121 and Louisiana Revised Statutes Annotated, Article 9, Chapter 373 and 374].

ALIMONY/MAINTENANCE/SPOUSAL SUPPORT: During the divorce proceeding, either spouse may be ordered to pay temporary alimony. Permanent periodic alimony may be granted to the spouse who is without fault and without sufficient means for support. Such alimony shall not exceed one-third of the other spouse's income unless the alimony is to be paid in a lump-sum payment. The factors considered are: (1) the effect of child custody on the spouse's earning capacity; (2) the time necessary to acquire sufficient education and training to enable the spouse to find appropriate employment; (3) the income, means, and assets of the spouses, and the liquidity of the assets; (4) the comparative financial obligations of the spouses; (5) the age and health of the spouses; (6) duration of marriage; (7) tax consequences; and (8) any other relevant circumstances. Permanent alimony may be revoked on remarriage or co-habitation or death. [Louisiana Civil Code Annotated, title V, Chapter 111, 112, 115].

SPOUSE'S NAME: A spouse may have his or her former name restored upon divorce. Case law notes the allowance of resumption of a wife's maiden name. In addition, a person may generally petition the court for change of name. [Louisiana Statutes Annotated, Article 13-4751; and Louisiana Case Law].

CHILD CUSTODY: Joint or sole custody is awarded based on the best interests of the child. The following order of preference is established: (1) to both parents; (2) to either parent (without regard to race or sex of the parents); (3) to the person or persons with whom the child has been living; or (4) to any other person that the court feels suitable and able to provide an adequate and stable environment for the child. Unless shown otherwise or unless the parents agree otherwise, joint custody is presumed to be in the best interests of the child, and will be awarded based on the following factors: (1) physical, emotional, mental, religious, and social needs of the child; (2) capability and desire of each parent to meet the child's needs; (3) preference of the child, if the child is of sufficient age and capacity; (4) the love and affection existing between the child and each parent; (5) the length of time the child has lived in a stable, satisfactory environment and the desirability of maintaining continuity; (6) the desire and ability of each parent to allow an open and loving frequent relationship between the child and the other parent; (7) the wishes of the parents; (8) the child's adjustment to his or her home, school, and community; (9) the mental and physical health of all individuals involved; (10) the permanence as a family unit of the existing or proposed custodial home; (11) the distance between the potential residences; (12) the moral fitness of the parents; and (13) any other relevant factor. The conduct of the proposed guardian is to be considered only as it bears on his or her relationship with the child. The parents must submit a plan for joint custody which designates: (1) the child's residence, (2) the rights of access and communication between the parents and child; and (3) child support amounts. A parent not granted custody is entitled to visitation rights unless that parent has subjected the child to physical or sexual abuse. [Louisiana Civil Code Annotated, Articles 131, 132, 133, and 134 and Louisiana Case Law].

CHILD SUPPORT: Both parents are obligated to support any children of a marriage. The factors for consideration listed in the statute are: (1) the needs of the child; and (2) the actual resources of each parent. In addition, Louisiana has adopted detailed Child Support Guideline provisions which are contained in the statute. These guidelines are presumed to be correct, unless one of the following factors make the guidelines unjust or not in the best interests of the child: (1) extraordinary medical expenses of the child or parent responsible for support payments; (2) the permanent or temporary total disability of the parent responsible for support; (3) the need for immediate or temporary support; (4) an extraordinary community debt of the parents; (5) that the combined income of the parents is less than that in the guideline charts; (6) obligation to support other dependents; (7) any other factor which would make application of the guidelines not in the best interest of the child. [Louisiana Revised Statutes Annotated, Article 9; Sections 315.1 and Louisiana Civil Code Annotated, Title V, Article 141].

PREMARITAL AGREEMENTS: Louisiana has no specific statutes pertaining to premarital agreements.

MAINE

RESIDENCY REQUIREMENTS AND WHERE TO FILE: Either spouse must be a resident of Maine, or the marriage or the grounds for divorce must have occurred in Maine. Otherwise, a person filing for divorce must be a resident of Maine for 6 months immediately prior to filing. The divorce may be filed for in the District Court in the county where either spouse resides. However, the defendant spouse has the right to have the proceeding moved to Superior Court. [Maine Revised Statutes Annotated: Title 4, Chapter 5, Section 155; and Title 19-A, Chapter 29, Section 901].

LEGAL GROUNDS FOR DIVORCE: No-Fault: Irreconcilable marital differences. [Maine Revised Statutes Annotated: Title 19-A, Chapter 29, Section 902].

General: (1) impotence; (2) adultery; (3) alcoholism and/or drug addiction; (4) confinement for incurable insanity for 7 consecutive years; (5) desertion for 3 years; (6) cruelty or abuse; and (7) nonsupport whereby a spouse is able to provide support but grossly, wantonly, or cruelly refuses or neglects to provide suitable maintenance for the complaining spouse. [Maine Revised Statutes Annotated: Title 19-A, Chapter 29, Section 902].

NAME OF COURT IN WHICH TO FILE FOR DIVORCE: District Court or Superior Court. "State of Maine, _____ Court, _____ County." [Maine Revised Statutes Annotated: Title 19-A, Chapter 29, Sections 902].

DOCUMENT CAPTION INFORMATION: Complaint for Divorce. "In Re: the Marriage of: _____, Plaintiff and _____, Defendant." Final document title: Judgement of Divorce.

LEGAL SEPARATION: Legal separation will be granted if spouses are or desire to be living apart with just cause for more than 60 days. If there are minor children of the marriage, mediation between the spouses is required prior to a legal separation. [Maine Revised Statutes Annotated: Title 19-A, Chapter 27, Section 851].

SIMPLIFIED OR SPECIAL DIVORCE PROCEDURES: If the divorce is not contested, testimony of a corroborating witness is not necessary. [Maine Revised Statutes Annotated: Title 19-A, Chapter 29, Section 726].

MEDIATION OR COUNSELING REQUIREMENTS: Mediation is mandatory in Maine if: one of the spouses denies that there are irreconcilable differences; or it is a contested divorce and children are involved. In addition, at any time a court may order mediation. [Maine Revised Statutes Annotated: Title 19-A, Chapter 29, Sections 251, and 902].

PROPERTY DISTRIBUTION: Maine is an "equitable distribution" state. Each spouse retains his or her individual property, including (1) any gifts or inheritances; (2) any property acquired prior to marriage; and (3) any increase in the value of property listed in (1) or (2) or property acquired in exchange for property listed in (1) or (2). The marital property is divided between the spouses after considering the following factors: (1) the contribution of each spouse to the acquisition of the marital property, including the contribution of each spouse as homemaker; (2) the value of each spouse's property; and (3) the economic circumstances of each spouse at the time the division of property is to become effective, including the desirability of awarding the family home to the spouse having custody of any children. Marital fault is not a factor. [Maine Revised Statutes Annotated: Title 19-A, Chapter 29, Section 953].

ALIMONY/MAINTENANCE/SPOUSAL SUPPORT: Either spouse may be ordered to pay a reasonable amount of alimony. The court may also order that a spouse's real estate be awarded to the other spouse for life as alimony. The court may also order that a lump-sum be paid to the other spouse as alimony. The factors for consideration set out in the statute are: (1) the duration of the marriage; (2) the age of the spouses; (3) the standard of living established during the marriage; (4) the ability of each spouse to pay; (5) the employment history and employment potential of each spouse; (6) the income history and income potential of each spouse; (7) the education and training of each spouse; (8) the provisions for retirement and health insurance benefits for each spouse; (9) the tax consequences of the division of marital property, including the tax consequences of the sale of the marital home; (10) the health and disabilities of each spouse; (11) the tax consequences of an alimony award; (12) the contributions of either spouse as homemaker; (13) the contributions of either spouse to the education or earning potential to the other spouse; (14) economic misconduct of either spouse resulting in the diminution of marital property or income; and (15) any other factors the court considers to be appropriate under the circumstances. [Maine Revised Statutes Annotated: Title 19-A, Chapter 29, Section 951].

SPOUSE'S NAME: During or after a divorce or annulment, and upon request, a spouse may have their name changed. [Maine Revised Statutes Annotated: Title 19-A, Chapter 29, Section 1051].

CHILD CUSTODY: Based on the best interests of the child, three types of custody may be awarded: (1) Responsibilities for the child's welfare are divided, either exclusively or proportionately. The responsibilities to be divided are: primary physical residence, parent-child contact, support, education, medical and dental care, religious upbringing, travel boundaries and expenses, and any other aspects. A parent awarded responsibility for any aspect may be required to inform the other parent of any major changes. (2) Parental responsibilities are shared. Most or all of the responsibilities are made on the basis of joint decisions and the parents retain equal parental rights and responsibilities. (3) One parent is granted full and exclusive rights and responsibility for the child's welfare, except for the responsibility of child support.

The factors to be considered are: (1) the age of the child; (2) the capability and desire of each parent to meet the child's needs; (3) the preference of the child, if the child is of sufficient age and capacity; (4) the length of time the child has lived in a stable, satisfactory environment and the desirability of maintaining continuity; (5) the desire and ability of each parent to allow an open and loving frequent relationship between the child and the other parent; (6) the child's adjustment to his or her home, school, and community; (7) the relationship of the child with parents, siblings, and other significant family members; (8) the stability of the home environment likely to be offered by each parent; (9) a need to promote continuity and stability in the life of the child; (10) the parent's capacity and willingness to cooperate; (11) methods for dispute resolution; (12) the effect on the child of one parent having sole authority over his or her upbringing; (13) the existence of any domestic violence or child abuse; (14) any other factors having a reasonable bearing on the child's upbringing. No preference is to be given because of parent's sex or because of the child's age or sex. In any child custody case, the court may order an investigation of the parents and child by the Department of Human Services. [Maine Revised Statutes Annotated: Title 19-A, Chapter 29, Sections 1501 and 1653].

CHILD SUPPORT: Either or both parents may be ordered to pay child support, regardless of any marital fault. An order for support may require that a parent be responsible for an insurance policy covering the child's medical, hospital, and other health care expenses. There are official Child Support Guidelines contained in the statute. These Guidelines are presumed to be correct unless there is a showing that the amount would be unjust or inappropriate or not in the best interests of the child under the particular circumstances in a case. There are also official child support guideline forms in use. Deviation from the guidelines is allowed under the following circumstances: (1) the non-primary residential caretaker is providing residential care over

30% of the time; (2) the number of children requiring support is over 6; (3) child support, spousal support, and property division is being decided at the same time; (4) the financial resources of the child; (5) the financial resources and needs of each parent, including any nonrecurring income not included in the definition of gross income; (6) the standard of living the child would have had if the marriage had continued; (7) the physical and emotional condition of the child; (8) the educational needs of the children; (9) inflation in relation to the cost of living; (10) income and financial contributions of a spouse of each parent; (11) other dependents of the parent required to pay support; (12) the tax consequences of a support award; (13) health insurance premiums of over 15% of the support award; (14) whether any of the children are over 12 years old; (15) the cost of transportation of any child; and (16) a finding that the application of the support guidelines would be unjust, inappropriate or not in the child's best interest. [Maine Revised Statutes Annotated: Title 19-A, Chapter 29, Sections 2001-2009].

PREMARITAL AGREEMENTS: The agreement must be in writing and signed by both parties and is enforceable without consideration. The agreement may be amended or revoked only by a written agreement signed by the parties and this amendment is enforceable without consideration. The agreement is not enforceable if the party proves that (1) the party did not execute the agreement voluntarily; (2) the agreement was unconscionable when executed in that the party was not provided a fair and reasonable disclosure of the property or financial obligations of the other party, the party did not voluntarily or expressly waive the disclosure of this information, did not have adequate knowledge concerning this information. If the agreement modifies or terminates spousal support, the party may be required to provide that support. If the marriage is determined to be void, the agreement is enforceable only to the extent necessary to avoid an inequitable result. [Maine Revised Statutes Annotated; Title 19-A, Chapter 21, Sections 603, 607, 608, 609].

MARYLAND

RESIDENCY REQUIREMENTS AND WHERE TO FILE: If the grounds for divorce occurred outside of Maryland, one of the spouses must have lived in Maryland for at least 1 year prior to filing for divorce. Otherwise, either spouse may file for divorce in Maryland. If insanity is the grounds for divorce, the residency requirement is increased to 2 years. The divorce may be filed for in a county where either spouse resides. [Annotated Code of Maryland; Family Law, Title 7, Section 7-103; and Maryland Rules, Rule S70].

LEGAL GROUNDS FOR (ABSOLUTE) DIVORCE: No-Fault: (1) the spouses have voluntarily lived separate and apart for 1 year without interruption or cohabitation and there is no reasonable expectation of reconciliation; or (2) the spouses have lived separate and apart without interruption for 2 years. [Annotated Code of Maryland; Family Law, Title 7, Section 7-103].

General: (1) adultery; (2) deliberate desertion for 12 months with no chance for reconciliation; (3) confinement for incurable insanity of at least 3 years; (4) conviction of a felony or a misdemeanor with at least a 3-year sentence and after 1 year having been served; and (5) cruel and inhumane treatment with no reasonable expectation of reconciliation. [Annotated Code of Maryland; Family Law, Title 7, Section 7-103].

NAME OF COURT IN WHICH TO FILE FOR DIVORCE: Circuit Court. "In the Circuit Court for _____, Maryland."

DOCUMENT CAPTION INFORMATION: Bill for Divorce. "In Re: the Marriage of: _____, Plaintiff and _____, Defendant." Final document title: Decree of Divorce. [Maryland Rules, Rule S72].

LEGAL SEPARATION: The grounds for a legal separation (limited divorce) are: (1) willful desertion; (2) cruel and inhuman treatment; (3) voluntary separation and living separate and apart without cohabitation. The legal separation may be temporary or permanent. The spouses must make a good-faith effort to reconcile their difference. [Annotated Code of Maryland; Family Law, Title 7, Section 7-102].

79

SIMPLIFIED OR SPECIAL DIVORCE PROCEDURES: Summary divorces are not permitted in Maryland. However, marital settlement agreements are specifically authorized by statute and may be used for full corroboration of a plaintiff's testimony that a separation was voluntary if (1) the agreement states that the spouses voluntarily agreed to separate and (2) the agreement was signed under oath before the application for divorce was filed. In addition, each spouse must file a Financial Statement Affidavit and a Joint Statement of Marital and Non-Marital Property. The form for the Joint Property Statement is contained in Maryland Rule S74. Finally, in a default situation, the divorce may be granted only upon actual testimony of the plaintiff spouse. [Annotated Code of Maryland; Courts and Judicial Procedure, Section 3-409; and Title 8, Section 8-104 and Maryland Rules, Rules S73 and S74].

MEDIATION OR COUNSELING REQUIREMENTS: Maryland specifically declares that it is in the best interests of children that there be mediated resolutions of parental disputes regarding custody. In cases where the custody of a child is in dispute, the court may order the parents to attempt to mediate that issue, unless there is a history of physical or sexual abuse of the child. [Maryland Rules, Rule S73A].

PROPERTY DISTRIBUTION: Maryland is an "equitable distribution" state. The spouses retain their separate property, including (1) any gifts and inheritances; (2) property acquired prior to the marriage; and (3) property which is directly traceable to property listed in (1) or (2). Marital property, including retirement benefits and military pensions, is then divided on an equitable basis. The court may order a division of the property, a sale of the property and a division of the proceeds, or a money award as an adjustment of the values. The court may award the family home to either party. The following factors are considered: (1) monetary and non-monetary contributions of each spouse to the acquisition of the marital property, including the contribution of each spouse as homemaker; (2) value of each spouse's property; (3) economic circumstances of each spouse at the time the division of property is to become effective; (4) length of the marriage; (5) whether the property award is instead of or in addition to alimony; (6) how and by whom the property was acquired, including any retirement, profit-sharing, or deferred compensation plans; (7) circumstances that contributed to the estrangement of the spouses; (8) age, physical and mental condition of the spouses; and (9) any other factor necessary to do equity and justice between the spouses. [Annotated Code of Maryland; Family Law, Title 8, Sections 8-202, 8-203, and 8-205].

ALIMONY/MAINTENANCE/SPOUSAL SUPPORT: Either spouse may be awarded alimony based on the following factors: (1) time necessary to acquire sufficient education and training to enable the spouse to find appropriate employment, and that spouse's future earning capacity; (2) standard of living established during the marriage; (3) duration of the marriage; (3) ability of the spouse from whom support is sought to meet his or her needs while meeting those of the other spouse; (4) financial resources of the spouse seeking alimony, including that spouse's marital property and ability to meet his or her needs independently; (5) comparative financial resources of the spouses, including their comparative earning abilities in the labor market; (6) contribution of each spouse to the marriage, including services in homemaking, child care, education, and career building of the other spouse; (7) age of the spouses; (8) physical and emotional conditions of the spouses; (9) any mutual agreement between the spouses concerning financial or service contributions by one spouse with the expectation of future reciprocation or compensation by the other; (10) ability of the spouse seeking alimony to become self-supporting; (11) the circumstances which lead to the breakdown of the marriage; and (12) any other factor the court deems just and equitable. [Annotated Code of Maryland; Family Law, Title 11, Section 11-106].

SPOUSE'S NAME: Either spouse's former or birth name may be restored if the purpose is not illegal, fraudulent, or immoral. [Annotated Code of Maryland; Family Law, Title 7, Section 7-105].

CHILD CUSTODY: Joint or sole custody may be awarded to either or both parents, based on the best interests of the child. Custody may be denied if the child has been abused by the parent seeking custody. There are no other factors for consideration set out in the statute. The court shall attempt to allow the child to live in the environment and community that are familiar to the child and will generally allow the use and possession of the family home by the person with custody of the child(ren). [Annotated Code of Maryland; Family Law, Title 7, Sections 5-203, 8-208, and 9-101; and Maryland Case Law].

CHILD SUPPORT: Child support may be awarded. There are specific child support guidelines and charts supplied in the statute which are presumed to be correct. However, the amount may be adjusted if it is inappropriate or unjust under the circumstances of the case. In determining whether the amount would be unjust, the court may consider: (1) the terms of any marital settlement agreement between the parents, including any provisions for payments of marital debts, mortgages, college education expenses, the right to occupy the family home, and any other financial terms; and (2) the presence in the household of either parent of other children that the parent has a duty to support. The family home may be awarded to the parent who has custody of a child to enable the child to continue to live in the environment and community that are familiar to the child. [Annotated Code of Maryland; Family Law, Title 7, Sections 12-101, 12-201, 12-202, 12-203, 12-204 and 8-206].

PREMARITAL AGREEMENTS: Maryland has no specific statutes pertaining to premarital agreements.

MASSACHUSETTS

RESIDENCY REQUIREMENTS AND WHERE TO FILE: If the grounds for divorce occurred in Massachusetts, one spouse must be a resident. If the grounds occurred outside of the state, the spouse filing must have been a resident for 1 year. The divorce should be filed for in the county in which the spouses last lived together. If neither spouse currently lives in that county then the divorce may be filed for in a county where either spouse currently resides. [Massachusetts General Laws Annotated; Chapter 208, Sections 4, 5, and 6].

LEGAL GROUNDS FOR DIVORCE: No-Fault: Irretrievable breakdown of the marriage (May be filed for either with or without a separation agreement. For no-fault divorce filed in conjunction with a separation agreement, see below under Simplified Or Special Divorce Procedures.) [Massachusetts General Laws Annotated; Chapter 208, Sections 1, 1A, and 1B].
    General: (1) impotence; (2) imprisonment for over 5 years; (3) adultery; (4) alcoholism and/or drug addiction; (5) desertion for 1 year before the filing for divorce; (6) cruel and inhuman treatment; and (7) nonsupport whereby a spouse is able to provide support but grossly, wantonly, or cruelly refuses or neglects to provide suitable maintenance for the complaining spouse. [Massachusetts General Laws Annotated; Chapter 208, Sections 1, 1A, 1B and 2].

NAME OF COURT IN WHICH TO FILE FOR DIVORCE: Probate Court for the Commonwealth of Massachusetts. "Commonwealth of Massachusetts, The Trial Court, The Probate and Family Court Department, _____ Division." [Massachusetts General Laws Annotated; Chapter 208, Section 6B].

DOCUMENT CAPTION INFORMATION: For fault-based divorce: Complaint for Divorce; "In Re: the Marriage of _____, Plaintiff and _____, Defendant." For no-fault divorce with or without a separation agreement: Petition for Divorce: "In Re: the Marriage of _____, Petitioner (or Co-Petitioner, if with a separation agreement) and _____, Respondent" (or Co-Petitioner, if with a separation agreement). [See next page under Simplified Or Special Divorce Procedures]. Final document title: Judgement of Divorce.

LEGAL SEPARATION: The grounds for legal separation are: (1) a spouse fails without cause to provide support; (2) desertion; or (3) gives the other spouse justifiable cause to live apart. The court may award support to the spouse and children living apart. If the grounds for legal separation occurred in Massachusetts, one spouse must be a resident. If the grounds occurred outside of the state, the spouse filing must have been a resident for 1 year. [Massachusetts General Laws Annotated; Chapter 208, Section 20].

SIMPLIFIED OR SPECIAL DIVORCE PROCEDURES: An action for divorce on the grounds of irretrievable breakdown of the marriage may be instituted by filing: (1) a petition signed by both spouses; and (2) a sworn affidavit that an irretrievable breakdown of the marriage exists; and (3) a notarized separation agreement signed by both spouses. A marital settlement agreement is an acceptable substitute for a separation agreement. No summons will be required. Such petitions are to be given a speedy hearing. Marital fault is not to be considered in any decision of the court on property division or maintenance. In addition, there are sample divorce forms for use in divorces set out in the Massachusetts Rules of Court Appendix of Forms. A Financial Statement must be filed in all divorce cases. There is an official Child Support Guidelines Worksheet contained in the Appendix of Forms. Finally, in every action for divorce, a Public Health Statistical Report must be filed by each spouse. Copies of this form are available from the offices of the Registers of Probate. [Massachusetts General Laws Annotated; Chapter 208, Sections 1A and Massachusetts Rules of Court; Appendix of Forms].

MEDIATION OR COUNSELING REQUIREMENTS: In cases where "irreconcilable differences" are used as the grounds for divorce, the court may refer the spouses and children for marriage and family counseling. [Massachusetts General Laws Annotated; Chapter 208, Sections 1A and Massachusetts Rules of Court].

PROPERTY DISTRIBUTION: Massachusetts is an "equitable distribution" state. The court may divide all of the spouse's property, including any gifts and inheritances, based on the following factors: (1) the contribution of each spouse to the acquisition, preservation, or appreciation in value of the property, including the contribution of each spouse as homemaker; (2) the length of the marriage; (3) the age and health of the spouses; (4) the occupation of the spouses; (5) the amount and sources of income of the spouses; (6) the vocational skills of the spouses; (7) the employability of the spouses; (8) the liabilities and needs of each spouse and the opportunity of each for further acquisition of capital assets and income; (9) the conduct of the parties during the marriage (if the grounds for divorce are fault-based); and (10) any health insurance coverage. Fault is not a factor if the grounds for the divorce are irretrievable breakdown of the marriage filed in conjunction with a separation/settlement agreement. [Massachusetts General Laws Annotated; Chapter 208, Sections 1A and 34].

83

ALIMONY/MAINTENANCE/SPOUSAL SUPPORT: Either spouse may be ordered to pay maintenance to the other. The factors to be considered are: (1) the contribution of each spouse to the acquisition, preservation, or appreciation in value of any property, including the contribution of each spouse as homemaker; (2) the length of the marriage; (3) the age and health of the spouses; (4) the occupation of the spouses; (5) the amount and sources of income of the spouses; (6) the vocational skills of the spouses; (7) the employability of the spouses; (8) the liabilities and needs of each spouse and the opportunity of each for further acquisition of capital assets and income; (9) the conduct of the parties during the marriage (if the grounds for divorce are fault-based); (10) any health insurance coverage; and (11) the present and future needs of any children of the marriage. Fault is not a factor if the grounds for the divorce are irretrievable breakdown of the marriage filed in conjunction with a separation/settlement agreement. Health insurance coverage may be ordered to be provided as part of the maintenance award. [Massachusetts General Laws Annotated; Chapter 208, Sections 1A, and 34].

SPOUSE'S NAME: The wife may be restored to the use of her former or maiden name. [Massachusetts General Laws Annotated; Chapter 208, Section 23].

CHILD CUSTODY: Custody may be awarded to either or both parents or to a third party. If there is no marital misconduct, the rights of each parent to custody shall be deemed to be equal. The happiness and welfare of the child shall be the factors that the court considers. In making this consideration, the court shall consider whether or not the child's present or past living conditions adversely affect his physical, mental, moral, or emotional health. Joint custody may be awarded if both parents agree and unless the court finds that joint custody is not in the best interests of the child. If the issue of custody is contested and the parents desire some form of shared custody, a shared parenting plan must be submitted to the court. Provisions in a Marital Settlement Agreement relating to child custody will fulfill this requirement. [Massachusetts General Laws Annotated; Chapter 208, Sections 28 and 31].

CHILD SUPPORT: The court may order either parent to provide maintenance, support (including health insurance), and education for any minor child. There are official Child Support Guidelines. These Guidelines are presumed to be correct unless there is a showing that the amount would be unjust or inappropriate under the particular circumstances in a case. Reasons for deviation from the Guidelines are: (1) the parent to pay support has other minor children, and there are insufficient financial resources available; (2) the parent to pay support has extraordinary expenses (travel-related visitation expenses, uninsured medical expenses, etc.) (3) other unusual circumstances. There is an official Child Support Guidelines Worksheet contained in the Appendix of Forms. [Massachusetts General Laws Annotated; Chapter 208, Section 28 and Massachusetts Rules of Court; Appendix of Forms].

PREMARITAL AGREEMENTS: Massachusetts allows premarital agreements that provide where any real or personal property or any right of action which either party may have may remain in the possession or become the property of that spouse. A schedule of the property to be affected must be attached to the agreement and is to be recorded in the registry of deeds either before the marriage or within 90 days thereafter. If the agreement is not recorded, it is void. [Massachusetts General Laws Annotated; Chapter 209, Sections 25 and 26].

MICHIGAN

RESIDENCY REQUIREMENTS AND WHERE TO FILE: Immediately prior to filing for divorce, one of the spouses must have been a resident of Michigan for 180 days and a resident of the county where the divorce is filed for 10 days. However, a person may file for divorce in any county in the state without meeting the 10-day residency requirement if the defendant was born in or is a citizen of a foreign country and there are minor children in the marriage that are at risk of being taken out of the country by the defendant. [Michigan Compiled Laws Annotated; Section 552.9].

LEGAL GROUNDS FOR DIVORCE: No-Fault: A breakdown of the marriage relationship to the extent that the objects of matrimony have been destroyed and there remains no reasonable likelihood that the marriage can be preserved. [Michigan Compiled Laws Annotated; Section 552.6]

General: A breakdown of the marriage relationship to the extent that the objects of matrimony have been destroyed and there remains no reasonable likelihood that the marriage can be preserved is the only grounds for divorce in Michigan. [Michigan Compiled Laws Annotated; Section 552.6].

NAME OF COURT IN WHICH TO FILE FOR DIVORCE: Circuit Court. "State of Michigan, _____ Judicial Circuit, _____ County." [Michigan Compiled Laws Annotated; Section 552.6].

DOCUMENT CAPTION INFORMATION: Complaint for Divorce. "In Re: the Marriage of: _____, Plaintiff and _____, Defendant." Final document title: Judgment of Divorce.

LEGAL SEPARATION: The only grounds for legal separation (separate maintenance) in Michigan is a breakdown of the marriage relationship to the extent that the objects of matrimony have been destroyed and there remains no reasonable likelihood that the marriage can be preserved. There is no residency requirement specified in the statute. [Michigan Compiled Laws Annotated; Section 552.7].

SIMPLIFIED OR SPECIAL DIVORCE PROCEDURES: There are mandatory official approved and simplified (fill-in-the-blank) forms available for all phases of the divorce process. These forms are contained in the official Michigan Supreme Court Administrative Office Forms Book and should be available from the clerk of the Circuit Court in any Michigan county. In addition, the Michigan Friend of the Court Bureau is to supply each party in a divorce case with a pamphlet discussing the court procedures, the rights and responsibilities of the parties, the availability of mediation, human services, and joint custody. [Michigan Compiled Laws Annotated; Section 552.505].

MEDIATION OR COUNSELING REQUIREMENTS: Voluntary mediation services are available in all situations involving custody and visitation of children. [Michigan Compiled Laws Annotated; Section 552.513].

PROPERTY DISTRIBUTION: Michigan is an "equitable distribution" state. The court may divide the all of the spouse's property, including any gifts or inheritances, in a just and reasonable manner, if it appears that the spouse contributed to the acquisition, improvement, or accumulation of the property. The factors to be considered are: (1) the contribution of each spouse to the acquisition of the marital property, including the contribution of each spouse as homemaker; (2) the length of the marriage; (3) any retirement benefits, including social security, civil service, military and railroad retirement benefits; (4) any prior marriage of each spouse; (5) the circumstances that contributed to the estrangement of the spouses; (6) the source of the property; (7) the cause of the divorce; and (8) each spouse's financial circumstances and rights to any insurance policies. [Michigan Compiled Laws Annotated; Sections 552.19, 552.101, and 552.401 and Michigan Case Law].

ALIMONY/MAINTENANCE/SPOUSAL SUPPORT: Either spouse may be ordered to pay alimony. The alimony may be awarded if the property awarded to a spouse is insufficient to allow that spouse suitable support and maintenance. Factors for consideration specified in the statute are: (1) the ability of either spouse to pay; (2) the character and situation of the spouses; and (3) all other circumstances of the case. All payments of child support shall be ordered to be made through the Michigan Friend of the Court Bureau. [Michigan Compiled Laws Annotated; Sections 552.13, 552.23, and 552.452].

SPOUSE'S NAME: At the wife's request, the court may restore the birth or former name, if there is no fraudulent intent. [Michigan Compiled Laws Annotated; Section 552.391].

CHILD CUSTODY: Sole or joint custody is awarded based on the best interests of the child and on the following factors: (1) moral character and prudence of the parents; (2) physical, emotional, mental, religious, and social needs of the child; (3) capability and desire of each parent to meet the child's emotional, educational, and other needs; (4) preference of the child, if the child is of sufficient age and capacity; (5) the love and affection and other

87

emotional ties existing between the child and each parent; (6) the length of time the child has lived in a stable, satisfactory environment and the desirability of maintaining continuity; (7) the desire and ability of each parent to allow an open and loving frequent relationship between the child and the other parent; (8) the child's adjustment to his or her home, school, and community; (9) the mental and physical health of all individuals involved; (10) the permanence as a family unit of the proposed custodial home or homes; (11) any evidence of domestic violence; and (12) any other factors.

If joint custody is an issue, the court will consider all of the above factors and the following additional factors: (1) whether the parents will be able to cooperate and generally agree concerning important decisions affecting the welfare of the child; and (2) if the parents agree on joint custody. [Michigan Compiled Laws Annotated; Sections 552.16, 722.23 and 722.26a].

CHILD SUPPORT: Either parent may be ordered to provide a just and proper amount of child support. There is a Child Support Formula to be used as a guideline and it is presumed to be correct unless shown to be unjust or inappropriate under the circumstances in a particular case. The court may require the parent providing support to file a bond guaranteeing the support payments. Support may include health care, dental care, child care, and education of the child. The Judgement of Divorce must include a provision that requires one or both of the parents to provide health care coverage, if such coverage is available at a reasonable cost as a benefit of employment. All payments of child support shall be ordered to be made through the Michigan Friend of the Court Bureau. Each parent will be required to keep the Michigan Friend of the Court Bureau informed of their address, sources of income, and health insurance coverage. [Michigan Compiled Laws Annotated; Sections 552.15, 552.16, and 552.452].

PREMARITAL AGREEMENTS: Michigan has no specific statutes pertaining to premarital agreements.

MINNESOTA

RESIDENCY REQUIREMENTS AND WHERE TO FILE: One of the spouses must have been a resident of Minnesota for at least 180 days immediately before the petition for dissolution of marriage is filed. The dissolution of marriage may be filed for in a county where either spouse resides. [Minnesota Statutes Annotated; Chapters 518.07 and 518.09].

LEGAL GROUNDS FOR DISSOLUTION OF MARRIAGE: No-Fault: Irrevocable breakdown of the marriage shown by (1) living separate and apart for 180 days; or (2) serious marital discord adversely affecting the attitude of one or both of the spouses toward the marriage. [Minnesota Statutes Annotated; Chapters 518.06 and 518.13].

General: Irrevocable breakdown of the marriage is the only grounds for dissolution of marriage in Minnesota. [Minnesota Statutes Annotated; Chapter 518.06].

NAME OF COURT IN WHICH TO FILE FOR DISSOLUTION OF MARRIAGE: County Court or District Court. "State of Minnesota, District Court, County of _____, _____ Judicial District."

DOCUMENT CAPTION INFORMATION: Petition for Dissolution of Marriage. "In Re: the Marriage of: _____, Petitioner [or Co-Petitioner if the petition is filed jointly] and _____, Respondent [or Co-Petitioner if the petition is filed jointly.]" [See below under Simplified Or Special Dissolution Of Marriage Procedures]. Final document title: Decree of Dissolution of Marriage.

LEGAL SEPARATION: The grounds for a legal separation in Minnesota are that it will be granted if the court finds that the spouses need a legal separation. One of the spouses must have been a resident of Minnesota for at least 6 months before the petition for legal separation is filed. [Minnesota Statutes Annotated; Chapter 518.06 and 518.07].

SIMPLIFIED OR SPECIAL DISSOLUTION OF MARRIAGE PROCEDURES: The petition may be brought by both spouses jointly as Co-Petitioners. This eliminates the need for service of process or the use of a summons. [Minnesota Statutes Annotated; Chapters 518.09 and 518.11].

MEDIATION OR COUNSELING REQUIREMENTS: Mediation may be ordered in cases in which the custody of children is contested, unless there is a history of physical or sexual child abuse. [Minnesota Statutes Annotated; Chapter 518.619].

PROPERTY DISTRIBUTION: Minnesota is an "equitable distribution" state. Each spouse retains his or her non-marital (separate) property, consisting of: (1) property acquired prior to the marriage; (2) any gifts or inheritances; or (3) property exchanged for or an increase in value of such non-marital property. All other marital property, including any pension and retirement plans, is divided, without regard to fault, after a consideration of the following factors: (1) the contribution of each spouse to the acquisition of the marital property, including the contribution of each spouse as homemaker; (2) the economic circumstances of each spouse at the time the division of property is to become effective; (3) the length of the marriage; (4) the age and health of the spouses; (5) the occupation of the spouses; (6) the amount and sources of income of the spouses; (7) the vocational skills of the spouses; (8) the employability of the spouses; (9) the liabilities and needs of each spouse and the opportunity of each for further acquisition of capital assets and income; (10) any prior marriage of each spouse; and (11) any other factor necessary to do equity and justice between the spouses. [Minnesota Statutes Annotated; Chapter 518.58].

ALIMONY/MAINTENANCE/SPOUSAL SUPPORT: Either spouse may be awarded maintenance, without regard to marital fault, if the spouse seeking maintenance: (1) lacks sufficient property to provide for reasonable needs considering the standard of living attained during the marriage; or (2) is unable to provide adequate self-support, considering the standard of living attained during the marriage, through appropriate employment; or (3) is the custodian of a child whose condition or circumstances make it appropriate that the custodian not be required to seek employment outside the home. The award of maintenance is based on a consideration of the following factors: (1) the sacrifices the homemaker has made in terms of earnings, employment, experience, and opportunities; (2) the time necessary to acquire sufficient education and training to enable the spouse to find appropriate employment, and that spouse's future earning capacity and the probability of completing education and training and becoming fully or partially self-supporting; (3) the standard of living established during the marriage; (4) the duration of the marriage and, in the case of a homemaker, the length of absence from employment and the extent to which any education, skills, or experience have become outmoded and earning capacity has become permanently diminished; (5) the ability of the spouse from whom support is sought to meet his or her needs while meeting those of the spouse seeking support; (6) the financial resources of the spouse seeking maintenance, including marital property apportioned to such spouse and such spouse's ability to meet his or her needs independently; (7) the contribution of each spouse to the marriage, including services rendered in homemaking, child care, education, and career building of the other spouse; (8) the age of the spouses; (9) the physical and emotional conditions of the spouses; (10) any loss of earnings, seniority, retirement benefits or other employment opportunities foregone by the spouse seeking maintenance; and (11) any other factor the court deems just and equitable. If the spouse receives public aid, the payments are to be made through the public aid agency. [Minnesota Statutes Annotated; Chapters 518.551 and 518.552].

SPOUSE'S NAME: Upon request, either spouse may change his or her name, unless there is intent to mislead or defraud. [Minnesota Statutes Annotated; Chapter 518.27].

CHILD CUSTODY: Joint or sole custody may be awarded. Sole custody will be awarded based on the best interests of the child and the following: (1) the child's cultural background; (2) physical and mental health of all parties; (3) capability and desire of each parent to give the child love, affection and guidance, and to continue raising the child in the child's culture and religion or creed, if any; (4) preference of the child, if the child is of sufficient age and capacity; (5) the length of time the child has lived in a stable, satisfactory environment and the desirability of maintaining continuity; (6) the wishes of the parents; (7) the child's adjustment to his or her home, school, and community; (8) the mental and physical health of all individuals involved; (9) the relationship of the child with parents, siblings, and other significant family members; (10) the conduct of the proposed guardian only as it bears on his or her relationship with the child; (11) the stability of the home environment likely to be offered by each parent; (12) a need to promote continuity and stability in the life of the child; (13) the effect of any child or spouse abuse on the child; (14) the child's primary caretaker; and (15) any other factors. The primary caretaker factor is not a presumption in favor of the primary caretaker, but is only one factor in the decision.

If both parents request joint custody, there is a presumption that such an arrangement will be in the best interests of the child, unless there has been any spousal abuse. If there has been any history of spousal abuse, there is a presumption that joint custody is not in the best interests of the child. Joint custody will be based on a consideration of the above factors and the following: (1) dispute resolution methods; (2) the effect of one parent having custody; and (3) the ability of the parents to cooperate and make decisions jointly. If both parents seek custody of a child who is too young to express a preference, the "primary caretaker" is to be awarded custody. [Minnesota Statutes Annotated; Chapter 518.17 and Minnesota Case Law].

CHILD SUPPORT: In determining child support, the following factors are considered: (1) the financial resources of the child; (2) the financial resources of the custodial parents; (3) the standard of living the child would have enjoyed if the marriage had not been dissolved; (4) the physical and emotional conditions and educational needs of the child; (5) the amount of public aid received by the child; (6) any income tax consequences of the payment of support; and (7) any debt of the parents. Misconduct of a parent in the marriage is not to be considered. If the parent to receive the support payments is receiving or has applied for public aid, the support payments must be made to the public agency responsible for child support enforcement in Minnesota. There are official child support guidelines contained in Minnesota Statutes Annotated; Chapter 518.551. [Minnesota Statutes Annotated; Chapters 518.551 and 518.552].

PREMARITAL AGREEMENTS: The agreement must be in writing, executed in the presence of two witnesses and acknowledged by the parties, and executed before someone who has the authority to administer an oath. The agreement can be amended or revoked after marriage. If the agreement conveys or determines rights to property, the agreement may be filed in every county where the property is located. If the agreement is not recorded, it is void. There must be a full and fair disclosure of the earnings and property of each party and the parties must have had an opportunity to consult with legal counsel. [Minnesota Statutes Annotated; Chapter 519.11].

MISSISSIPPI

RESIDENCY REQUIREMENTS AND WHERE TO FILE: One of the spouses must have been a resident for at least 6 months, and not have secured residency for the purpose of obtaining a divorce. A member of the armed services and his or her spouse are considered residents if stationed in Mississippi. A divorce on the grounds of irreconcilable differences should be filed for in: (1) the county where either spouse resides, if both spouses are residents of Mississippi; or (2) the county where one spouse resides if the other spouse is a non-resident of Mississippi. A divorce sought on fault-based grounds should be filed for in: (1) the county where the defendant resides if he or she is a resident of Mississippi; or (2) the county where the plaintiff resides if the defendant is a non-resident of Mississippi; or (3) the county where the spouses last lived prior to separating, if the plaintiff is still a resident of the county in which the suit is filed. [Mississippi Code Annotated; Section 93, Chapters 5-5 and 5-11].

LEGAL GROUNDS FOR DIVORCE: No-Fault: Irreconcilable differences. (See also below under Simplified or Special Divorce Procedures). [Mississippi Code Annotated; Section 93, Chapters 5-1, 5-2, and 5-7].

General: (1) impotence; (2) adultery; (3) imprisonment; (4) alcoholism and/or drug addiction; (5) confinement for incurable insanity for at least 3 years before the divorce is filed; (6) wife is pregnant by another at the time of marriage without husband's knowledge; (7) willful desertion for at least 1 year; (8) cruel and inhuman treatment; (9) spouse lacked mental capacity at the time of the marriage; (10) incest; and (11) marriage to some other person at the time of the current marriage. In addition, an affidavit must be filed stating that there is no collusion between the spouses. [Mississippi Code Annotated; Section 93, Chapters 5-1 and 5-7].

NAME OF COURT IN WHICH TO FILE FOR DIVORCE: Chancery Court. "Chancery Court of _____ County, State of Mississippi." [Mississippi Code Annotated; Section 93, Chapter 5-7].

DOCUMENT CAPTION INFORMATION: Bill of Complaint for Divorce. "In Re: the Marriage of: _____, Plaintiff and _____, Defendant." Final document title: Decree of Divorce.

LEGAL SEPARATION: There are provisions in Mississippi for separate maintenance. [Mississippi Code Annotated; Section 93, Chapter 5-23].

SIMPLIFIED OR SPECIAL DIVORCE PROCEDURES: A no-fault divorce on the
grounds of irreconcilable differences will be granted if: (1) a joint bill of complaint for divorce is filed by both the husband and wife; or (2) a bill of complaint has been filed and (a) the defendant has entered an appearance by
written waiver of process; or (b) has been personally served with the divorce
papers. In addition, if there is a written agreement between the spouses for
the care and custody of any children and for the division of all property, the
court may incorporate such an agreement into the divorce judgement. If the
spouses can not agree on the terms of an agreement, they must consent to the
divorce in writing and consent to allow the court to decide all contested
issues. There is a 60 day waiting period after filing before a hearing may be
scheduled. A bill filed meeting these qualifications will be taken as proved
and no testimony or proof will be required at the hearing. However, if the
defendant denies that there are irreconcilable differences, the divorce may
not be granted on these grounds. [Mississippi Code Annotated; Section 93,
Chapter 5-2].

MEDIATION OR COUNSELING REQUIREMENTS: There is no legal provision
in Mississippi for mediation

PROPERTY DISTRIBUTION: Mississippi is a "title" state. Each spouse retains
his or her property for which they have title. There are no statutory provisions
in Mississippi for considerations regarding property division. However, Mississippi has judicially adopted the "equitable division" systems of property
division. Recent court decisions have allowed for a wife's contributions to the
acquisition of assets to provide the court with authority to divide any jointly
accumulated assets on an "equitable" basis. A 1994 case (Ferguson v. Ferguson)
spelled out a set of factors for the equitable division of marital property: (1) a
spouse's substantial contribution to the accumulation of property; (2) the degree to which a spouse has previously expended or disposed of any marital
property; (3) the market and emotional value of the property in question; (4)
the value of any non-marital or separate property; (5) the tax consequences of
the division of property; (6) the extent to which property division may elimi-
nate the need for alimony or any other future friction between the parties; (7)
the needs of the party, considering income, assets, and earning capacity; and
(8) any other equitable factors. [Mississippi Case Law].

ALIMONY/MAINTENANCE/SPOUSAL SUPPORT: Either spouse may be
awarded maintenance if it is equitable and just. There are no other factors for
consideration specified in the statute. However, a 1996 case (Parsons v. Parsons) spelled out a set of factors for consideration: (1) the spouse's income
and expenses; (2) the spouse's health and earnings; (3) the spouse's needs,

obligations, and assets; (4) the presence of any children; (5) the spouse's ages; (6) the standard of living during the marriage; (7) any tax consequences; (8) any marital fault; (9) any wasteful dissipation of assets; (10) length of the marriage; and (11) any other just and equitable factors. [Mississippi Code Annotated; Section 93, Chapter 5-23 and Mississippi Case Law].

SPOUSE'S NAME: Either spouse may petition the court for a name change. [Mississippi Code Annotated; Section 93, Chapter 17-1].

CHILD CUSTODY: Joint or sole child custody is awarded based on the best interests of the child. There are no specific factors for consideration in the statute. The court may award: (1) joint physical and legal custody to one or both parents; (2) physical custody to both parents and legal custody to one parent; (3) legal custody to both parents and physical custody to one parent; or (4) custody to a third party if the parents have abandoned the child or are unfit. If irreconcilable differences are the grounds for divorce, joint custody may be awarded if both parents apply for joint custody. If both parents apply for joint custody, there is a presumption that joint custody is in the best interests of the child. Otherwise, either parent may apply for joint custody. If both parents are fit and the child is 12 or older, the child may choose the parent he or she wishes to live with. If child abuse is alleged by either parent, the court shall order an investigation by the Mississippi Department of Public Welfare. [Mississippi Code Annotated; Section 93, Chapters 5-23, 5-24, and 11-65].

CHILD SUPPORT: Child support may be ordered as the court finds just and equitable. Where both parents have income or estates, each parent may be ordered to provide support in proportion to his or her relative financial ability. A parent may be required to provide health insurance coverage for the child, if such insurance coverage is available at a reasonable cost through an employer or organization. Bond or sureties may be required to guarantee payments. [Mississippi Code Annotated; Section 93, Chapters 5-23, and 11-65].

PREMARITAL AGREEMENTS: Mississippi has no specific statutes pertaining to premarital agreements.

MISSOURI

RESIDENCY REQUIREMENTS AND WHERE TO FILE: One of the spouses must be a resident of Missouri for 90 days before filing for dissolution of marriage. The dissolution of marriage should be filed in the county where the Plaintiff resides. In addition, there is a 30-day waiting period after filing before a dissolution of marriage will be granted. [Annotated Missouri Statutes; Title 30, Sections 452.300 and 452.305].

LEGAL GROUNDS FOR DISSOLUTION OF MARRIAGE: No-Fault: Irretrievable breakdown of the marriage and no reasonable likelihood that the marriage can be preserved. [Annotated Missouri Statutes; Title 30, Section 452.305].

General: Irretrievable breakdown of the marriage with no reasonable likelihood that the marriage can be preserved is the only grounds for dissolution of marriage in Missouri. [Annotated Missouri Statutes; Title 30, Section 452.305].

NAME OF COURT IN WHICH TO FILE FOR DISSOLUTION OF MARRIAGE: Circuit Court. "In the Circuit Court of _____ County, Missouri."

DOCUMENT CAPTION INFORMATION: Petition for Dissolution of Marriage. "In Re: the Marriage of: _____, Plaintiff [or Co-Plaintiff if the petition is filed jointly] and _____, Defendant [or Co-Plaintiff if the petition is filed jointly]." [See below under Simplified Or Special Dissolution Of Marriage Procedures]." Final document title: Decree of Dissolution. [Annotated Missouri Statutes; Title 30, Section 452.300].

LEGAL SEPARATION: The grounds for legal separation in Missouri are an irretrievable breakdown of the marriage, which may include the following factors: (1) adultery; (2) abandonment for six months; (3) separation 12 months before filing the petition; (4) spousal behavior that the other spouse can not reasonably be expected to live with; and (5) living separate and apart continuously for 24 months. One of the spouses must be a resident of Missouri for 90 days before filing for legal separation. [Annotated Missouri Statutes; Title 30, Sections 452.305 and 452.320].

SIMPLIFIED OR SPECIAL DISSOLUTION OF MARRIAGE PROCEDURES: Missouri allows for a joint petition by both spouses to be filed. In such cases, each spouse should be titled as a "Co-Plaintiff." Settlement agreements are expressly authorized by statute in Missouri. In addition, some counties have approved pre-printed forms for filing for dissolution of marriage which are available upon request from the court clerk. [Annotated Missouri Statutes; Title 30, Sections 452.320 and 452.325].

MEDIATION OR COUNSELING REQUIREMENTS: The court can delay a divorce proceeding for 30-180 days and suggest that the spouses seek counseling. [Annotated Missouri Statutes; Title 30, Section 452.320].

PROPERTY DISTRIBUTION: Missouri is an "equitable distribution" state. Each spouse retains his or her separate property obtained prior to the marriage, including any gifts or inheritances. In addition, any property exchanged for separate property or interest obtained from holding separate property remains as separate. Commingled property does not become marital solely by virtue of the act of commingling. Marital property (all property acquired after the marriage whether held jointly or individually, except if (1) gift or inheritance, (2) received in exchange for non-marital property, (3) an increase in non-marital property, or (4) property excluded by a written agreement between the spouses) is divided after a consideration of the following factors: (1) the contribution of each spouse to the acquisition of the marital property, including the contribution of each spouse as homemaker; (2) the value of each spouse's property; (3) the economic circumstances of each spouse at the time the division of property is to become effective; (4) the conduct of the spouses during the marriage generally and as it relates to the disposition of their property; (5) the desirability of awarding the family home to the spouse having custody of the children; and (6) any custodial arrangements for children. [Annotated Missouri Statutes; Title 30, Section 452.330 and Missouri Case Law].

ALIMONY/MAINTENANCE/SPOUSAL SUPPORT: Either spouse may be awarded maintenance if that spouse can show: (1) an inability to support his or herself; and (2) a lack of sufficient property (including his or her share of any marital property) to provide for his or her own needs; or (3) that the spouse seeking support is the custodian of a child whose condition or circumstances make it appropriate for that spouse not to seek outside employment. The following factors are considered: (1) the time necessary to acquire sufficient education and training to enable the spouse to find appropriate employment, and that spouse's future earning capacity; (2) the standard of living established during the marriage; (3) the duration of the marriage; (4) the ability of the spouse from whom support is sought to meet his or her needs while meeting those of the spouse seeking support; (5) the financial resources of the spouse seeking maintenance, including marital property apportioned to such spouse and such spouse's ability to meet his or her needs independently; (6)

the age of the spouses; (7) the physical and emotional conditions of the spouses; (8) the obligations, assets, and separate property of the spouses; (9) the comparative earning capacities of each spouse; and (10) the conduct of the spouses during the marriage. The court may order the payments to be made through the circuit clerk. [Annotated Missouri Statutes; Title 30, Sections 452.335 and 452.345].

SPOUSE'S NAME: A spouse may petition the court for a change of name. A public notice of any name change should be published in a local newspaper in the county where the person resides. [Annotated Missouri Statutes; Title 36, Sections 527.270 and 527.290].

CHILD CUSTODY: Joint or sole custody is awarded based on the best interests of the child and upon consideration of the following factors: (1) the preference of the child; (2) the wishes of the parents; (3) the child's adjustment to his or her home, school, and community; (4) the mental and physical health of all individuals involved; (5) any history of child or spouse abuse; (6) the child's need for a continuing relationship with both parents; (7) both parents willingness and ability to perform parental obligations; (8) the intention of either parent to relocate his or her residence outside Missouri; (9) which parent is more likely to allow the child frequent and meaningful contact with the other parent; and (10) the relationship of the child with parents, siblings, and other significant family members. Domestic violence against a child is a bar to custody. No preference is to be given because of parent's sex, age or financial status, or the child's age, or sex. There is now a legislative encouragement of joint custody or arrangements which will encourage the parents to both share in the decision-making responsibility of caring for the child. An award of joint custody must include a joint custody plan. A parent not granted custody is entitled to reasonable visitation. [Annotated Missouri Statutes; Title 30, Sections 452.375 and 452.400 and Missouri Case Law].

CHILD SUPPORT: Either or both parents may be ordered to provide child support. The following factors are considered: (1) the father's primary responsibility for the support of his child; (2) the financial resources and needs of the child; (3) the standard of living the child would have enjoyed if the marriage had not been dissolved; (4) the physical and emotional conditions and educational needs of the child; and (5) the financial resources, needs, and obligations of both the noncustodial and the custodial parent. A parent may be required to provide health insurance coverage for any children if such coverage is available at a reasonable cost from an employer, union, or other organization. There are official child support guidelines contained in the statute which are presumed to be correct unless shown to be unjust or inappropriate under the particular circumstances of the case. The court may order the payments to be made through the circuit clerk. [Annotated Missouri Statutes; Title 30, Sections 452.340 and 452.345].

PREMARITAL AGREEMENTS: The agreement must be in writing, acknowledged by each of the parties or proved by one or more witnesses. The agreement is not valid unless recorded in the recorders office. [Annotated Missouri Statutes; Title 30, Chapter 451, Sections 220 and 240].

MONTANA

RESIDENCY REQUIREMENTS AND WHERE TO FILE: One of the spouses must be a resident of Montana for 90 days immediately prior to filing. The dissolution of marriage should be filed for in the county where the petitioner has been a resident for the previous 90 days. [Montana Code Annotated; Section 25, Title 2-118; and Section 40, Title 4-104].

LEGAL GROUNDS FOR DISSOLUTION OF MARRIAGE: No-Fault: Irretrievable breakdown of the marriage, and serious marital discord which adversely affects the attitude of both spouses towards the marriage and no reasonable prospect of reconciliation, and living separate and apart for 180 days prior to filing. All three of these factors must be met to satisfy the grounds for dissolution of marriage. [Montana Code Annotated; Section 40, Title 4-104].

General: Irretrievable breakdown of the marriage and living separate and apart for 180 days prior to filing are the only grounds for dissolution of marriage in Montana. [Montana Code Annotated; Section 40, Title 4-104].

NAME OF COURT IN WHICH TO FILE FOR DISSOLUTION OF MARRIAGE: District Court. "District Court for the State of Montana and for the County of _____."

DOCUMENT CAPTION INFORMATION: Petition for Dissolution of Marriage. "In Re: the Marriage of: _____, Petitioner [or Co-Petitioner if the petition is filed jointly] and _____, Respondent [or Co-Petitioner if the petition is filed jointly.]" [See below under Simplified Or Special Dissolution Of Marriage Procedures]. Final document title: Decree of Dissolution of Marriage. [Montana Code Annotated; Section 40, Titles 1-105 and 4-103].

LEGAL SEPARATION: Irretrievable breakdown of the marriage is the only grounds for legal separation in Montana. One of the spouses must be a resident of Montana for 90 days immediately prior to filing for legal separation. [Montana Code Annotated; Section 40, Title 4-104].

SIMPLIFIED OR SPECIAL DISSOLUTION OF MARRIAGE PROCEDURES: Joint petitions for dissolution of marriage are allowed. In such cases, both spouses should be titled as "Co-Petitioners" on the petition. In addition, separation or settlement agreements are specifically authorized by law. [Montana Code Annotated; Section 40, Title 4-107].

MEDIATION OR COUNSELING REQUIREMENTS: If there are minor children or one spouse denies that the marriage is irretrievably broken, the court may delay the proceedings for 30 to 60 days and refer the spouses to one of the following: (1) a psychiatrist, (2) a physician, (3) an attorney, (4) a social worker, (5) a pastor or director of any religious denomination to which the spouses belong, or (6) any other person who is competent and qualified in personal counseling. [Montana Code Annotated; Section 40, Titles 3-121, and 3-124].

PROPERTY DISTRIBUTION: Montana is an "equitable distribution" state. All of the spouse's property, including any held prior to the marriage and any gifts and inheritances, is divided by the court, without regard to marital misconduct, based on consideration of the following factors: (1) the contribution of each spouse to the acquisition of the marital property, including the contribution of each spouse as homemaker; (2) the length of the marriage; (3) the age and health of the spouses; (4) the occupation of the spouses; (5) the amount and sources of income of the spouses; (6) the vocational skills of the spouses; (7) the employability of the spouses; (8) the liabilities and needs of each spouse and the opportunity of each for further acquisition of capital assets and income; (9) the time necessary for a spouse to acquire sufficient education to enable the spouse to find appropriate employment; (10) any premarital agreement; (11) any prior marriage of each spouse; (12) whether the property award is instead of or in addition to maintenance; and (13) any custodial provisions for the children. [Montana Code Annotated; Section 40, Title 4-202].

ALIMONY/MAINTENANCE/SPOUSAL SUPPORT: Either spouse may be awarded maintenance if that spouse can show: (1) an inability to support his or herself; and (2) a lack of sufficient property (including his or her share of any marital property) to provide for his or her own needs; or (3) that the spouse seeking support is the custodian of a child whose condition or circumstances make it appropriate for that spouse not to seek outside employment. The award is made without regard to marital fault, based on the following factors: (1) the time necessary to acquire sufficient education and training to enable the spouse to find appropriate employment, and that spouse's future earning capacity; (2) the standard of living established during the marriage; (3) the duration of the marriage; (4) the ability of the spouse from whom support is sought to meet his or her needs while meeting those of the spouse seeking support; (5) the financial resources of the spouse seeking maintenance, including marital property apportioned to such spouse and any child support and such spouse's ability to meet his or her needs independently; (6) the age of the spouses; and (7) the physical and emotional conditions of the spouses. [Montana Code Annotated; Section 40, Title 4-203].

SPOUSE'S NAME: Upon the wife's request, her former or maiden name will be restored. [Montana Code Annotated; Section 40, Title 4-108].

CHILD CUSTODY: "Parenting" is now the legal terminology in use in Montana to describe the concept of custody. "Parenting Plans" are now the Montana description of child custody arrangements. Sole or joint parenting is awarded based on the best interests of the child and upon a consideration of the following factors: (1) the preference of the child; (2) the wishes of the parents; (3) the child's adjustment to his or her home, school, and community; (4) the mental and physical health of all individuals involved; (5) any history of child or spouse abuse; (6) any chemical dependency or abuse by a parent; (7) the relationship of the child with parents, siblings, and other significant family members; (8) the continuity and stability of the child's care; (9) the developmental needs of the child; (10) whether a parent has failed to pay any of the child's birth-related costs; (11) whether the child has frequent and continuing contact with both parents [a consideration of any spousal or child abuse by either parent or anyone residing in a parent's household is considered also]; (12) any adverse effects on the child resulting from one parent's continuous and annoying efforts to amend parenting plans [annoying is meant to refer to efforts to (a) amend a parenting plan within 6 months of a prior plan and (b) efforts to amend a final parenting plan without having made a good-faith effort to comply with the plan; and (13) whether a parent has failed to financially support the child. The parent's must submit a parenting plan to the court; although they may choose to submit a temporary or "interim" parenting plan A parent's sex is not to be considered. [Montana Code Annotated; Section 40, Titles 4-104, 4-108, and 4-212].

CHILD SUPPORT: Either or both parents may be ordered to pay child support, based on a consideration of the following factors: (1) the financial resources of the child; (2) the standard of living the child would have enjoyed if the marriage had not been dissolved; (3) the physical and emotional conditions and educational and medical needs of the child; (4) the financial resources, needs, and obligations of both the noncustodial and the custodial parent; (5) the age of the child; (6) the cost of any day care; (7) the parenting plan for the child; (8) the needs of any other person that a parent is obligated to support; and (9) the provision of health and medical insurance for the child. A portion of the parent's property may be set aside in a trust fund for the support of the children. A parent may be ordered to provide health insurance coverage for a child if such coverage is available at a reasonable cost. There are uniform child support guidelines adopted by the department of public health and human services that are to be considered by the court. Child support payments may be required to be made through the department of health and human services. [Montana Code Annotated; Section 40, Title 4-204 and Title 5-209].

PREMARITAL AGREEMENTS: The agreement must be in writing and signed by both parties and is enforceable without consideration. The agreement is not enforceable if the party proves (1) the agreement was not executed voluntarily; (2) the agreement was unconscionable when executed; (3) that before the execution of the agreement the person wasn't provided a fair and reasonable disclosure of the property or financial obligations of the other party, did not voluntarily waive any right to the disclosure of these obligations, did not have adequate knowledge of these obligations; (4) a provision of the agreement modifies or eliminates alimony and that modification causes the party to be eligible for public assistance. If the marriage is determined to be invalid, the agreement is enforceable only to the extent necessary to avoid an inequitable result. [Montana Code Annotated; Section 40, Titles 2-604, 2-608 and 2-609].

NEBRASKA

RESIDENCY REQUIREMENTS AND WHERE TO FILE: (1) one of the spouses must have been a resident of Nebraska for at least 1 year; or (2) the marriage was performed in Nebraska and one of the spouses has lived in Nebraska for the entire marriage. The dissolution of marriage may be filed for in a county where either spouse resides. There is a 30-day waiting period after service of the petition for dissolution of marriage on the respondent before the case can be decided in court. [Revised Statutes of Nebraska; Chapter 42-342, 42-348, 42-349, and 42-354].

LEGAL GROUNDS FOR DISSOLUTION OF MARRIAGE: No-Fault: Irretrievable breakdown of the marriage. [Revised Statutes of Nebraska; Chapter 42-361].

General: Spouse lacked mental capacity to consent (including temporary incapacity resulting from drug or alcohol use). [Revised Statutes of Nebraska; Chapter 42-362].

NAME OF COURT IN WHICH TO FILE FOR DISSOLUTION OF MARRIAGE: District Court. "In the District Court for _____ County, Nebraska." [Revised Statutes of Nebraska; Chapter 42-353, Chapter 25-2740].

DOCUMENT CAPTION INFORMATION: Petition for Dissolution of Marriage. "In Re: the Marriage of: _____, Petitioner [or Co-Petitioner if the petition is filed jointly] and _____, Respondent [or Co-Petitioner if the petition is filed jointly]." [See below under Simplified Or Special Dissolution Of Marriage Procedures]. Final document title: Decree of Dissolution of Marriage.

LEGAL SEPARATION: Irretrievable breakdown of the marriage is the only grounds for a legal separation in Nebraska. There are no residency requirements specified in the statute. If the residency requirements for dissolution of marriage are met after the petition for legal separation has been filed, the spouse filing may change the proceeding to a proceeding for dissolution of marriage. [Revised Statutes of Nebraska; Chapter 42-350].

SIMPLIFIED OR SPECIAL DISSOLUTION OF MARRIAGE PROCEDURES: Joint petitions for dissolution of marriage may be filed by both spouses. In such cases, the spouses should be referred to as "Co-Petitioners" on the court documents. In addition, marital settlement agreements are specifically authorized by law. [Revised Statutes of Nebraska; Chapter 42-361 and 42-366].

MEDIATION OR COUNSELING REQUIREMENTS: A dissolution of marriage will not be granted until every reasonable effort for a reconciliation has been made. If it appears to the court that there is some reasonable possibility of reconciliation, dissolution of marriage actions may be transferred to a conciliation court or the spouses may be referred to a qualified marriage counselor, family service agency, or other agency which provides conciliation services. Official conciliation counselors are available in counties of over 250,000 persons. [Revised Statutes of Nebraska; Chapter 42-360 and 42-808].

PROPERTY DISTRIBUTION: Nebraska is an "equitable distribution" jurisdiction. The spouses retain their separate property acquired prior to the marriage. All of the spouse's marital property, including any gifts and inheritances acquired during the marriage, may be divided, based on a consideration of the following factors: (1) the contribution of each spouse to the acquisition of the marital property, including the contribution of each spouse as homemaker; (2) the economic circumstances of each spouse at the time the division of property is to become effective; (3) the length of the marriage; and (4) any custodial provisions for the children. [Revised Statutes of Nebraska; Chapter 42-365].

ALIMONY/MAINTENANCE/SPOUSAL SUPPORT: Either spouse may be ordered to pay reasonable spousal support, without regard to marital fault, based on a consideration of the following factors: (1) the circumstances of both spouses; (2) the duration of the marriage; (3) the contribution of each spouse to the marriage, including services rendered in homemaking, child care, education, and career building of the other spouse; (4) any interruption of personal careers or education; and (5) the ability of the supported spouse to engage in gainful employment without interfering with the interests of any minor children in his or her custody. Reasonable security for the payments may be required. [Revised Statutes of Nebraska; Chapter 42-365].

SPOUSE'S NAME: Either spouse may include a request to restore his or her former name in the petition for dissolution of marriage. [Nebraska Case Law].

CHILD CUSTODY: Joint or sole custody of children is determined according to the best interests of the child and based on a consideration of the following factors: (1) the general health, welfare, and social behavior of the child; (2) the preference of the child, if the child is of sufficient age and capacity; (3) the child's relationship with each parent prior to the filing for dissolution of marriage; and (4) any credible evidence of child or spousal abuse. No preference

105

is to be given because of parent's sex. Joint custody may be awarded if both parents agree. [Revised Statutes of Nebraska; Chapter 42-364].

CHILD SUPPORT: The amount of child support is determined based on a consideration of the earning capacity of each parent. There are official Supreme Court child support guidelines which should be available from the clerk of the court. [Revised Statutes of Nebraska; Chapter 42-364].

PREMARITAL AGREEMENT: The agreement must be in writing and signed by both parties. The agreement is not enforceable if it is proven that (1) the agreement was not executed voluntarily; (2) the agreement is unconscionable in that there was no fair and reasonable disclosure of the property or financial obligations of the other party, did not voluntarily waive the right to the disclosure of this information, did not have adequate knowledge of these obligations; (3) a provision of the agreement modifies or eliminates alimony and that modification causes that person to be eligible for public assistance. If the marriage is determined to be void, the agreement is enforceable only to the extent necessary to avoid an inequitable result. [Revised Statutes of Nebraska; Chapter 42, Sections 1003, 1006, and 1007].

NEVADA

RESIDENCY REQUIREMENTS AND WHERE TO FILE: The divorce may be filed in the county: (1) where either spouse resides; or (2) where the spouses last lived together; or (3) where the cause of the divorce took place; or (4) where the plaintiff resided for 6 weeks immediately prior to filing for divorce. One of the spouses must have been a resident of Nevada for at least 6 weeks prior to filing for divorce, unless the cause for the divorce took place in the county in Nevada where the spouses actually lived at the time of the happening of the cause. [Nevada Revised Statutes; Chapter 125; Section 020].

LEGAL GROUNDS FOR DIVORCE: No-Fault: (1) incompatibility; or (2) living separate and apart without cohabitation for 1 year. [Nevada Revised Statutes; Chapter 125; Sections 010].

General: Insanity which existed for at least 2 years before filing for the divorce. [Nevada Revised Statutes; Chapter 125; Section 010].

NAME OF COURT IN WHICH TO FILE FOR DIVORCE: District Court. "In the District Court for _____ County, Nevada." [Nevada Revised Statutes; Chapter 125; Section 020].

DOCUMENT CAPTION INFORMATION: Complaint for Divorce. "In Re: the Marriage of: _____, Plaintiff and _____, Defendant." Final document title: Decree of Divorce.

LEGAL SEPARATION: If a spouse has any of the grounds for divorce or if he or she has been deserted for over 90 days, a suit for separate maintenance of his or herself and any children may be filed. In addition, the spouses may agree to an immediate separation and make appropriate provisions for spousal and child support. There is no residency requirement specified in the statute. [Nevada Revised Statutes; Chapter 125; Section 190].

SIMPLIFIED OR SPECIAL DIVORCE PROCEDURES: There are two provisions for summary divorce in Nevada. First, a summary divorce may be granted if the following conditions are met: (1) either spouse has been a resident of the state for at least 6 weeks; (2) the spouses are incompatible or have lived separate and apart without cohabitation for 1 year; (3) there are no minor children (born or adopted) and the wife is not pregnant, or the spouses have signed an agreement specifying the custody and support of the children; (4) there is no community or joint property or the spouses have signed an agreement regarding the division of their property and the assumption of their liabilities and have signed any deeds, titles, or other evidences of transfer of property; (5) both spouses waive their rights to spousal support (maintenance) or the spouses have signed an agreement specifying the amount of spousal support; (6) both spouses waive (a) their rights to notice of entry of the final decree of divorce, (b) their rights to appeal the divorce, (c) their rights to request findings of fact and conclusions of law in the divorce proceeding, and (d) their rights to a new trial; (7) both spouses want the court to enter the decree of divorce. A Summary Proceeding for Divorce is begun by filing a joint petition, signed under oath, together with an Affidavit of Corroboration of Residency by a witness.

In addition, a spouse may apply for a divorce by default by affidavit. In such situations, oral testimony will not normally be required. If there is a marital settlement agreement, it should be identified in the affidavit and attached to it when filed. The affidavit should state that: (1) the residency requirements have been met; (2) all of the information in the petition is correct and true on the personal knowledge of the person signing the affidavit; (3) that the affidavit contains only facts that would be admissible into evidence; (4) give factual support for each allegation in the application; and (5) establish that the person signing the affidavit is competent to testify.

Each divorce filed must also contain a Civil Cover sheet, a Verification of Pleadings, a request for submission, and an Affidavit of Residency. Finally, there are specific provisions authorizing separation agreements and marital settlement agreements. [Nevada Revised Statutes; Chapter 123; Sections 020 and 090; and Chapter 125; Sections 181-184].

MEDIATION OR COUNSELING REQUIREMENTS: There are no legal provisions in Nevada for divorce mediation.

PROPERTY DISTRIBUTION: Nevada is a "community property" state. The spouses retain all of their separate property, acquired prior to the marriage or by gift or inheritance. The court will divide all of the spouse's community property and all of the property held jointly by the spouses on or after July 1, 1979, including any military retirement benefits. The following factors are considered: (1) the economic circumstances of each spouse at the time the division of property is to become effective; (2) how and by whom the property was acquired; (3) the merits of each spouse; and (4) the burdens imposed upon either spouse for the benefit of the children. Marital fault is not mentioned as a factor. Either spouse's property is also then subject to distribution for alimony or child support. Separate property which one spouse contributed to purchase or improve community property may be returned to the contributing spouse. [Nevada Revised Statutes; Chapter 125; Section 150].

ALIMONY/MAINTENANCE/SPOUSAL SUPPORT: Unless there is a pre-marital agreement, either spouse may be awarded alimony, without regard to marital fault. The alimony may be a lump-sum or periodic payments. The award of alimony must be just and equitable, and consider (1) the respective merits of the spouses; (2) the condition in which they will be left by the divorce; (3) who acquired the property to be used for alimony; (4) and if there are burdens imposed upon the property for the benefit of any children. In addition the court shall consider a spouse's need for alimony for the purpose of obtaining training or education relating to a job, profession, or career. Other factors which the court is to consider are: (1) whether the spouse who would pay the alimony has obtained greater job skills or education during the marriage; and (2) whether the spouse who would receive alimony provided financial support while the other spouse obtained job skills or education. Alimony may be provided for a limited time period for job training, career testing, and education. [Nevada Revised Statutes; Chapter 125; Section 150].

SPOUSE'S NAME: For a reasonable cause, the court will restore the wife's former name. [Nevada Revised Statutes; Chapter 125; Section 130].

CHILD CUSTODY: Joint or sole custody is awarded based on the best interests of the child and upon the following factors: (1) the preference of the child, if the child is of sufficient age and capacity; (2) the wishes of the parents. No preference is to be given because of parent's sex; (3) whether either parent has committed domestic violence; and (4) other relevant factors. There is a presumption of joint custody if both parents have signed an agreement for joint custody or both agree to joint custody in open court. There is also a presumption that it is not in the best interests of a child to have custody awarded to a parent who has committed domestic violence. [Nevada Revised Statutes; Chapter 125; Sections 480 and 490].

CHILD SUPPORT: Temporary (during the divorce proceeding) and permanent child support may be granted. There are official Child Support percentages contained in Nevada Revised Statutes; Chapter 125B, Section 070. These Guidelines are presumed to be correct unless there is a showing that the needs of the child would not be met under the particular circumstances in a case. Factors for deviation from the guideline percentages are: (1) the cost of health insurance; (2) the cost of child care; (3) any special educational needs of the child; (4) the age of the child; (5) the responsibility of the parents for the support of others; (6) the value of services contributed by the parents; (7) any public aid paid to the child; (8) any pregnancy expenses; (9) any visitation travel expenses; (10) the amount of time the child spends with each parent; (11) the relative income of each parent; and (12) any other necessary expenses. [Nevada Revised Statutes; Chapter 125; Section 230 and Chapter 125B, Section 070, 080, and 090].

PREMARITAL AGREEMENT: The agreement must be in writing and signed by both parties and is enforceable without consideration. The agreement is not enforceable if the party proves that (1) the execution of the agreement was not voluntary; (2) the agreement was unconscionable when executed; (3) before execution of the agreement the party was not provided a fair and reasonable disclosure of the property or financial obligations of the other party, did not waive disclosure of these obligations, did not have adequate knowledge of these obligations; (4) a provision modifies or eliminates alimony or support and that modification causes one party to be eligible for public assistance. If the marriage is determined to be void, the agreement is only enforceable to the extent necessary to avoid an inequitable result. [Nevada Revised Statues; Chapter 123A, Sections 040, 080, and 090].

NEW HAMPSHIRE

RESIDENCY REQUIREMENTS AND WHERE TO FILE: (1) Both spouses must be residents of the state when the divorce is filed for; or (2) the spouse filing for divorce must have been a resident of New Hampshire for 1 year immediately prior to filing for divorce and the other spouse was personally served with process within the state; or (3) the cause of divorce must have arisen in New Hampshire and one of the spouses must be living in New Hampshire when the divorce is filed for. The divorce may be filed for in a county where either spouse resides. [New Hampshire Revised Statutes Annotated; Chapters 458:5, 458:6, and 458.9].

LEGAL GROUNDS FOR DIVORCE: No-Fault: Irreconcilable differences which have caused the irremediable breakdown of the marriage. [New Hampshire Revised Statutes Annotated; Chapter 458:7].

General: (1) impotence; (2) adultery; (3) abandonment and not been heard of for 2 years; (4) imprisonment with a sentence of more than 1 year served; (5) physical abuse or reasonable apprehension of physical abuse; (6) desertion without support of spouse by husband for 2 years; (7) cruel and inhuman treatment; (8) habitual intemperance (drunkenness) for 2 years; (9) living separate and apart without cohabitation (wife left without husband's consent for 2 years); (10) mental abuse; (11) when either spouse has joined a religious society which professes that the relationship of the husband and wife is unlawful and refuses to cohabit with the other for 6 consecutive months; (12) when the wife of any citizen of New Hampshire leaves the state without her husband's consent and lives elsewhere for 10 consecutive years without returning to claim her marriage rights; and (13) when the wife lives in New Hampshire for 2 years and her husband becomes the citizen of a foreign country without supporting the wife. [New Hampshire Revised Statutes Annotated; Chapter 458:7, 458:7a, and 458:26].

NAME OF COURT IN WHICH TO FILE FOR DIVORCE: Superior Court. "The State of New Hampshire, Superior Court in and for _____."

DOCUMENT CAPTION INFORMATION: Petition for Divorce. "In Re: the Marriage of _____, Petitioner and _____, Respondent." Final document title: Decree of Divorce.

LEGAL SEPARATION: The grounds for legal separation (limited divorce) in New Hampshire are the same as for divorce. (1) The spouse filing for legal separation must have been a resident of New Hampshire for 1 year; or (2) the cause of legal separation must have arisen in New Hampshire and one of the spouses must be living in New Hampshire when the action for legal separation is filed for. [New Hampshire Revised Statutes Annotated; Chapters 458:5, 458:6, 458:7, 458:7a, and 458:26].

SIMPLIFIED OR SPECIAL DIVORCE PROCEDURES: There are no legal provisions in New Hampshire for simplified divorce procedures.

MEDIATION OR COUNSELING REQUIREMENTS: At either spouse's request or if the court feels that there is a reasonable chance at reconciliation, it may delay the divorce proceedings and order the spouses to submit to marriage counseling. There are also provisions for voluntary marital mediation of issues involved in the divorce. [New Hampshire Revised Statutes Annotated; Chapters 458:7B and 458:15-a].

PROPERTY DISTRIBUTION: New Hampshire is an "equitable distribution" state. The court will divide all of the spouse's property, including (1) gifts; (2) inheritances; (3) property acquired prior to the marriage; and (4) any retirement or pension benefits, as is equitable and just. An equal division is presumed to be equitable. The factors for consideration specified in the statute are: (1) the length of the marriage; (2) the age and health of the spouses; (3) the occupation of the spouses; (4) the vocational skills of the spouses; (5) the employability of the spouses; (6) the value of each spouse's property; (7) the amount and sources of income of the spouses; (8) the liabilities and needs of each spouse; (9) the opportunity of each for further acquisition of capital assets and income; (10) the ability of the custodial parent to engage in gainful employment without interfering with the interests of any minor children in custody; (11) the need of the custodial parent to occupy or own the marital residence and any household furnishings; (12) the actions of either spouse during the marriage which contributed to the increase or decrease in value of any property; (13) any significant disparity between the spouses in relation to the contribution of each spouse to the acquisition of the marital property, including the contribution of each spouse to the care and education of the children and the care and management of the home; (14) the expectation of any retirement or pension benefits; (15) the federal income tax consequences of the court's division of the property; (16) any marital fault if such fault caused the breakdown of the marriage and caused pain and suffering or economic loss; (17) the value of any property acquired prior to marriage or exchanged for property acquired prior to marriage; (18) the value of any gifts or inheritances; (19) any direct or indirect contribution to the education or career development of the other spouse; (20) any interruption in education or career opportunities to benefit the other's career, the marriage, or any children; (21)

the social and economic status of each spouse; (22) any other relevant factor. [New Hampshire Revised Statutes Annotated; Chapter 458:16-a].

ALIMONY/MAINTENANCE/SPOUSAL SUPPORT: Either spouse may be ordered to pay support to the other if: (1) the spouse in need lacks sufficient income or property to provide for reasonable needs, taking into account the standard of living during the marriage; and (2) the spouse to pay is able to meet his or her reasonable needs, taking into account the standard of living during the marriage; and (3) the spouse in need is unable to support him or herself at a reasonable standard of living or is the custodian of a child whose condition or circumstances make it appropriate that the custodian not seek employment outside the home. The factors for consideration are: (1) the duration of the marriage; (2) the age of the spouses; (3) the physical and emotional conditions of the spouses; (4) the vocational skills and employability of the spouse seeking support; (5) the tax consequences to each spouse; (6) the amount and sources of income of the spouses; (7) the occupation of the spouses; (8) the value of each spouse's property; (9) the liabilities and needs of each spouse; (10) the opportunity of each for further acquisition of capital assets and income; (11) any marital fault if such fault caused the breakdown of the marriage and caused pain and suffering or economic loss; (12) the contribution of each spouse to the acquisition, preservation, or appreciation in value of the marital property, including any non-economic contributions of each spouse to the family unit; and (13) the social and economic status of each spouse. [New Hampshire Revised Statutes Annotated; Chapter 458:19].

SPOUSE'S NAME: A spouse's former name may be restored in a divorce. [New Hampshire Revised Statutes Annotated; Chapter 458:24].

CHILD CUSTODY: Joint legal custody (joint responsibility for all parental rights and decisions, except physical custody) is presumed to be in the best interests of the child unless there has been child abuse by one of the parents. Custody is awarded based on a consideration of the following factors: (1) preference of the child; (2) the education of the child; (3) any findings or recommendations of a neutral mediator; and (4) any other factors. No preference is given to either parent based on the parent's sex. Repeated and unwarranted interference by a parent with primary custody with the visitation rights of the other parent is now a factor in modifying custody arrangements. [New Hampshire Revised Statutes Annotated; Chapter 458:17].

CHILD SUPPORT: The court may order reasonable provisions for the support and education of a child. There are specific child support guidelines set out in the statute. There is a presumption that the amount set forth in the guidelines is correct, unless it is shown that the amount is unjust or inappropriate under the particular circumstances of a case. The factors for consideration for adjusting the amount up or down which are specified in the statute are: (1) any

113

extraordinary medical, dental, or educational expenses of the child; (2) a significantly higher or lower income of either parent; (3) the economic conse-quences of the presence of any stepparents or stepchildren; (4) any extraordi-nary costs associated with physical custody; (5) the economic consequences to either parent of the disposition of the marital home; (6) any state or federal tax consequences; (7) any split or shared custody arrangements; and (8) any other significant factor. The court may order health insurance coverage as a method of support. There are also provisions for wage assignments and wage withholding to secure the payment of any child support. [New Hampshire Revised Statutes Annotated; Chapters 458:17, 458:18, 458-C:1-5].

PREMARITAL AGREEMENT: New Hampshire has no specific statutes pertain-ing to premarital agreements.

NEW JERSEY

RESIDENCY REQUIREMENTS AND WHERE TO FILE: (1) One of the spouses must be a resident of New Jersey for at least 1 year prior to filing for divorce; or (2) when the cause for divorce is adultery and took place in New Jersey, one of the spouses must have been a resident (no time limit). The divorce may be filed for in any county in New Jersey. [New Jersey Statutes Annotated; Title 2A, Chapters 34-8 and 34-10].

LEGAL GROUNDS FOR DIVORCE: No-Fault: Living separate and apart for 18 months and no reasonable prospect of reconciliation. [New Jersey Statutes Annotated; Title 2A, Chapter 34-2].

General: (1) adultery; (2) imprisonment for 18 months; (3) unnatural sexual behavior before or after marriage; (4) alcoholism and/or drug addiction; (5) willful desertion for 1 year; (6) cruel and inhuman treatment; (7) separation for 2 years caused by confinement for mental illness; and (8) extreme cruelty. [New Jersey Statutes Annotated; Title 2A, Chapter 34-2].

NAME OF COURT IN WHICH TO FILE FOR DIVORCE: Superior Court. "Superior Court of New Jersey, Chancery Division, Family Part, _____ County." [New Jersey Statutes Annotated; Title 2A, Chapter 34-8].

DOCUMENT CAPTION INFORMATION: Complaint for Divorce. "In Re: the Marriage of: _____, Plaintiff and _____, Defendant." Final document title: Judgement of Divorce.

LEGAL SEPARATION: The grounds for legal separation (or a divorce from bed and board) are the same as for divorce. One of the spouses must be a resident of New Jersey for at least 1 year prior to filing for legal separation or when the cause for legal separation is adultery and took place in New Jersey, one of the spouses must have been a resident (no time limit). [New Jersey Statutes Annotated; Title 2A, Chapter 34-2].

SIMPLIFIED OR SPECIAL DIVORCE PROCEDURES: The filing of an acknowledgment of service of process or appearance is specifically authorized. Also, there is a required Case Information Statement which must be filed as shown

115

in New Jersey Civil Practice Rules, Appendix V. [New Jersey Statutes Annotated; Title 2A, Chapter 34-11].

MEDIATION OR COUNSELING REQUIREMENTS: There are no legal provisions in New Jersey for divorce mediation.

PROPERTY DISTRIBUTION: New Jersey is an "equitable distribution" state. A spouse's separate property acquired before a marriage is retained by that spouse. All of the spouse's other property (except that acquired by gift and inheritance) is divided equitably, based on the following factors: (1) the value of each spouse's marital property; (2) the value of the separate property of the spouses; (3) the length of the marriage; (4) the age and health of the spouses; (5) the amount and sources of income of the spouses; (6) the liabilities and needs of each spouse and the opportunity of each for further acquisition of capital assets and income; (7) the standard of living established during the marriage; (8) how and by whom the property was acquired; (9) the tax consequences to each spouse; (10) the contribution of each spouse to the acquisition of the marital property, including the contribution of each spouse as homemaker; (11) the economic circumstances of each spouse at the time the division of property is to become effective; (12) any written agreement between the spouses; (13) the income and earning capacity of the spouses; (14) the educational background, training, employment skills of the spouses; (15) any custodial responsibilities; (16) the length of absence from the job market; (17) the time and expense necessary to enable the spouse to acquire sufficient education or training to enable the spouse to become self-supporting at a standard of living reasonably comparable to that enjoyed during the marriage; (18) the need for the parent with custody of any children to own or occupy the marital residence; (19) the need to create a trust fund for the future medical or educational needs of a spouse or children; (20) contribution by each party to the education, training or earning power of the other; (21) the extend to which a party deferred achieving his or her career goals; and (22) any other factor necessary to do equity and justice between the spouses. [New Jersey Statutes Annotated; Title 2A, Chapter 34-23.1].

ALIMONY/MAINTENANCE/SPOUSAL SUPPORT: Either spouse may be ordered to pay alimony, without regard to marital fault, based on the following factors: (1) the duration of the marriage; (2) the actual needs, obligations, and ability to pay of each spouse; (3) the standard of living established during the marriage; (4) the time and expense necessary to acquire sufficient education and training to enable the spouse to find appropriate employment, and that spouse's future earning capacity; (5) the age of the spouses; (6) the physical and emotional conditions of the spouses; (7) the earning capacities, educational levels, vocational skills, and employability of the spouses; (8) the length of absence from the job market; (9) any child custodial responsibilities of the spouse seeking alimony; (10) the availability of training and employment;

116

(11) the opportunity for the future acquisition of capital and income; (12) the history of financial and non-financial contributions of each spouse to the marriage, including the contribution of each spouse to the care and education of children and interruption of personal careers or educational opportunities; (13) the equitable distribution of property and any payouts from this property, if a consideration of this income is fair and just (however, income from retirement benefits which are treated as an asset for purposes of equitable distribution are not to be considered); and (14) and any other factor the court deems just and equitable. [New Jersey Statutes Annotated; Title 2A, Chapter 34-23].

SPOUSE'S NAME: The court may allow either spouse to use his or her former name. [New Jersey Statutes Annotated; Title 2A, Chapter 34-21].

CHILD CUSTODY: Sole or joint custody may be awarded based on the following factors: (1) the physical, emotional, mental, religious, and social needs of the child; and (2) the preference of the child, if the child is of sufficient age and capacity. No preference is to be given because of parent's sex. A father may not forcibly take a minor child from a mother's actual physical custody. [New Jersey Statutes Annotated; Title 2A, Chapter 34-23 and New Jersey Case Law].

CHILD SUPPORT: The court may award child support for the care, maintenance, and education of a child. The factors for consideration specified in the statute are: (1) the needs of the child; (2) the standard of living and economic circumstances of both parents; (3) the financial resources, needs, and obligations of both the noncustodial and the custodial parent; (4) the earning ability of each parent, including educational background, training, employment skills, work experience, custodial responsibility for the children, cost of child care, and the length and cost of education and training to obtain employment; (5) the need and capacity of the child for education, including higher education; (6) the age and health station of the child and the parents; (7) the income, assets, and earning ability of the child; (8) the responsibility of the parents for the support of others; (9) reasonable debts and liabilities of each child and parent; and (10) any other relevant factors. There are specific New Jersey Supreme Court child support guidelines contained in New Jersey Civil Practice Rules, Appendix IX. [New Jersey Statutes Annotated; Title 2A, Chapter 34-23].

PREMARITAL AGREEMENT: The agreement shall be in writing with a statement of assets attached to it, signed and is enforceable without consideration. The agreement can be amended or revoked only by a written agreement signed by the parties and is enforceable without consideration. The agreement is not enforceable if it is proven that (1) the agreement was not executed voluntarily; (2) the agreement was unconscionable at the time enforcement is sought or (3) that party before execution was not provided a full and fair disclosure of the earnings, property and financial obligations of the other party, did not voluntarily waive the right to the disclosure of this information, did not have adequate knowledge of these obligations or did not consult with independent counsel and did not voluntarily waive the opportunity to consult with independent counsel. If the marriage is determined to be void, the agreement is enforceable only to the extent necessary to avoid an inequitable result. [New Jersey Statutes Annotated; Title 37, Chapters 2-33, 2-37, 2-38, and 2-39].

NEW MEXICO

RESIDENCY REQUIREMENTS AND WHERE TO FILE: One of the spouses must have been a resident of New Mexico for at least 6 months immediately preceding the filing for dissolution of marriage and have a home in New Mexico. The dissolution of marriage may be filed in any county where either spouse resides. [New Mexico Statutes Annotated; Article 4, Section 40-4-5].

LEGAL GROUNDS FOR DISSOLUTION OF MARRIAGE: No-Fault: Incompatibility because of discord and conflicts of personalities such that the legitimate ends of the marriage relationship have been destroyed preventing any reasonable expectation of reconciliation. [New Mexico Statutes Annotated; Article 4, Sections 40-4-1 and 40-4-2].

General: (1) adultery; (2) abandonment; (3) cruel and inhuman treatment; and (4) incompatibility. [New Mexico Statutes Annotated; Article 4, Section 40-4-1].

NAME OF COURT IN WHICH TO FILE FOR DISSOLUTION OF MARRIAGE: District Court. "State of New Mexico, In the District Court, _____ County."

DOCUMENT CAPTION INFORMATION: Petition for Dissolution of Marriage. "In Re: the Marriage of: _____, Petitioner and _____, Respondent." Final document title: Decree of Dissolution of Marriage.

LEGAL SEPARATION: If the spouses have permanently separated and do not live together or cohabit, either spouse may begin proceedings for property division, child custody and support, and maintenance, without asking for a dissolution of marriage. One of the spouses must have been a resident of New Mexico for at least 6 months immediately preceding the filing for legal separation and have a home in New Mexico. [New Mexico Statutes Annotated; Article 4, Sections 40-4-3, 40-4-5].

SIMPLIFIED OR SPECIAL DISSOLUTION OF MARRIAGE PROCEDURES: Marital settlement agreements and contracts for separation are specifically authorized by law and must be in writing. Any marital settlement agreements should be recorded in the county where the any real estate may be that is

119

affected by the agreement. [New Mexico Statutes Annotated; Article 4, Sections 40-2-4 and 40-2-5].

MEDIATION OR COUNSELING REQUIREMENTS: If domestic relations mediation programs have been established in the county where the dissolution of marriage is filed for, parents may request the use of such programs, or the court may order the parents to enter the program. [New Mexico Statutes Annotated; Article 4, Section 40-12-5].

PROPERTY DISTRIBUTION: New Mexico is a "community property" state. Each spouse retains his or her separate property acquired prior to the marriage, designated as separate property by a written agreement, and any gifts or inheritances. New Mexico has a "quasi-community" property which includes: All property, except separate property, which a spouse acquires outside of New Mexico which would have been community property if they had acquired it in New Mexico. "Quasi-community" property is treated like standard community property if both parties are domiciled in New Mexico at the time of dissolution. The spouse's community property is to be divided equally between the spouses. Marital fault is not considered. There are no factors for consideration set out in the statute. [New Mexico Statutes Annotated; Article 4, Sections 40-3-8 and 40-4-7].

ALIMONY/MAINTENANCE/SPOUSAL SUPPORT: Either spouse may be awarded a just and proper amount of maintenance, without regard to marital fault. The factors that the court will consider are: (1) duration of the marriage; (2) spouse's current and future earning capacities; (3) good faith efforts of the spouses to maintain employment or become self-supporting; (4) needs and obligations of each spouse; (5) age and health of the spouses; (6) amount of property that each spouse owns; (7) spouses standard of living during the marriage; (8) medical and life insurance maintained during the marriage; (9) assets of the spouses, including any income-producing property (However, requiring a spouse to sell assets shall not be considered unless there are exceptional circumstances); (10) each spouse's liabilities; and (11) any marital separation or settlement agreements. [New Mexico Statutes Annotated; Article 4, Section 40-4-7 and New Mexico Case Law].

SPOUSE'S NAME: The court may order the restoration of a spouse's former name. [New Mexico Statutes Annotated; Article 4, Section 40-8-1].

CHILD CUSTODY: Joint or sole child custody is to be determined according to the best interests of the child. There is a presumption that joint custody is in the best interests of the child. The factors for consideration are: (1) the wishes of the child; (2) the wishes of the parents; (3) relationship of the child with parents, siblings, and other significant family members; (4) child's adjustment to his or her home, school, and community; and (5) the mental and physical

120

health of all individuals involved. If a minor is 14 years old or older, the court may consider the wishes of the minor. In addition, the factors that are considered for joint custody are as follows: (1) ability of the parents to cooperate and make decisions jointly; (2) physical proximity of the parents to each other as this relates to the practical considerations of where the child will reside; (3) whether an award of joint custody will promote more frequent or continuing contact between the child and each of the parents; (4) love, affection, and other emotional ties existing between the parents and the child; (5) capacity and disposition of the parents to provide the child with food, clothing, medical care, and other material needs; (6) whether each parent is willing to accept all the responsibilities of parenting, including a willingness to accept or relinquish care at specified times; (7) whether each parent is able to allow the other to provide care without intrusion; and (8) the suitability of a parenting plan for the implementation of joint custody. [New Mexico Statutes Annotated; Article 4, Sections 40-4-1-9.1 and 40-4-9].

CHILD SUPPORT: Either parent may be ordered to provide child support, based on a consideration of the financial resources of that parent. Any welfare benefits are not considered. Specific child support guidelines and worksheets are provided. Separate worksheets are provided for determining child support amounts for parents with visitation and for parents with shared responsibility. Shared responsibility or joint custody is defined as each parent having the child in their home at least 35% of the time during a year. Chid Support Guidelines are contained in New Mexico Statutes Annotated; Article 4, Section 40-4-11.1. These guidelines are presumed to be correct unless there is a showing that the amount of support would be unjust or inappropriate under the particular circumstances of a case, specifically (1) any extraordinary uninsured medical, dental, or counseling expenses for the child of over $100.00 per year; (2) any extraordinary educational expenses for the child; (3) any transportation and communication expenses for long-distance visitation or time sharing; or (4) substantial hardship for either parent or the child. The assignment and withholding of wages to secure the payment of child support payments may be ordered. [New Mexico Statutes Annotated; Article 4, Sections Section 27-2-27, 40-4-7 40-4-11 and 40-4-11.1]

PREMARITAL AGREEMENT: The agreement must be in writing, signed by both parties, and acknowledged. The agreement is enforceable without consideration. The agreement is not enforceable if (1) not executed voluntarily; (2) was unconscionable when executed and the person was not provided a fair and reasonable disclosure of the property or financial obligations of the other party, did not voluntarily waive any right to the disclosure of this information, and did not have adequate knowledge of these obligations. If the marriage is determined to be void, the agreement is enforceable only to the extent necessary to avoid an inequitable result. [New Mexico Statues Annotated; Sections 40-3A-3, 40-3A-7 and 40-3A-8].

NEW YORK

RESIDENCY REQUIREMENTS AND WHERE TO FILE: If only one spouse resides in New York at the time of filing the divorce, the residency requirement is 2 years. However, the requirement is reduced to 1 year if: (1) the spouses were married in New York and either spouse is still a resident; or (2) they once resided in New York and either spouse is still a resident; or (3) the grounds for divorce arose in New York. In addition, there is no residency time limit requirement if both of the spouses were residents of New York at the time of filing the divorce and the grounds for divorce arose in New York. The divorce may be filed for in a county where either spouse resides. [Consolidated Laws of New York Annotated; Domestic Relations Law, Volume 8, Sections 230 and 231; and New York Civil Practice Laws and Rules, Rule 503].

LEGAL GROUNDS FOR DIVORCE: No-Fault: (1) living separate and apart for 1 year under the terms of a separation agreement which is in writing and signed and notarized. (Proof of compliance with the terms of the settlement agreement must be submitted when the divorce is filed). In addition, a copy of the agreement or a brief memorandum of the agreement must be filed in the office of the clerk of the county; or (2) living separate and apart for 1 year under the terms of a judicial separation decree. [Consolidated Laws of New York Annotated; Domestic Relations Law, Volume 8, Section 170].

General: (1) adultery; (2) abandonment for 1 year; (3) imprisonment for 3 or more consecutive years; and (4) cruel and inhuman treatment. [Consolidated Laws of New York Annotated; Domestic Relations Law, Volume 8, Section 170].

NAME OF COURT IN WHICH TO FILE FOR DIVORCE: Supreme Court. "Supreme Court of the State of New York, _____ County."

DOCUMENT CAPTION INFORMATION: Complaint for Divorce. "In Re: the Marriage of: _____, Plaintiff and _____, Defendant." Final document title: Judgment of Divorce.

LEGAL SEPARATION: The grounds for legal separation (separation from bed and board) in New York are: (1) adultery; (2) abandonment; (3) imprisonment for 3 or more consecutive years; (4) neglect of and failure to provide support for a wife; and (5) cruel and inhuman treatment. If only one spouse resides in New York at the time of filing the legal separation, the residency requirement is 2 years. However, the requirement is reduced to 1 year if: (1) the spouses were married in New York and either spouse is still a resident; or (2) they once resided in New York and either spouse is still a resident; or (3) the grounds for legal separation arose in New York. In addition, there is no residency time limit requirement if both of the spouses were residents of New York at the time of filing the legal separation and the grounds for legal separation arose in New York. [Consolidated Laws of New York Annotated; Domestic Relations Law, Volume 8, Sections 200, 230, and 231].

SIMPLIFIED OR SPECIAL DIVORCE PROCEDURES: A summary divorce may be granted in New York if: (1) the spouses lived apart for 1 year according to the terms of a separation decree or a separation agreement; and (2) satisfactory proof is submitted to the court that the spouse seeking the divorce has substantially performed all the terms and conditions of the separation decree or separation agreement. There are sample divorce forms contained in the statute (Forms 1 and 12 for no-fault grounds), including the language necessary to state specific grounds and residency requirements. In addition, New York requires a financial disclosure to be filed in every divorce action. [Consolidated Laws of New York Annotated; Domestic Relations Law, Volume 8, Sections 170 and 236].

MEDIATION OR COUNSELING REQUIREMENTS: There are no legal provisions in New York for divorce mediation.

PROPERTY DISTRIBUTION: New York is an "equitable distribution" state. Separate property, including property acquired before a marriage and any gifts or inheritances whenever acquired, is to remain with the spouse who owns it. Separate property also includes any increase in value or property acquired in exchange for separate property. Marital property acquired during the marriage will be equitably divided between the spouses, based on the following factors: (1) the contribution of each spouse to the acquisition of the marital property, including the contribution of each spouse as homemaker; (2) the value of each spouse's property at the time of the marriage and at the time of filing for divorce; (3) the probable future economic circumstances of each spouse; (4) the length of the marriage; (5) the age and health of the spouses; (6) the amount and sources of income of the spouses; (7) the present and potential earning capability of each spouse; (8) the potential loss of inheritance or pension rights upon dissolution of the marriage; (9) whether the property award is instead of or in addition to maintenance; (10) custodial provisions for the children and the need for a custodial parent to occupy the marital home; (11) the type of marital property in question (whether it is liquid or non-liquid); (12) the impossibility or difficulty of evaluating an interest in an asset such as a business, profession, or corporation and the desirability of keeping such an asset intact and free from interference by the other spouse; (13) the tax consequences to each party; (14) the wasteful dissipation of assets; (15) any transfer of property made in anticipation of divorce; (16) any equitable claim that a spouse has in marital property, including joint efforts and expenditures, and contribution and services as a spouse, parent, wage earner, and homemaker, and to the career and career potential of the other spouse; and (17) any other factor necessary to do equity and justice between the spouses. Marital fault may be considered. Financial disclosure of assets and income are mandatory. [Consolidated Laws of New York Annotated; Domestic Relations Law, Volume 8, Section 236, Part B].

ALIMONY/MAINTENANCE/SPOUSAL SUPPORT: Either spouse may be awarded maintenance, without regard to marital fault, based on a consideration of the following factors: (1) the income and property of the spouses, including any marital property divided as a result of the dissolution of marriage; (2) any transfer of property made in anticipation of divorce; (3) the duration of the marriage; (4) the wasteful dissipation of marital property; (5) the contribution of each spouse to the marriage and the career of the other spouse, including services rendered in homemaking, child care, education, and career building of the other spouse; (6) the tax consequences to each spouse; (7) any custodial and child support responsibilities; (8) the ability of the spouse seeking support to become self-supporting and the time and training necessary; (9) any reduced lifetime earning capacity as the result of having foregone or delayed education, training, employment, or career opportunities during the marriage; (10) whether the spouse from whom maintenance is sought has sufficient property and income to provide maintenance for the other spouse; and (11) any other factor the court deems just and equitable. [Consolidated Laws of New York Annotated; Domestic Relations Law, Volume 8, Section 236, Part B].

SPOUSE'S NAME: At the wife's request, upon divorce the court may restore her maiden or other former name. [Consolidated Laws of New York Annotated; Domestic Relations Law, Volume 8, Section 240a].

CHILD CUSTODY: Joint or sole child custody is to be determined according to the best interests of the child. Neither parent is entitled to a preference. There are no factors specified in the statute. [Consolidated Laws of New York Annotated; Domestic Relations Law, Volume 8, Section 240 and New York Case Law].

CHILD SUPPORT: Either or both parents may be ordered to pay child support necessary for the support, maintenance, and education of the child. Health insurance coverage may be ordered to be provided. Marital misconduct of either parent is not to be considered. There are specific child support guidelines which are presumed to be correct, unless there is a showing that the amount of support would be unjust or inappropriate. The factors to be considered in determining the inappropriateness or justness of an award of support are: (1) the financial resources of the child; (2) the standard of living the child would have enjoyed if the marriage had not been dissolved; (3) the physical and emotional health of the child and any special needs or aptitudes of the child; (4) the financial resources, needs, and obligations of both the noncustodial and the custodial parent; (5) the tax consequences to each parent; (6) the non-monetary contributions that the parents will make towards the care and well-being of the child; (7) the educational needs of either parent; (8) whether one parent's income is substantially less than the other parent's; (8) the needs of other children of the non-custodial parent; (9) if the child does not receive public aid: any extraordinary expenses required for the non-custodial parent to exercise visitation rights; and (10) any other relevant factors. Security may be required for the payments. [Consolidated Laws of New York Annotated; Domestic Relations Law, Volume 8, Sections 32, 33, 236-Part B, 240, and 243 and New York Case Law].

PREMARITAL AGREEMENT: New York has no specific statutes pertaining to premarital agreements.

NORTH CAROLINA

RESIDENCY REQUIREMENTS AND WHERE TO FILE: Either spouse must have been a resident of North Carolina for at least 6 months prior to filing for divorce. Divorce may be filed for in the county of residence of either spouse. [General Statutes of North Carolina; Chapter 50, Sections 50-8, 1-82].

LEGAL GROUNDS FOR DIVORCE: No-Fault: Living separate and apart without cohabitation for 1 year. [General Statutes of North Carolina; Chapter 50, Section 50-6]

General: (1) confinement for incurable insanity for 3 years; or (2) incurable mental illness based on examinations for 3 years. [General Statutes of North Carolina; Chapter 50, Sections 50-5.1].

NAME OF COURT IN WHICH TO FILE FOR DIVORCE: Superior Court or District Court. "In the General Court of Justice, _____ Division, North Carolina, _____ County."

DOCUMENT CAPTION INFORMATION: Complaint for Divorce. "In Re: the Marriage of: _____, Plaintiff and _____, Defendant." Final document title: Decree of Divorce.

LEGAL SEPARATION: The grounds for legal separation (divorce from bed and board) are as follows: (1) abandonment; (2) adultery; (3) alcoholism and/or drug addiction; (4) cruel and inhuman treatment endangering the life of the spouse; (5) personal indignities rendering life burdensome and intolerable; and (6) turning a spouse out-of-doors. Either spouse must have been a resident of North Carolina for at least 6 months prior to filing for divorce from bed and board. [General Statutes of North Carolina; Chapter 50, Sections 50-7 and 50-8].

SIMPLIFIED OR SPECIAL DIVORCE PROCEDURES: There are no legal provisions in North Carolina for simplified divorce procedures. However, pre-marital and marital property settlement agreements are specifically recognized as valid. The payment or non-payment of alimony may be the subject of a marital settlement agreement. [General Statutes of North Carolina; Chapter 50, Sections 16.6(b) and 20].

MEDIATION OR COUNSELING REQUIREMENTS: If child custody is a contested issue, the court may order the parents to submit to mandatory mediation of that issue. [General Statutes of North Carolina; Chapter 50, Section 50-13.1].

PROPERTY DISTRIBUTION: North Carolina is an "equitable distribution" state. Separate property, including (1) any property acquired before the marriage; (2) any gifts and inheritances acquired during the marriage; (3) any property acquired in exchange for separate property; (4) any increase in the value of separate property; and (5) the expectation of a nonvested pension, retirement or other deferred compensation rights, will be retained by the spouse who owns it. Marital property (property acquired by either or both spouses during the marriage and before the separation, including any pension or retirement fund benefits) will be divided equally unless the court finds that an equal division is not fair. The division is based on the following factors: (1) any direct or indirect contributions to the career or education of the other spouse; (2) any depletion or waste of property; (3) the net value of the property; (4) the liquid or non-liquid character of the property; (5) the contribution of each spouse to the acquisition of the marital property, including the contribution of each spouse as homemaker; (6) the economic circumstances of each spouse at the time the division of property is to become effective; (7) any increase or decrease in the value of the separate property of the spouse during the marriage or the depletion of the separate property for marital purposes; (8) the length of the marriage; (9) the age and health of the spouses; (10) the federal income tax consequences of the court's division of the property; (11) liabilities of the spouses; (12) any retirement benefits, including social security, civil service, military and railroad retirement benefits; (13) any prior alimony or child support obligations of each spouse; (14) the desirability of the spouse with custody of any children occupying the marital residence; (15) any other factor necessary to do equity and justice between the spouses; and (16) interest in keeping an asset or interest in a business, corporation, or profession intact and free from claim or interference by the other party. [General Statutes of North Carolina; Chapter 50, Section 50-20].

ALIMONY/MAINTENANCE/SPOUSAL SUPPORT: Either spouse may be awarded alimony. The factors for consideration are: (1) the standard of living established during the marriage; (2) the comparative financial resources of the spouses, including their comparative earning abilities in the labor market and their incomes; (3) the mental, physical and emotional conditions of the spouses; (4) the marital misconduct of the spouses; (5) the ages of the spouses; (6) the contribution of one spouse to the education, training, or earning power of the other spouse; (7) the effect of a spouse having primary custody of a child; (8) the relative education of the spouses and the time necessary for a spouse to acquire sufficient education or training to become self-sufficient; (9) the contribution of a spouse as a homemaker; (10) the tax consequences; (11) the

127

ability of the spouse to pay; (12) separate and marital debt; (13) expenses needed to support each party; (14) obligations to support others; (15) property brought to the marriage; (16) the relative needs of the spouses; and (17) any other factor the court deems just and equitable. The court may require bond for security for the alimony payments. [General Statutes of North Carolina; Chapter 50, Sections 50-16.2A, 50-16.3A, 50-16.7].

SPOUSE'S NAME: Upon request, the court may allow either spouse to resume the use of his or her former or maiden name. A woman may also make application to the clerk of the court for resumption of the use of her maiden or former name. [General Statutes of North Carolina; Chapter 50, Section 50-12].

CHILD CUSTODY: Joint or sole child custody is determined according to the interests and welfare of the child. There is no presumption that either parent is better suited to have custody. The court is to consider all relevant factors including acts of domestic violence and the safety of the child. [General Statutes of North Carolina; Chapter 50, Section 50-13.2].

CHILD SUPPORT: Both parents are primarily responsible for the support of a minor child and either parent may be ordered to pay child support. The factors to be considered are: (1) the needs of the child; (2) the earnings, conditions, and accustomed standard of living of the child; (3) the child care and homemaker contributions of each parent; (4) any joint or shared custody arrangements; (5) the parents ability to pay; (6) the parent's own special needs, such as unusual medical expenses; (7) any types of other support provided to the child, such as a residence, payment of a mortgage, payment of medical expenses, provisions for health insurance, or lump sum payments; (8) a parent's prior child support or alimony obligations; and (9) any other relevant factors. There are official child support guidelines which are presumed to be correct, unless there is a showing that the amount of support would be unjust or inappropriate. Child support worksheets are also provided Child support payments may be required to be paid through the clerk of the court. Income withholding may be used if child support payments become delinquent. Child support obligations may be required to be secured by a bond or mortgage. The court may require a parent to provide health insurance coverage for a child. [General Statutes of North Carolina; Chapter 50, Section 50-13.4; Child Support Guidelines and Worksheets are contained in the Annotated Rules of North Carolina].

PREMARITAL AGREEMENT: The agreement must be in writing and signed by both parties and is enforceable without consideration. The agreement will not be enforced if it is proven that (1) the agreement was not executed voluntarily; (2) the agreement was unconscionable when executed and before execution the party was not provided a fair and reasonable disclosure of the property or financial obligations of the other party, did not voluntarily waive any right to the disclosure of these obligations, did not have adequate knowledge of these obligations; (3) a provision of the agreement modifies or eliminates spousal support which causes that party to be eligible for public assistance at the time of separation or divorce. If the marriage is determined to be void, the agreement is enforceable only to the extent necessary to avoid an inequitable result. [General Statutes of North Carolina; Chapter 52B, Sections 52B-3, 52B-7 and 52B-8].

NORTH DAKOTA

RESIDENCY REQUIREMENTS AND WHERE TO FILE: The spouse filing for divorce must be a resident of North Dakota for at least 6 months prior to the filing of the divorce or the entry of the final divorce. If the defendant is a resident of North Dakota, the divorce must be filed in the county where the defendant resides. If the defendant is not a resident, the divorce may be filed for in any county that the plaintiff designates in the complaint. [North Dakota Century Code; Chapters 14-05-17 and 28-04-05].

LEGAL GROUNDS FOR DIVORCE: No-Fault: Irreconcilable differences. [North Dakota Century Code; Chapter 14-05-03].
General: (1) adultery; (2) confinement for incurable insanity for a period of 5 years; (3) conviction of a felony; (4) willful desertion; (5) cruel and inhuman treatment; (6) willful neglect; and (7) habitual intemperance (drunkenness). [North Dakota Century Code; Chapter 14-06-01].

NAME OF COURT IN WHICH TO FILE FOR DIVORCE: District Court. "State of North Dakota, County of _____, In the District Court, _____ Judicial District."

DOCUMENT CAPTION INFORMATION: Complaint for Divorce. "In Re: the Marriage of: _____, Plaintiff and _____, Defendant." Final document title: Decree of Divorce.

LEGAL SEPARATION: The grounds for legal separation (separation from bed and board) in North Dakota are: (1) irreconcilable differences; (2) adultery; (3) confinement for incurable insanity for a period of 5 years; (4) conviction of a felony; (5) willful desertion; (6) cruel and inhuman treatment; (7) willful neglect; and (8) habitual intemperance (drunkenness). The spouse filing for legal separation must be a resident of North Dakota for at least 6 months prior to the entry of the legal separation or commencement of the action. [North Dakota Century Code; Chapters 14-05-03, 14-06-01, and 14-06-06].

SIMPLIFIED OR SPECIAL DIVORCE PROCEDURES: Separation agreements are specifically authorized by statute. [North Dakota Century Code; Chapter 14-07-07].

MEDIATION OR COUNSELING REQUIREMENTS: In an action for divorce or legal separation where child support or child custody is an issue, the court may order the parents to submit to mediation, unless there has been physical or sexual abuse of a spouse or child. [North Dakota Century Code; Chapter 14-09.1-02].

PROPERTY DISTRIBUTION: North Dakota is an "equitable distribution" state. All of the spouse's property, including gifts, inheritances, and any property acquired prior to the marriage, will be equitably distributed as the court feels is just and proper. There are no factors for consideration specified in the statute. [North Dakota Century Code; Chapter 14-05-24].

ALIMONY/MAINTENANCE/SPOUSAL SUPPORT: Either spouse may be required to make allowances for the support of the other spouse for his or her entire life or a shorter period. All of the circumstances of the situation may be considered. There are no other specific factors for consideration set out in the statute. Support payments may be required to be made through the clerk of the court. [North Dakota Century Code; Chapter 14-05-24].

SPOUSE'S NAME: Upon request, a wife's former or maiden name may be restored. [North Dakota Case Law].

CHILD CUSTODY: Child custody is awarded according to the best interests and welfare of the child, and based on the following factors: (1) moral fitness of the parents; (2) capability and desire of each parent to meet the child's needs; (3) preference of the child, if the child is of sufficient age and capacity; (4) the love and affection existing between the child and each parent; (5) the length of time the child has lived in a stable, satisfactory environment and the desirability of maintaining continuity; (6) the child's adjustment to his or her home, school, and community; (7) the mental and physical health of the parents; (8) the stability of the home environment likely to be offered by each parent; (9) the child's interaction with anyone who resides with a parent, including such person's history of violence of any type; (10) any spouse or child abuse or sexual abuse or history of domestic violence or violence of any type; (11) the capacity and disposition of the parents to give the child love, affection, guidance, and continue the child's education; (12) the permanence, as a family unit, of the proposed or existing custodial home; (13) the making of any false accusations by one parent against the other; and (14) any other factors. Any evidence of child or spouse abuse or domestic violence creates a presumption that custody or visitation with that parent would not be in the best interests of the child. If there is any evidence of sexual abuse of a child, the court is required to prohibit any visitation or contact with that parent unless the parent has completed counseling and the court determines that supervised visitation is in the best interests of the child. Both parents are considered to be equally entitled to custody of a child. [North Dakota Century Code; Chapters 14-05-22, 14-09-06, 14-09-06.1 and 14-09-06.2].

CHILD SUPPORT: Either parent may be ordered to pay child support. The amount awarded will be based on consideration of the amount that is needed to give the child support and an education suitable to the child's circumstances. There are specific child support guidelines that the court will consider which have been prepared by the North Dakota Department of Human Services. Until June 30, 1999, child support payments are required to be paid through the state disbursement office. All child support orders will be reviewed every 3 years, unless neither parent requests such a review. [North Dakota Century Code; Chapters 14-09-08, 14-09-08.1, 14-09-08.4, and 14-09-09.7]

PREMARITAL AGREEMENT: The agreement must be in writing and signed by both parties and enforceable without consideration. The agreement is not enforceable if proven that (1) the agreement was not executed voluntarily; (2) the agreement was unconscionable when executed and before execution of the agreement, the party was not provided fair and reasonable disclosure of the other party's financial or property obligations, did not voluntarily waive disclosure of these obligations and did not have notice of them; (3) if the agreement modifies or eliminates spousal support and that causes the other party to be eligible for public assistance. If a court finds that to enforce the agreement would be unconscionable, it may refuse to enforce it. If the marriage is determined to be void, the agreement is enforceable only to the extent necessary to avoid an inequitable result. [North Dakota Century Code; Chapters 14-3.1-03, 14-3.1-06, 14-3.1-07, and 14-3.1-08].

OHIO

RESIDENCY REQUIREMENTS AND WHERE TO FILE: The spouse filing for divorce or dissolution of marriage must have been a resident of Ohio for at least 6 months and a resident of the county for at least 90 days immediately prior to filing. [Ohio Revised Code Annotated; Section 3105.03 and Ohio Rules of Civil Procedure, Rule 3].

LEGAL GROUNDS FOR DIVORCE/DISSOLUTION OF MARRIAGE: No-Fault: (1) incompatibility, unless denied by the other spouse; or (2) living separate and apart without cohabitation and without interruption for 1 year. [Ohio Revised Code Annotated; Section 3105.01].

General: (1) adultery; (2) imprisonment; (3) willful desertion for 1 year; (4) cruel and inhuman treatment; (5) bigamy; (6) habitual intemperance (drunkenness); (7) when a final divorce decree has been obtained outside of the state of Ohio that does not release the other spouse from the obligations of the marriage inside the state of Ohio; (8) fraud; and (9) neglect. [Ohio Revised Code Annotated; Section 3105.01].

NAME OF COURT IN WHICH TO FILE FOR DIVORCE/DISSOLUTION OF MARRIAGE: Court of Common Pleas. "In the Court of Common Pleas of _____ County, Ohio."

DOCUMENT CAPTION INFORMATION: Petition for Dissolution of Marriage (See below under Summary Divorce); or Complaint for Divorce. "In Re: the Marriage of: _____, Petitioner if in Petition for Dissolution of Marriage; or Plaintiff if in Complaint for Divorce and _____, Co-Petitioner if in Petition for Dissolution of Marriage; or Defendant in Complaint for Divorce." Final document title: Decree of Dissolution of Marriage; or Decree of Divorce. [See below under Simplified Or Special Dissolution Of Marriage Procedures].

LEGAL SEPARATION: Legal separation may be sought for the following grounds: (1) adultery; (2) imprisonment; (3) willful desertion for 1 year; (4) cruel and inhuman treatment; (5) bigamy; (6) habitual intemperance (drunkenness); (7) when a final divorce decree has been obtained outside of the state of Ohio that does not release the other spouse from the obligations of the

133

marriage inside the state of Ohio; (8) fraud; (9) neglect; (10) incompatibility; or (11) living separate and apart without cohabitation and without interruption for 1 year. [Ohio Revised Code Annotated; Sections 3105.01 and 3105.17].

SIMPLIFIED OR SPECIAL DIVORCE/DISSOLUTION OF MARRIAGE PROCEDURES: Both spouses may jointly file a petition for dissolution of marriage. The petition must: (1) be signed by both spouses; (2) have attached to it a separation agreement which provides for (a) division of property, (b) spousal support (including, if the spouses desire, the authorization of the court to modify any spousal support terms), and (c) custody, visitation, and child support, if there are any minor children. Between 30 and 90 days after filing such a petition, both spouses must appear in court and state under oath that he or she: (1) voluntarily signed the agreement; (2) is satisfied with the agreement; and (3) seeks dissolution of the marriage. In addition, settlement agreements are also authorized by statute and may be used in a divorce proceeding. A sample divorce complaint form is contained in Ohio Rules of Civil Procedure, Appendix of Forms, Form #20. In addition, separation agreements are specifically authorized. Finally, there may be local court rules which apply to divorce proceedings in Ohio. [Ohio Revised Code Annotated; Sections 3105.03, 3105.10, 3105.61-65 and Ohio Rules of Civil Procedure, Appendix of Forms].

MEDIATION OR COUNSELING REQUIREMENTS: At the request of either spouse or on the court's own initiative, the court may order the spouses to undergo conciliation procedures for up to 90 days. The court will set forth the procedures and name the conciliator. In addition, the court may order that parents attend mediation sessions on issues of child custody and visitation matters. [Ohio Revised Code Annotated; Sections 3105.091 and 3117.01+].

PROPERTY DISTRIBUTION: Ohio is an "equitable division" state. Each spouse retains her or his separate property, including gifts, inheritances, property acquired prior to the marriage, income or appreciation of separate property, and individual personal injury awards. An equitable division of all of the spouse's marital property acquired during the marriage, is allowed based on the following factors: (1) the desirability of awarding the family home, or right to reside in it, to the spouse with custody of the children; (2) the liquidity of the property to be distributed; (3) the financial resources of both spouses; (4) the economic desirability of retaining an asset intact; (5) the tax consequences of the division; (6) the duration of the marriage; (7) the costs of any sale of an asset, if a sale is necessary for division purposes; (8) any division made in a separation agreement; and (9) any other relevant factor. The division of the marital property will be equal, unless such a division would be inequitable. Marital fault is not a consideration. The amount of any spousal support award is not to be considered in the division of property. [Ohio Revised Code Annotated; Section 3105.171].

ALIMONY/MAINTENANCE/SPOUSAL SUPPORT: Either spouse may be awarded reasonable spousal support, in lump sum or in periodic payments, based on a consideration of the following factors: (1) whether the spouse seeking support is the custodian of a child whose condition or circumstances make it appropriate for that spouse not to seek outside employment; (2) the earning ability of both spouses; (3) the income of both spouses, including marital property apportioned to each spouse and each spouse's ability to meet his or her needs independently; (4) the needs and obligations of each spouse; (5) the contribution of each spouse to the education, earning ability, and career building of the other spouse, including the spouse's contribution to the earning of a professional degree by the other spouse; (6) the age of the spouses; (7) the physical, mental, and emotional conditions of the spouses; (8) the relative assets and liabilities of the spouses, including any court-ordered payments; (9) the educational level of each spouse at the time of the marriage and at the time the action for support is commenced; (10) the standard of living during the marriage; (11) any pension or retirement benefits of either spouse; (12) the duration of the marriage; (13) the tax consequences of the award; (14) the time and expense necessary for the spouse seeking support to acquire education, training, or job experience to obtain appropriate employment; (15) the lost income producing capacity of either spouse resulting from marital responsibilities; (16) any other relevant factor. Marital fault is not a consideration. The court may require a spouse to provide health insurance coverage for the other spouse. [Ohio Revised Code Annotated; Sections 3105.18, 3105.71, and 3105.171].

SPOUSE'S NAME: Upon request, the court will restore a person's former or maiden name. [Ohio Revised Code Annotated; Sections 3105.16 and 3105.34].

CHILD CUSTODY: Shared parenting or sole child custody may be awarded according to the best interests of the child. Factors to be considered are: (1) the preference of the child, if the child is of sufficient age and capacity; (2) the child's adjustment to his or her home, school, and community; (3) the mental and physical health of all individuals involved; (4) the relationship of the child with parents, siblings, and other significant family members; (5) whether one parent has willfully denied visitation to the other parent; (6) any child or spousal abuse; (7) whether either parent lives or intends to live outside of Ohio; (8) the ability of the parents to cooperate and make joint decisions; (9) the health and safety of the child; (10) any history of child abuse, spouse abuse, domestic violence by a parent or anyone who is or will be a member of the household where the child will reside, or parental kidnapping; (11) the geographic proximity of the parents to each other as it relates to shared parenting; (12) the child's and parent's available time; (13) the child's available time to spend with any siblings; (14) any failure to pay child support; and (15) any other relevant factors. Both parents are considered to have equal rights to custody. In addition, for shared parenting to be awarded, both parents must request it and submit a plan for shared parenting. The financial status of a parent is not to be considered for allocating any parental rights and responsibilities. The court may require an investigation of the parents and any evidence of neglect or child or spousal abuse will be considered against the granting of shared parenting or such parent being granted the status as residential parent. [Ohio Revised Code Annotated; Sections 3105.21, 3109.03, 3109.04, and 3109.051].

CHILD SUPPORT: Either or both parents may be ordered to pay child support. Marital misconduct is not to be considered in this award. Health care insurance may be ordered to be provided for the child and the spouse. Child support payments may be ordered to be paid through the state child support agency. There are official child support guidelines that are presumed to be correct unless there is a showing that the amount of the support award would be unjust or inappropriate under the particular circumstances of a case. Factors which may be considered in adjusting a child support amount are: (1) special or unusual needs of a child; (2) obligations for other minor or handicapped children; (3) other court-ordered payments; (4) extended visitation or extraordinary costs for visitation; (5) mandatory wage deductions (including union dues); (6) disparity in income between the parent's households; (7) benefits that either parent receives from remarriage or sharing living expenses with others; (8) the amount of taxes paid by a parent; (9) significant contributions from a parent (including lessons, sports equipment, or clothing); (10) the financial resources and earning capacity of the child; (11) the standard of living and circumstances of each parent and the standard of living the child would have enjoyed if the marriage had not been dissolved; (12) the physical and emotional conditions and needs of the child; (13) the medical and educational needs of the child; (14) the relative financial resources, other assets and resources, needs, and obligations of both the noncustodial and the custodial parent; (15) the need and capacity of the child for an education and the educational opportunities of the child; (16) the age of the child; (17) the earning ability of each parent; (18) the responsibility of each parent for the support of others; (19) the value of services contributed by the custodial parent; and (20) any other relevant factor. A child support computation worksheet is also contained in the statute. [Ohio Revised Code Annotated; Sections 3105.71, 3113.215, and 3113.217].

PREMARITAL AGREEMENT: Ohio has no specific statutes pertaining to premarital agreements.

OKLAHOMA

RESIDENCY REQUIREMENTS AND WHERE TO FILE: Either spouse must have been a resident of Oklahoma for 6 months immediately prior to filing for divorce. The divorce may be filed for in the county in which the plaintiff has been a resident for 30 days or in the county where the defendant resides. [Oklahoma Statutes Annotated; Title 43, Sections 102 and 103].

LEGAL GROUNDS FOR DIVORCE: No-Fault: Incompatibility. [Oklahoma Statutes Annotated; Title 43, Section 101].

General: (1) impotence; (2) adultery; (3) abandonment for 1 year; (4) imprisonment; (5) confinement for incurable insanity for 5 years; (6) cruel and inhuman treatment; (7) fraud; (8) habitual intemperance (drunkenness); (9) the wife pregnant by another at the time of the marriage; (10) gross neglect; and (11) a foreign divorce which is not valid in Oklahoma. [Oklahoma Statutes Annotated; Title 43, Section 101].

NAME OF COURT IN WHICH TO FILE FOR DIVORCE: District Court. "State of Oklahoma, In the District Court, _____ County."

DOCUMENT CAPTION INFORMATION: Petition for Divorce. "In Re: the Marriage of: _____, Plaintiff and _____, Defendant." Final document title: Decree of Divorce.

LEGAL SEPARATION: A spouse may sue the other spouse for alimony without filing for divorce. The grounds for requesting non-divorce-based alimony are: (1) impotence; (2) adultery; (3) abandonment for 1 year; (4) imprisonment; (5) confinement for incurable insanity for 5 years; (6) cruel and inhuman treatment; (7) fraud; (8) habitual intemperance (drunkenness); (9) the wife pregnant by another at the time of the marriage; (10) gross neglect; and (11) incompatibility. [Oklahoma Statutes Annotated; Title 43, Sections 101 and 129].

SIMPLIFIED OR SPECIAL DIVORCE PROCEDURES: Separation agreements are specifically authorized by statute. [Oklahoma Statutes Annotated; Title 43, Section 205].

MEDIATION OR COUNSELING REQUIREMENTS: The court may appoint an arbitrator for joint custody disputes which take place after a divorce. [Oklahoma Statutes Annotated; Title 43, Section 109].

PROPERTY DISTRIBUTION: Oklahoma is an "equitable distribution" state. Each spouse is entitled to keep: (1) the property owned by him or her before the marriage; and (2) any gifts or inheritances acquired during the marriage. All property held or acquired jointly during the marriage will be divided between the spouses in a just and reasonable manner. A portion of the jointly-held property may be set aside to one spouse for the support of any children who may live with that spouse. The only factors for consideration set out in the statute are: (1) the way in which the property in question was held; and (2) the time and manner of the acquisition of the property. Marital fault is not a factor. [Oklahoma Statutes Annotated; Title 43, Section 121].

ALIMONY/MAINTENANCE/SPOUSAL SUPPORT: Alimony may be awarded to either spouse. The award may be in money or property, in lump sum or installments, having regard for the value of the property at the time of the award. Marital fault is not a consideration. There are no other factors for consideration set out in the statute. Alimony payments may be required to be paid through the clerk of the court. [Oklahoma Statutes Annotated; Title 43, Sections 121 and 136].

SPOUSE'S NAME: Upon request, a wife may have her former or maiden name restored upon divorce. [Oklahoma Statutes Annotated; Title 43, Section 121].

CHILD CUSTODY: Joint or sole child custody may be awarded based on the best interests of the child, and upon a consideration of the preference of the child, if the child is of sufficient age to form an intelligent preference. When it is in the best interests of the child, the court shall assure that children have frequent and continuing contact with both parents and encourage the parents to share the rights and responsibilities of child rearing. However, there is neither a preference for or against joint or sole custody. In determining custody, the court shall consider which parent is likely to allow frequent contact with the other parent. There is no preference either for or against private, public, or home schooling of children. The sex of the parent is not to be taken into consideration. The court may require that the parents submit a joint custody plan to the court if joint custody is desired. [Oklahoma Statutes Annotated; Title 10, Section 21.1 and Title 43, Section 109 and 112].

CHILD SUPPORT: The parent awarded custody of the child must provide for the education and support of the child to the best of his or her ability. If such support is inadequate, the non-custodial parent must assist in the support to the best of his or her ability. A portion of the non-custodial parents property may be set aside for the custodial parent's use in supporting the child. The only factors for consideration set out in the statute are: (1) the income and means of the parents; and (2) the property and assets of the parents. There are official child support guidelines and forms provided by the Oklahoma Department of Human Services. The amount of support as shown by the guidelines is presumed to be correct unless it is shown to be unjust, unreasonable, inappropriate, or inequitable under the particular circumstances of a case. Child support computation forms are available from the clerk of the court. Child support payments may be required to be paid through the clerk of the court. Security or bond may be required for the payments and income withholding may be used to guarantee the payments. [Oklahoma Statutes Annotated; Title 43, Sections 110, 112, 118, 119, 121, and 136; and Title 56, Sections 235+].

PREMARITAL AGREEMENT: Oklahoma has no specific statutes pertaining to premarital agreements.

OREGON

RESIDENCY REQUIREMENTS AND WHERE TO FILE: If the marriage was not performed in Oregon, one of the spouses must have been a resident of Oregon for 6 months immediately prior to filing. If the marriage was performed in Oregon and either of the spouses is a resident at the time of filing, there is no durational residency requirement. The dissolution of marriage may be filed in a county where either spouse resides. There is a 90-day waiting period before a hearing will be scheduled which begins after the respondent has been served with papers or has filed an Appearance. [Oregon Revised Statutes; Sections 14.070, 107.065, and 107.075].

LEGAL GROUNDS FOR DISSOLUTION OF MARRIAGE: No-Fault: Irreconcilable differences between the spouses which have caused the irretrievable breakdown of the marriage. Misconduct of the spouses will only be considered when child custody is an issue or if necessary to prove irreconcilable differences. [Oregon Revised Statutes; Section 107.025 and 107.036].

General: (1) consent to marriage was obtained by fraud or force; (2) minor married without lawful consent; (3) spouse lacked mental capacity to consent. [Oregon Revised Statutes; Section 107.015]

NAME OF COURT IN WHICH TO FILE FOR DIVORCE: Circuit Court. "In the Circuit Court for the State of Oregon for the County of _____."

DOCUMENT CAPTION INFORMATION: Petition for Dissolution of Marriage. "In the Matter of the Marriage of: _____, Petitioner [or Co-Petitioner if the petition is filed jointly] and _____, Respondent [or Co-Petitioner if the petition is filed jointly]." [See below under Simplified Or Special Dissolution Of Marriage Procedures]. Final document title: Decree of dissolution of Marriage.

TITLE OF FINAL DISSOLUTION OF MARRIAGE PAPERS: Decree of Dissolution of Marriage.

LEGAL SEPARATION: The grounds for legal separation (separation from bed and board) in Oregon are irreconcilable differences between the spouses which have caused the irretrievable breakdown of the marriage. The spouses may enter a separation agreement to live apart for at least 1 year. At least one of the spouses must be a resident of Oregon when the action for legal separation is filed. The legal separation may be filed for in a county where either spouse lives. [Oregon Revised Statutes; Sections 14.070, 107.025, 107.075, 107.455, and 107.475].

SIMPLIFIED OR SPECIAL DISSOLUTION OF MARRIAGE PROCEDURES: The spouses may qualify for a summary dissolution of marriage procedure if the following qualifications are met: (1) the residency requirements are fulfilled; (2) There are no minor children and the wife is not pregnant; (3) the marriage is not over 10 years in length; (4) neither spouse owns any real estate; (5) there are no unpaid debts in excess of $15,000 incurred by either or both spouses during the marriage; (6) the total value of all of the spouse's personal property is less than $30,000, excluding any unpaid balances on loans; (7) the petitioner waives the right to spousal support (alimony); (8) the petitioner waives the right to any pendente lite orders, except for the prevention of spouse abuse (temporary court orders pending the final divorce); (9) the petitioner knows of no other pending domestic relations suit in Oregon or any other state. There are specific mandatory forms for filing for summary dissolution of marriage that are available from the clerk of the court in each circuit. Separation agreements are also expressly authorized. In addition, in all other cases, the spouses can jointly file for a dissolution of marriage. [Oregon Revised Statutes; Sections 107.055, 107.065, 107.085, 107.105, 107.485+].

MEDIATION OR COUNSELING REQUIREMENTS: Certain Oregon courts offer conciliation services. If a court does offer such services, either spouse or the court may delay the dissolution of marriage proceedings for 45 days while a reconciliation or settlement is attempted. In addition, if child custody or child support issues are contested, the court will refer the parents to mediation for up to 90 days. [Oregon Revised Statutes; Sections 107.179, 107.540, and 107.550].

PROPERTY DISTRIBUTION: Oregon is an "equitable distribution" state. All of the spouses property is subject to division by the court, including any gifts, inheritances, and property acquired prior to the marriage. Regardless of whether the property is held jointly or individually, there is a presumption that the spouses contributed equally to the acquisition of any property, unless shown otherwise. All property will be divided, without regard to any fault of the spouses, based on the following factors: (1) the cost of any sale of assets; (2) the amount of taxes and liens on the property; (3) the contribution of each spouse to the acquisition of the marital property, including the contribution of each spouse as homemaker; (4) any retirement benefits, including social security, civil service, military and railroad retirement benefits; (5) any life insurance coverage; and (6) whether the property award is instead of or in

141

addition to spousal support. [Oregon Revised Statutes; Sections 107.036 and 107.105].

ALIMONY/MAINTENANCE/SPOUSAL SUPPORT: Either spouse may be ordered to pay spousal support to the other spouse, without regard to marital fault. The factors for consideration are: (1) the need for and the time necessary to acquire sufficient education and training to enable the spouse to find appropriate employment to become self-supporting, and that spouse's future earning capacity; (2) the standard of living during the marriage; (3) the duration of the marriage; (4) the comparative financial resources of the spouses, including their comparative earning abilities in the labor market; (5) the tax consequences to each spouse; (6) the age of the spouses; (7) the physical and emotional conditions of the spouses; (8) the usual occupation of the spouses during the marriage; (9) the vocational skills and employability of the spouse seeking support; (10) any custodial and child support responsibilities; (11) the educational level of each spouse at the time of the marriage and at the time the divorce is filed for; (12) any life insurance; (13) the costs of health care; (14) the extent that a spouse's earning capacity is impaired due to absence from the job market to be homemaker and the extent that job opportunities are unavailable considering the age of the spouse and the anticipated length of time for appropriate training; and (15) the contribution of each spouse to the marriage, including services rendered in homemaking, child care, education, and career building of the other spouse; (16) any long term financial obligations, including legal fees; (17) any child support obligations; and (18) any other factor the court deems just and equitable. If a spouse has been out of the job market for a long time while acting as homemaker and the other spouse has an economically advantageous position due to joint efforts of both spouses, spousal support will be awarded as compensation. The spouse receiving spousal support must make a reasonable effort to become self-supporting within 10 years or the support may be terminated. The court may order the spouse to pay the support to carry life insurance with the other spouse as beneficiary. In addition, a spouse may have a right to continued health insurance coverage under the other spouse's policy. [Oregon Revised Statutes; Sections 107.036, 107.105, 107.412, and 743.600].

SPOUSE'S NAME: The spouses may resume the use of their prior names after a dissolution of marriage. [Oregon Revised Statutes; Section 107.105].

CHILD CUSTODY: Joint custody, joint responsibility for the child, and extensive contact between the child and both parents is encouraged. Joint or sole custody is determined based on the best interests of the child and the following factors: (1) the love and affection existing between the child and other family members; (2) the attitude of the child: (3) the length of time the child has lived in a stable, satisfactory environment and the desirability of maintaining continuity; (4) any spouse abuse; (5) the relationship of the child with

142

parents, siblings, and other significant family members; and (6) the parent's interests and attitudes towards the child. The conduct, income, social environment, and life style of the proposed guardian is to be considered only if it is shown to cause emotional or physical damage to the child. No preference is to be given because of parent's sex. The court will not order joint custody unless both parents agree to the terms of the custody. [Oregon Revised Statutes; Sections 107.105, 107.137, 107.169].

CHILD SUPPORT: Either parent may be ordered to pay child support, based on the following factors: (1) the needs of the child; (2) the parent's ability to pay support; (3) the standard of living the child would have enjoyed if the marriage had not been dissolved; (4) the physical and emotional conditions and educational needs of the child; (5) the relative financial means of the parents, including their income, resources, and property; (6) the potential earnings of the parents; (7) the needs of any other dependents of a parent; (8) the desirability of the parent having either sole custody or physical care of the child remaining in the home as a full-time parent; (9) the tax consequences to each parent; and (10) any other relevant factors. There are official child support scales and formulas available. The child support payments may be required to be paid through the clerk of the court. There may be court orders issued to withhold wages to pay for the child support. Every child support award must also contain provisions for the payment of any uninsured medical care for the child and the payment of health insurance for the child. The court may also order the parent required to pay support to maintain life insurance coverage with the child as beneficiary. [Oregon Revised Statutes; Sections 25.275, 25.280, 107.105, 107.106, and 107.820].

PREMARITAL AGREEMENT: The agreement must be in writing and signed by both parties and is enforceable without consideration. The agreement is not enforceable if it is proven that (1) the agreement was not executed voluntarily; (2) the agreement was unconscionable when executed and before execution, the party was not provided a fair and reasonable disclosure of the property or financial obligations of the other party, did not voluntarily waive disclosure of such obligations, and could not have had adequate knowledge of these obligations. If a provision of the agreement modifies or eliminates spousal support and that causes the party to be eligible for public assistance at the time of separation or divorce, the court may require the other party to provide support to the extent necessary to avoid eligibility. [Oregon Revised Statues, Section 108.705].

143

PENNSYLVANIA

RESIDENCY REQUIREMENTS AND WHERE TO FILE: Either spouse must have been a resident of Pennsylvania for at least 6 months before filing. The divorce may be filed for in a county where (1) the defendant resides; (2) the plaintiff resides, if the defendant does not live in Pennsylvania; (3) where the marriage home was, if the plaintiff continuously resided in the same county; (4) prior to 6 months after separation, and if the defendant agrees, where the plaintiff resides; (5) prior to 6 months after separation, and if neither spouse lives in the county of the marriage home, where either spouse lives; and (6) after 6 months after separation, where either spouse lives. [Pennsylvania Consolidated Statutes Annotated, Title 23, Section 3104].

LEGAL GROUNDS FOR DIVORCE: No-Fault: (1) irretrievable breakdown of the marriage with the spouses living separate and apart without cohabitation for 2 years; or (2) irretrievable breakdown of the marriage and the spouses have both filed affidavits that they consent to the divorce. In the case of no-fault ground #(2), 90 days must elapse after the filing for divorce before the court will grant a divorce. [Pennsylvania Consolidated Statutes Annotated, Title 23, Section 3301].

General: (1) adultery; (2) bigamy; (3) imprisonment for 2 or more years; (4) confinement for incurable insanity for 18 months; (5) willful desertion for 1 year; (6) cruel and inhuman treatment endangering the life of the spouse; and (7) personal indignities. [Pennsylvania Consolidated Statutes Annotated, Title 23, Section 3301 and Pennsylvania Case Law].

NAME OF COURT IN WHICH TO FILE FOR DIVORCE: Court of Common Pleas. "Court of Common Pleas, _____ County, Pennsylvania."

DOCUMENT CAPTION INFORMATION: Complaint for Divorce. "In Re: the Marriage of: _____, Plaintiff and _____, Defendant." Final document title: Decree of Divorce.

LEGAL SEPARATION: The spouses may enter into a binding separation agreement if it is made on reasonable terms. There is no residency requirement specified by statute. [Pennsylvania Consolidated Statutes Annotated, Title 23, Section 3301].

SIMPLIFIED OR SPECIAL DIVORCE PROCEDURES: The spouses may file for divorce on the grounds of irretrievable breakdown of the marriage and if both spouses consent to the divorce, it will be handled in an expedited manner. There are official sample forms for filing a complaint for divorce on the grounds of irretrievable breakdown of the marriage. There are also official forms available for filing the required affidavit of consent. There are also other sample divorce proceeding forms available in Pennsylvania Rules of Civil Procedure, Actions of Divorce of Annulment Section, Rule 1920.01+. In addition, separation agreements are expressly authorized. [Pennsylvania Consolidated Statutes Annotated, Title 23, Section 3301; and Pennsylvania Rules of Civil Procedure, Rules 1920.01+].

MEDIATION OR COUNSELING REQUIREMENTS: If the court determines that there is a reasonable prospect for reconciliation, it may order the spouses to seek counseling for a period of between 90 and 120 days. Upon the request of one of the spouses, three counseling sessions may be required. If no reconciliation is reached, and one of the spouses states that the marriage is irretrievably broken, a divorce may be granted. Counseling sessions may also be ordered by the court in conjunction with child custody and are mandatory if a parent has been convicted of a violent or abusive crime. [Pennsylvania Consolidated Statutes Annotated, Title 23, Section 3302 and 5303].

PROPERTY DISTRIBUTION: Pennsylvania is an "equitable distribution" state. Separate property that is (1) acquired prior to the marriage; (2) acquired in exchange for any separate property; (3) any gifts and inheritances; and (4) any property designated as separate in a valid agreement between the spouses, will be retained by the spouse owning it. All other marital property will be divided equitably, without regard to any marital misconduct, based on the following factors: (1) the contribution or dissipation of each spouse to the acquisition, preservation, depreciation, or appreciation of the marital property, including the contribution of each spouse as homemaker; (2) the age and health of the spouses; (3) the sources of income of the spouses; (4) the value of each spouse's property; (5) the economic circumstances of each spouse at the time the division of property is to become effective; (6) the length of the marriage; (7) the tax consequences to each spouse; (8) the occupation of the spouses; (9) the amount and sources of income of the spouses, including retirement and any other benefits; (10) the vocational skills of the spouses; (11) the employability of the spouses; (12) the liabilities and needs of each spouse and the opportunity of each for further acquisition of capital assets and income; (13) the standard of living established during the marriage; (14) any contributions toward the education, training, or increased earning power of the other spouse; (15) any prior marital obligations; and (16) whether the person will have custody of any dependent minor children. The court may require a spouse purchase or maintain life insurance and name the other spouse as beneficiary. Both spouses will be required to submit an inventory and appraisal of their property. [Pennsylvania Consolidated Statutes Annotated, Title 23, Sections 3501 and 3502].

ALIMONY/MAINTENANCE/SPOUSAL SUPPORT: Alimony may be awarded to either spouse if necessary. In determining the alimony award, the following factors are considered: (1) whether the spouse seeking alimony lacks sufficient property to provide for his or her own needs; (2) whether the spouse is unable to be self-supporting through appropriate employment; (3) whether the spouse seeking alimony is the custodian of a child; (4) the time necessary to acquire sufficient education and training to enable the spouse to find appropriate employment, and that spouse's future earning capacity; (5) any tax consequences; (6) the standard of living established during the marriage; (7) the duration of the marriage; (8) the financial resources of the spouse seeking alimony, including marital property apportioned to such spouse and such spouse's ability to meet his or her needs independently; (9) the comparative financial resources of the spouses, including their comparative earning abilities in the labor market; (10) the needs and obligations of each spouse; (11) the contribution of each spouse to the marriage, including services rendered in homemaking, child care, education, and career building of the other spouse; (12) the age of the spouses; (13) the physical, mental, and emotional conditions of the spouses; (14) the probable duration of the need of the spouse seeking support and alimony; (15) the educational level of each spouse at the time of the marriage and at the time the action for alimony is commenced; (16) the conduct of the spouses during the marriage; (17) the spouse's sources of income, including medical, insurance, retirement benefits, inheritances, assets and liabilities, and any property brought into the marriage by either spouse; (18) any marital misconduct; and (19) any other factor the court deems just and equitable. There are official spousal support guidelines now in use in Pennsylvania and these are presumed to be correct unless there is a showing that the amount would be unjust of inappropriate under the particular circumstances of a case. Alimony payments may be ordered to be paid through the Domestic Relations Section of the court. [Pennsylvania Consolidated Statutes Annotated, Title 23, Sections 3701, 3702, 3704, 3706, 4322].

SPOUSE'S NAME: Any person may resume the use of his or her former or maiden name upon divorce. A written notice to that effect must be filed in the office of the clerk of the court where the divorce was entered. [Pennsylvania Consolidated Statutes Annotated, Title 54, Section 704].

CHILD CUSTODY: Joint (shared) or sole custody may be awarded based on the best interests of the child, and upon a consideration of the following factors: (1) which parent is more likely to encourage, permit, and allow frequent and continuing contact, including physical access between the other parent and the child; and (2) whether either parent has engaged in any violent, criminally sexual, abusive, or harassing behavior. Both parents may be required to attend counseling sessions regarding child custody. The recommendations of the counselor may be used in determining child custody. In shared custody situations, the court may also require the parents to submit a written plan for child custody to the court. [Pennsylvania Consolidated Statutes Annotated, Title 23, Sections 5302, 5303, 5304, 5305, and 5306].

CHILD SUPPORT: Either or both parents may be ordered to provide child support according to their ability to pay. The factors for consideration set out by statute are: (1) the net income of the parents; (2) the earning capacity of the parents; (3) the assets of the parents; (4) any unusual needs of the child or the parents; and (5) any extraordinary expenses. Child support payments may be ordered to be paid through the Domestic Relations Section of the court. There are official child support guidelines available and these are presumed to be correct unless there is a showing that the amount would be unjust of inappropriate under the particular circumstances of a case. The court may require that health insurance coverage be provided for any child if it is available at a reasonable cost. [Pennsylvania Consolidated Statutes Annotated, Title 23, Sections 4322 and Pennsylvania Case Law].

PREMARITAL AGREEMENT: Pennsylvania has no specific statutes pertaining to premarital agreements.

RHODE ISLAND

RESIDENCY REQUIREMENTS AND WHERE TO FILE: Either spouse must have been a resident of Rhode Island for 1 year prior to filing for divorce. The divorce may be filed for in the county of residence of the plaintiff, unless the 1-year residency requirement has been satisfied by the defendant's residence. In such case, the divorce must be filed for in the county of the defendant's residence. [General Laws of Rhode Island; Title 15, Chapter 15-5-12].

LEGAL GROUNDS FOR DIVORCE: No-Fault: (1) irreconcilable differences which have caused the irremediable breakdown of the marriage; or (2) living separate and apart without cohabitation for 3 years. [General Laws of Rhode Island; Title 15, Chapters 15-5-1, 15-5-3, and 15-5-5].

General: (1) impotence; (2) adultery; (3) abandonment and presumed dead; (4) alcoholism and/or drug addiction; (5) confinement for incurable insanity; (6) failure to consummate marriage; (7) willful desertion for 5 years (or less within the discretion of the court); (8) cruel and inhuman treatment; (9) bigamy; (10) life imprisonment; (11) spouse is of unsound mind; (12) incest; and (13) gross neglect. [General Laws of Rhode Island; Title 15, Chapters 15-5-1 and 15-5-2; and Rhode Island Case Law].

NAME OF COURT IN WHICH TO FILE FOR DIVORCE: Family Court. "State of Rhode Island, Family Court, _____ Division."

DOCUMENT CAPTION INFORMATION: Complaint for Divorce. "In Re: the Marriage of: _____, Plaintiff and _____, Defendant." Final document title: Final Judgement of Divorce. [Rhode Island Rules of Procedure for Domestic Relations, Rule 7].

LEGAL SEPARATION: Legal separation (or divorce from bed and board) may be granted for the following reasons: (1) impotence; (2) adultery; (3) abandonment and presumed dead; (4) alcoholism and/or drug addiction; (5) confinement for incurable insanity; (6) failure to consummate marriage; (7) willful desertion for 5 years (or less within the discretion of the court); (8) cruel and inhuman treatment; (9) bigamy; (10) life imprisonment; (11) spouse is of unsound mind; (12) incest; (13) gross neglect; (14) irreconcilable differences which have caused the irremediable breakdown of the marriage; (15) living separate and apart without cohabitation for 3 years; and (16) any other cause which may seem to require a divorce from bed and board (legal separation). The spouse seeking legal separation must have been a resident for a period of time that the court deems proper. [General Laws of Rhode Island; Title 15, Chapters 15-5-1, 15-5-2, 15-5-3, 15-5-5, and 15-5-9; and Rhode Island Case Law].

SIMPLIFIED OR SPECIAL DIVORCE PROCEDURES: A court hearing will be required in all divorce cases. An official Financial Statement must be filed in all divorce cases. In addition an official Child Support Guidelines form must be filed in all cases involving minor children. Official sample forms are available for use in preparing the Complaint for Divorce and other documents are found in: Rhode Island Rules of Procedure for Domestic Relations, Appendix of Forms.

MEDIATION OR COUNSELING REQUIREMENTS: In cases which involve child custody or visitation, the court may direct the parents to participate in mediation in an effort to resolve any differences. There is an official Family Court counseling form which must be filed with the Complaint for Divorce. [General Laws of Rhode Island; Title 15, Chapter 15-5-29].

PROPERTY DISTRIBUTION: Rhode Island is an "equitable distribution" state. Separate property which a spouse owned prior to the marriage and any property which a spouse receives by gift or inherits (either before or during a marriage) is not subject to division. Any other property (including any income from separate property that was earned during the marriage) may be divided by the court. The following factors are considered: (1) the contribution of each spouse to the acquisition of the marital property, including the contribution of each spouse as homemaker; (2) the length of the marriage; (3) the conduct of the spouses during the marriage; (4) the health and ages of the spouses; (5) the amount and sources of income of the spouses; (6) the occupation and employability of each of the spouses; (7) the contribution by one spouse to the education, training, licensure, business, or increased earning power of the other; (8) the need of a custodial parent to occupy or own the marital residence and to use or own the household effects according to the best interests of any children; (9) either spouse's wasteful dissipation or unfair transfer of any assets in contemplation of divorce; (10) opportunity of each party for future acquisition of assets and income; and (11) any other factor which is just and proper. [General Laws of Rhode Island; Title 15, Chapter 15-5-16.1].

ALIMONY/MAINTENANCE/SPOUSAL SUPPORT: Either spouse may be awarded alimony after a divorce or legal separation. In determining the amount of alimony, the following factors are to be considered: (1) the extent to which either spouse is unable to support him or her self adequately because of their position as primary caretaker of a child whose age, condition, or circumstances make it appropriate that the parent not seek employment outside of the home; (2) the extent to which either party is unable to support him or her self adequately with consideration of the following factors: (a) the extent to which a spouse was absent from employment while fulfilling homemaking responsibilities; (b) the extent to which a spouse's education may have become outmoded and his or her earning capacity diminished: (c) the time and expense required for a supported spouse to acquire the appropriate education and training to develop marketable skills and become employed; (d) the probability, given the spouse's age and skills, of completing education and training and becoming self-supporting; (e) the standard of living during the marriage; (f) the opportunity for either spouse for the future acquisition of capital assets and income; (g) the ability of the supporting spouse to pay, taking into consideration the supporting spouse's (i) earning capacity; (ii) earned and unearned income; (iii) assets; (iv) debts; and (v) standard of living; (4) the length of the marriage; (5) the conduct of parties during marriage; (6) the age and health of parties; (7) the station, occupation, amount and sources of income; (8) the vocational skills, the employability of the parties; (9) the liabilities and needs of each party; and (10) any other factors which are just and proper. [General Laws of Rhode Island; Title 15, Chapters 15-5-16 and 15-5-16.1].

SPOUSE'S NAME: Any woman may request that her name be changed. [General Laws of Rhode Island; Title 15, Chapter 15-5-17].

CHILD CUSTODY: Child custody is determined according to the best interests of the child. Reasonable visitation should be granted to the non-custodial parent, unless it would be harmful to the child. There are no factors for consideration set out by statute. There is no specific provision for joint custody in Rhode Island. [General Laws of Rhode Island; Title 15, Chapter 15-5-16].

CHILD SUPPORT: Either parent may be ordered to provide child support, after a consideration of the following factors: (1) the financial resources of the child; (2) the standard of living the child would have enjoyed if the marriage had not been dissolved; (3) the physical and emotional conditions and educational needs of the child; (4) the earning potential of the parents; (5) any other dependents of the parents; (6) the financial resources, needs, and obligations of both the noncustodial and the custodial parent; and (7) any other factors. Family Court child support guidelines have been adopted. In order to guarantee child support payments, the court may require: (1) income or property assignments; (2) posting of bond; or (3) wage withholding. There is an official Child Support Guidelines Form which must be filed in cases involving minor children. [General Laws of Rhode Island; Title 15, Chapters 15-5-16.2, 15-5-16.6, and 15-9-1 and Rhode Island Rules of Procedure for Domestic Relations, Appendix of Forms].

PREMARITAL AGREEMENT: The agreement must be in writing and signed by both parties and is enforceable without consideration. The agreement is not enforceable if it is proven that (1) the agreement was not executed voluntarily; (2) the agreement was unconscionable when executed because the party was not provided a fair and reasonable disclosure of the property or financial obligations of the other party, did not voluntarily waive the disclosure of this information, did not have adequate knowledge of these obligations. These factors must proven by clear and convincing evidence. If a provision of the agreement modifies or eliminates spouse support and that causes the party to be eligible for public assistance, the court may require that party to provide support to the extent necessary to avoid that eligibility. If the marriage is determined to be void, the agreement is enforceable only to the extent necessary to avoid an inequitable result. [General laws of Rhode Island; Chapters 15-17-2, 15-17-6, and 15-17-7].

SOUTH CAROLINA

RESIDENCY REQUIREMENTS AND WHERE TO FILE: The spouse filing for divorce must have been a resident of South Carolina for at least 1 year, unless both spouses are residents, in which case the spouse filing must only have been a resident for 3 months. There is a required 90-day delay from the time of filing to the time of the final decree of divorce. The divorce may be filed for in: (1) the county where the defendant resides; (2) the county where the plaintiff resides if the defendant does not live in South Carolina; or (3) the county where the spouses last lived together if both still live in South Carolina. [Code of Laws of South Carolina; Chapter 3, Sections 20-3-30, 20-3-60, and 20-3-80].

LEGAL GROUNDS FOR DIVORCE: No-Fault: Living separate and apart without cohabitation for 1 year. [Code of Laws of South Carolina; Chapter 3, Section 20-3-10].

General: (1) adultery; (2) alcoholism and/or drug addiction; (3) physical abuse or reasonable apprehension of physical abuse; and (4) willful desertion for 1 year. [Code of Laws of South Carolina; Chapter 3, Section 20-3-10].

NAME OF COURT IN WHICH TO FILE FOR DIVORCE: Family Court. "State of South Carolina, The Family Court of the _____ Judicial Circuit." [Code of Laws of South Carolina; Chapter 3, Section 20-7-420].

DOCUMENT CAPTION INFORMATION: Complaint for Divorce. "In Re: the Marriage of: _____, Plaintiff and _____, Defendant." Final document title: Decree of Divorce.

LEGAL SEPARATION: South Carolina authorizes legal separation (separate maintenance). [Code of Laws of South Carolina; Chapter 3, Section 20-3-140].

SIMPLIFIED OR SPECIAL DIVORCE PROCEDURES: The court is authorized to develop and make available sample or mandatory forms for use in divorce matters. These may be available locally from the clerk of the court. [South Carolina Rules of Family Court, Rule 3].

MEDIATION OR COUNSELING REQUIREMENTS: The court may refer the spouses to a referee, who must make an honest effort to bring about a reconciliation between the spouses. In such cases, no divorce may be granted unless certified by the judge or the referee that the reconciliation efforts were unsuccessful. [Code of Laws of South Carolina; Chapter 3, Sections 20-3-90 and 20-7-850].

PROPERTY DISTRIBUTION: South Carolina is an "equitable distribution" state. Each spouse is entitled to keep his or her non-marital property, consisting of property: (1) which was acquired prior to the marriage; (2) acquired by gift or inheritance; (3) acquired in exchange for non-marital property; or (4) was acquired due to an increase in the value of any non-marital property. All other property acquired during the marriage is subject to division, based on a consideration of the following factors: (1) the duration of the marriage; (2) the age of the spouses; (3) any marital misconduct; (4) any economic misconduct; (5) the value of the marital property; (6) the contribution of each spouse to the acquisition of the marital property, including the contribution of each spouse as homemaker; (7) the income of each spouse; (8) the earning potential of each spouse and the opportunity for the future acquisition of capital assets; (9) the physical and emotional health of each spouse; (10) the needs of each spouse for additional training or education in order to achieve their earning potential; (11) the non-marital property of each spouse; (12) any retirement benefits; (13) whether alimony has been awarded; (14) the desirability of awarding the family home to the spouse having custody of any children; (15) the tax consequences; (16) any other support obligations of either spouse; (17) any marital debts of the spouses; (18) any child custody arrangements; and (19) any other relevant factors. [Code of Laws of South Carolina; Chapter 3, Sections 20-7-472 and 20-7-473].

ALIMONY/MAINTENANCE/SPOUSAL SUPPORT: Either spouse may be awarded alimony. The factors for consideration are: (1) the duration of the marriage and the ages of the spouses when married and when divorced; (2) the physical and emotional conditions of the spouses; (3) the educational background of each spouse, and the need of additional training or education to reach the spouse's income potential; (4) the employment history and earning capacity of each spouse; (5) the standard of living during the marriage; (6) the current and expected earnings of each spouse; (7) the marital and separate property of each spouse; (8) the custody of any children and its effect on the ability of the custodial spouse to work full-time; (9) any marital misconduct; (10) any tax consequences; (11) any prior support obligations; (12) current and anticipated expenses and needs of both spouses; and (13) any other relevant factors. The court may require the posting of bond as security for the payment of alimony and may require a spouse to carry life insurance and name the other spouse as beneficiary. [Code of Laws of South Carolina; Chapter 3, Sections 20-3-120, 20-3-130, 20-3-140 and South Carolina Case Law].

153

SPOUSE'S NAME: Upon request, the court may allow a woman to resume the use of her former or maiden name. [Code of Laws of South Carolina; Chapter 3, Section 20-3-180].

CHILD CUSTODY: In awarding child custody, the factors for consideration are as follows: (1) the circumstances of the spouses; (2) the nature of the case; (3) the religious faith of the parents and child; (4) the welfare of the child; and (5) the best spiritual and other interests of the child. The parents both have equal rights regarding any award of custody of children. [Code of Laws of South Carolina; Chapter 3, Sections 20-3-160, 20-7-100 and 20-7-1520].

CHILD SUPPORT: Both parents have joint responsibility for child support. The court may require income withholding for the guarantee of child support payments. There are official child support guidelines which are presumed to be correct unless one of the following factors requires a deviation from the amount: (1) educational expenses for the child or a spouse; (2) the equitable distribution of property; (3) any consumer debts; (4) if the family has more than 6 children; (5) unreimbursed extraordinary medical or dental expenses of either parent; (6) mandatory retirement deductions of either parent; (7) support obligations for other dependents; (8) unreimbursed extraordinary medical or dental expenses of the child; (9) other court ordered payments; (10) any available income of the child; (11) a substantial disparity in the income of the parents which make it impractical for the non-custodial parent to pay the guideline amount; (12) the effect of alimony on the circumstances; and (13) any agreements between the spouses, if in the best interests of the child. [Code of Laws of South Carolina; Chapter 3, Sections 20-3-160, 20-7-40, 20-7-100, 20-7-852, 20-7-1315, and 43-5-580; and South Carolina Case Law].

PREMARITAL AGREEMENT: South Carolina has no specific statutes pertaining to premarital agreements.

SOUTH DAKOTA

RESIDENCY REQUIREMENTS AND WHERE TO FILE: The spouse filing for divorce must be a resident of South Dakota or a member of the Armed Forces stationed in South Dakota at the time of the filing and must remain a resident until the divorce is final. There is no durational residency requirement. The divorce may be filed for in the county where either spouse resides, but the defendant has the right to have it transferred to his or her county of residence if desired. In addition, there is a 60-day waiting period after filing before a hearing will be held or the divorce will be granted. [South Dakota Codified Laws; Volume 9A, Title 25, Chapters 25-4-30, 25-4-30.1, and 25-4-34].

LEGAL GROUNDS FOR DIVORCE: No-Fault: Irreconcilable differences which have caused the irretrievable breakdown of the marriage. [South Dakota Codified Laws; Title 25, Chapters 25-4-2, 25-4-17.2, and 25-4-18].

General: (1) adultery; (2) confinement for incurable insanity for 5 years; (3) conviction of a felony; (4) willful desertion; (5) cruel and inhuman treatment; (6) willful neglect; (7) habitual intemperance (drunkenness); and (8) separation caused by misconduct. [South Dakota Codified Laws; Title 25, Chapters 25-4-2 and 25-4-18].

NAME OF COURT IN WHICH TO FILE FOR DIVORCE: Circuit Court. "State of South Dakota, County of _____, In the Circuit Court, _____ Judicial District."

DOCUMENT CAPTION INFORMATION: Complaint for Divorce. "In Re: the Marriage of: _____, Plaintiff and _____, Defendant." Final document title: Decree of Divorce.

LEGAL SEPARATION: The grounds for legal separation (separate maintenance) in South Dakota are: (1) adultery; (2) confinement for incurable insanity for 5 years; (3) conviction of a felony; (4) willful desertion; (5) cruel and inhuman treatment; (6) willful neglect; (7) habitual intemperance (drunkenness); and (8) irreconcilable differences which have caused the irretrievable breakdown of the marriage. The spouse filing for legal separation must be a resident of South Dakota or a member of the Armed Forces stationed in South Dakota at the

155

time of the filing and must remain a resident until the legal separation is final. [South Dakota Codified Laws; Title 25, Chapters 25-4-17.2 and 25-4-40].

SIMPLIFIED OR SPECIAL DIVORCE PROCEDURES: If both spouses consent to the use of "irreconcilable differences" as the grounds for divorce, the court may grant the divorce based entirely on affidavits of the spouses which establish the required residency and grounds for the divorce. In such cases, a personal appearance in court by either of the spouses will not generally be required. [South Dakota Codified Laws; Title 25, Chapters 25-4-17.3].

MEDIATION OR COUNSELING REQUIREMENTS: If the court determines that there is a reasonable possibility for reconciliation between the spouses, the divorce proceedings can be delayed for up to 30 days while the spouses seek counseling. [South Dakota Codified Laws; Title 25, Chapters 25-4-17.2].

PROPERTY DISTRIBUTION: South Dakota is an "equitable distribution" state. All of the spouse's property is equitably divided by the court. Marital fault is not to be considered unless it is relevant to the acquisition of property during the marriage. The only factor specified in the statute is a consideration of the circumstances of the spouses. South Dakota courts have interpreted this to include the following factors for consideration: (1) the contribution of each spouse to the acquisition of the marital property, including the contribution of each spouse as homemaker; (2) the value of each spouse's property; (3) the length of the marriage; (4) the age and health of the spouses; (5) the present and potential earning capability of each spouse; (6) the value of the property; and (7) the income-producing capacity of the spouse's assets. [South Dakota Codified Laws; Title 25, Chapters 25-4-44 and 25-4-45.1; and South Dakota Case Law].

ALIMONY/MAINTENANCE/SPOUSAL SUPPORT: Either spouse may be awarded maintenance for life or a shorter period. The only factor specified in the statute is a consideration of the circumstances of the spouses. South Dakota courts have interpreted this to include the following factors for consideration: (1) the duration of the marriage; (2) the ability of the spouse from whom support is sought to meet his or her needs while meeting those of the spouse seeking support; (3) the financial resources of the spouse seeking maintenance, including marital property apportioned to such spouse and such spouse's ability to meet his or her needs independently; (4) the comparative financial resources of the spouses, including their comparative earning abilities in the labor market; (5) the age of the spouses; (6) the physical and emotional conditions of the spouses; (7) the fault of the spouses during the marriage. Reasonable security may be required to guarantee the payment of maintenance. [South Dakota Codified Laws; Title 25, Chapters 25-4-42, 25-4-44, 25-4-45.1, 25-7A-20; and South Dakota Case Law].

SPOUSE'S NAME: Upon request or on the court's own initiative, a wife's former or maiden name may be restored. [South Dakota Codified Laws; Title 25, Chapter 25-4-47].

CHILD CUSTODY: Sole or joint child custody is to be awarded based on the discretion of the court and the best interests of the child. Fault is not to be considered unless it is relevant to the fitness of a parent to have custody. Neither parent is considered the preferred parent based on the parent's sex. The preference of the child may be considered. In joint custody decisions, the court may consider the expressed desires of the parents and the best interests of the child. No other specific factors are specified. [South Dakota Codified Laws; Title 25, Chapters 25-3-11, 25-4-25, 25-4-45, 25-4-45.1, and 25-5-7.1-7.3; and South Dakota Case Law].

CHILD SUPPORT: Either or both parents may be ordered to provide child support. There is an official child support obligation schedule set forth in the statute. Deviation from the official schedule may be based on a consideration of the following factors: (1) the financial condition of either parent that would make application of the schedule inequitable; (2) income tax consequences; (3) any special needs of the child; (4) income from other persons; (5) the effect of custody and visitation provisions; (6) agreements between the parents which provide other forms of support for the direct benefit of the child; (7) a voluntary reduction in the income of either parent; (8) any other support obligations of a parent. The support payments may be ordered to be paid through the court clerk. Wage withholding orders may also be ordered. [South Dakota Codified Laws; Title 25, Chapters 25-3-11, 25-4-38, and 25-7-6.2 to 25-7-6.12]

PREMARITAL AGREEMENT: The agreement must be in writing and signed by both parties and is enforceable without consideration. The agreement will not be enforced if it is proven that (1) the agreement was not executed voluntarily; (2) the agreement was unconscionable when executed and before execution, the party was not provided a fair and reasonable disclosure of the property or financial obligations of the other party, did not voluntarily waive the right to the disclosure of this information, and did not have knowledge of these obligations. If the marriage is determined to be void, the agreement is enforceable only to the extent necessary to avoid an inequitable result. [South Dakota Codified Laws; Title 25, Chapters 25-2-17, 25-2-21, and 25-2-22].

TENNESSEE

RESIDENCY REQUIREMENTS AND WHERE TO FILE: The spouse seeking divorce must have been a resident of Tennessee when the grounds for divorce arose. If the grounds for divorce arose outside of Tennessee and the petitioner resided outside of Tennessee, either spouse must have been a resident for 6 months prior to filing. The divorce may be filed for in any of the following counties: (1) the county in which both spouses lived at the time of their separation; (2) the county in which the respondent lives if he or she is a resident of Tennessee; or (3) the county in which the petitioner lives if the respondent is a non-resident of Tennessee. [Tennessee Code Annotated; Volume 6A, Title 36, Sections 36-4-104 and 36-4-105].

LEGAL GROUNDS FOR DIVORCE: No-Fault: (1) irreconcilable differences if (a) there has been no denial of this ground; or (b) the spouses submit a properly signed marital dissolution agreement [see below under Simplified or Special Divorce Procedures] or (c) this grounds for divorce is combined with a general fault-based grounds; or (2) living separate and apart without cohabitation for 2 years when there are no minor children. [Tennessee Code Annotated; Volume 6A, Title 36, Section 36-4-101 and 36-4-103].

General: (1) impotence; (2) adultery; (3) conviction of a felony and imprisonment; (4) alcoholism and/or drug addiction; (5) wife is pregnant by another at the time of marriage without husband's knowledge; (6) willful desertion for 1 year; (7) bigamy; (8) endangering the life of the spouse; (9) commission and/or conviction of an infamous crime; (10) refusing to move to Tennessee with a spouse and willfully absenting oneself from a new residence for 2 years; (11) cruel and inhumane treatment; (12) spouse has made life intolerable; (13) abandonment or kicking spouse out of the home and refusing to provide spousal support; and (14) living separate from each other for 2 or more years. [Tennessee Code Annotated; Volume 6A, Title 36, Section 36-4-101].

NAME OF COURT IN WHICH TO FILE FOR DIVORCE: Circuit Court or Chancery Court. "In the _____ Court of _____ County, Tennessee."

158

DOCUMENT CAPTION INFORMATION: Petition for Divorce. "In Re: the Marriage of: _____, Plaintiff and _____, Defendant." Final document title: Final Decree of Divorce.

LEGAL SEPARATION: The grounds for legal separation (divorce from bed and board) are the same as the grounds for a divorce. There is no residency requirement specified in the statute. [Tennessee Code Annotated; Volume 6A, Title 36, Sections 36-4-102, and 36-4-119].

SIMPLIFIED OR SPECIAL DIVORCE PROCEDURES: If the divorce is based on irreconcilable differences, the spouses may enter into a notarized marital settlement agreement. The agreement must: (1) make specific reference to a pending divorce by the name of the court and the docket number; or (2) state that the respondent is aware that a divorce will be filed for in the state of Tennessee; and (3) state that the respondent waives service of process and waives filing an answer. The waiver of service will be valid for 180 days after the respondent signs the agreement and will constitute a general appearance by the respondent and give the court personal jurisdiction over the respondent and will constitute a default judgement. The petition for divorce must have been on file for over 60 days before a hearing will be held if the spouses have no minor children and 90 days if they have any minor children. The spouses must make adequate and sufficient provisions in their marital settlement agreement for the care and custody of any minor children and for an adequate settlement of their property. The spouses may also make provisions in their settlement for alimony. A final decree may be entered without any corroborating proof or testimony by the petitioner or respondent. If the respondent contests or denies that there are irreconcilable differences, a divorce may not be granted on those grounds, unless there is a valid marital settlement agreement. Some counties may require the respondent to sign an appearance and waiver form before the court clerk for it to be valid. In addition, in any petition for divorce, the wife's maiden name must be stated and the race and color of each spouse must be stated. Financial affidavits may also be required. [Tennessee Code Annotated; Volume 6A, Title 36, Sections 36-4-103 and 36-4-116; and Tennessee Rules of Court].

MEDIATION OR COUNSELING REQUIREMENTS: Upon request, the court may delay a divorce proceeding to allow an attempt at reconciliation. In addition, in those cases which involve child custody considerations, the court may order either or both parents to an educational seminar concerning the effects of divorce on children. [Tennessee Code Annotated; Volume 6A, Title 36, Sections 36-4-126, 36-4-130, and 36-6-101].

PROPERTY DISTRIBUTION: Tennessee is an "equitable distribution" state. The separate property of each spouse is retained by that spouse. Separate property is property that was: (1) acquired prior to marriage; (2) by gift or inheritance; (3) in exchange for any separate property, or (4) obtained from income or appreciation of separate property, if the other spouse did not contribute to the preservation and appreciation. The marital property, including: (1) any property acquired during the marriage by either spouse; (2) any increase in value of any property to which the spouses contributed to the upkeep and appreciation; and (3) any retirement benefits, is divided by the court, without regard to any marital fault, and after a consideration of the following factors: (1) the contribution of each spouse to the acquisition, preservation, appreciation, or dissipation of the marital property, including the contribution of each spouse as homemaker, wage-earner, or parent; (2) the value of each spouse's property; (3) the economic circumstances of each spouse at the time the division of property is to become effective; (4) the length of the marriage; (5) the age and health of the spouses; (6) the vocational skills of the spouses; (7) the liabilities and needs of each spouse and the opportunity of each for further acquisition of capital assets and income; (8) the federal income tax consequences of the court's division of the property; (9) the present and potential earning capability of each spouse; (10) the tangible and intangible contributions made by one spouse to the education, training, or increased earning power of the other spouse; (11) the relative ability of each party for the future acquisition of capital and income; and (12) any other factor necessary to do equity and justice between the spouses. [Tennessee Code Annotated; Volume 6A, Title 36, Section 36-4-121].

ALIMONY/MAINTENANCE/SPOUSAL SUPPORT: Spousal support may take the form of lump sum, periodic, or rehabilitative support. Tennessee favors rehabilitative support; however, if this is not feasible, the court may grant long-term alimony, until the death or remarriage of the supported spouse. Spousal support may be awarded to either spouse, based on a consideration of the following: (1) the value of any separate property and the value of the spouses share of any marital property; (2) whether the spouse seeking alimony is the custodian of a child whose circumstances make it appropriate for that spouse not to seek outside employment; (3) the need for sufficient education and training to enable the spouse to find appropriate employment; (4) the standard of living during the marriage; (5) the duration of the marriage; (6) the comparative financial resources of the spouses, including their comparative earning abilities in the labor market and any retirement, pension, or profit-sharing benefits; (7) the needs and obligations of each spouse; (8) the tangible and intangible contributions of each spouse to the marriage, including services rendered in homemaking, child care, and contributions to the education, earning capacity, and career building of the other spouse; (9) the relative education and training of the spouses and the opportunity of each party to secure education and training; (10) the age of the spouses; (11) the physical and mental condition of the spouse; (12) the tax consequences to each spouse; (13) the usual occupation of the spouses during the marriage; (14) the vocational skills and employability of the spouse seeking alimony; (15) the conduct of the spouses during the marriage; and (16) any other factor the court deems just and equitable. The court may require that spousal support payments be made through the clerk of the court. Spousal support payments may include expenses of job training and education. [Tennessee Code Annotated; Volume 6A, Title 36, Section 36-5-101].

SPOUSE'S NAME: There is no statutory provision in Tennessee for the restoration of a wife's name upon divorce. However, case law provides that a wife may resume the use of her former or maiden name [Tennessee Case Law].

CHILD CUSTODY: Joint or sole custody is awarded according to the best interests of the child and considering the child's preference. There is a presumption that joint custody is in the best interests of the child when the parents have an agreement to that effect or agree in open court to joint custody. There is no presumption that either parent is more suited to obtain custody. However, if the child is of tender years, the sex of the parent seeking custody is a factor which may be taken into consideration. No other factors are listed in the statute. [Tennessee Code Annotated; Volume 6A, Title 36, Section 36-6-101].

CHILD SUPPORT: Either or both of the parents may be ordered to provide child support. The factors for consideration are as follows: (1) the financial resources of the child; (2) the standard of living the child would have enjoyed if the marriage had not been dissolved; (3) the physical and emotional conditions and educational needs of the child; (4) the financial resources, needs, and obligations of the parents; (5) the earning capacity of each parent; (6) the age and health of the child; (7) the monetary and non-monetary contributions of each parent to the well-being of the child; (8) any pension or retirement benefits of the parents; (9) whether the non-custodial parent's visitation is over 110 days per year or under 55 days per year; and (10) any other relevant factors. The court may require that health insurance coverage be provided for the child or that the spouse who is to pay the support maintain a life insurance policy for the benefit of the child. The court can require that the child support payments be paid through the clerk of the court. The posting of bond, wage assignments, and wage withholding may also be ordered. There are official Tennessee Supreme Court child support guidelines which are presumed to be correct unless there is a showing that the amount would be unjust or inappropriate under the particular circumstances of the case. Standardized forms for determining child support are also to be available. [Tennessee Code Annotated; Volume 6A, Title 36, Sections 36-5-101, 36-5-501, 36-5-604; and Tennessee Court Rules Annotated, Supreme Court Rules, Tennessee Uniform Administrative Rules Act, Title 4, Chapter 5].

PREMARITAL AGREEMENT: Tennessee has no specific statutes pertaining to premarital agreements.

TEXAS

RESIDENCY REQUIREMENTS AND WHERE TO FILE: One of the spouses must have resided in Texas for 6 months prior to filing and in the county where the divorce is filed for 90 days prior to filing. [Texas Codes Annotated; Family Code, Chapter 6.301].

LEGAL GROUNDS FOR DIVORCE: No-Fault: (1) the marriage has become insupportable because of discord or conflict of personalities that has destroyed the legitimate ends of the marriage relationship and prevents any reasonable expectation of reconciliation; or (2) living separate and apart without cohabitation for 3 years. [Texas Codes Annotated; Family Code, Chapters 6.001 and 6.006].

General: (1) adultery; (2) abandonment; (3) confinement for incurable insanity for 3 years; (4) conviction of a felony and imprisonment for over 1 year; and (5) cruel and inhuman treatment. [Texas Codes Annotated; Family Code, Chapters 6.001-6.008].

NAME OF COURT IN WHICH TO FILE FOR DIVORCE: District Court. "In the District Court of _____ County, Texas, _____ Judicial District."

DOCUMENT CAPTION INFORMATION: Petition for Divorce. "In the Matter of the Marriage of: _____, Petitioner and _____, Respondent." Final document title: Decree of Divorce. [Texas Codes Annotated; Family Code, Chapter 6.401].

LEGAL SEPARATION: Separation agreements are expressly authorized by statute. [Texas Codes Annotated; Family Code, Chapter 7.006].

SIMPLIFIED OR SPECIAL DIVORCE PROCEDURES: Separation agreements and property settlements are expressly authorized, including agreements regarding conservatorship and child support provisions. [Texas Codes Annotated; Family Code, Chapters 7.006].

MEDIATION OR COUNSELING REQUIREMENTS: It is the official policy of the state of Texas to promote amicable and non-judicial settlements of issues regarding children and families. Upon written agreement of the spouses or the court's own decision, the court may refer the divorce proceeding to mediation. The mediated settlement of the case is binding if it is signed by the spouses, any attorneys of the spouses, and provides that the agreement is not subject to revocation. In addition, upon request, the court can order both spouses to consult a marriage counselor. If the counselor's report indicates a reasonable expectation of reconciliation, the court can order further counseling for up to 60 additional days. Upon every filing for divorce, the court clerk is required to furnish a statement to the person filing regarding the availability of marital counseling services. In addition, if there has been a history of conflict and difficulties in resolving questions of access to any children, the court may order either parent to participate in counseling. [Texas Codes Annotated; Family Code, Chapters 102.0085, 153.010, 6.505 and 6.602].

PROPERTY DISTRIBUTION: Texas is a "community property" state. The "community" property, consisting of any other property acquired by either spouse during the marriage, will be divided equally, unless the court finds that equal division would be unjust. In addition, the court may divide property acquired by either spouse while residing outside of Texas which would have been community property if they had acquired it while residing in Texas. The only factors for consideration specified in the statute are a due regard for the rights of each party and any children. Any property possessed by either spouse during the marriage is presumed to be community property unless it can be shown that the property is actually separate property. A court can determine the rights of the spouses in any pension or retirement plan or their rights under any insurance policy. [Texas Codes Annotated; Family Code, Chapters 7.001-7.006].

ALIMONY/MAINTENANCE/SPOUSAL SUPPORT: The court may award maintenance for a spouse only if (1) the spouse from whom maintenance is requested has been convicted of family violence within 2 years before the suit for dissolution; or (2) the duration of the marriage was 10 years or longer and the spouse seeking maintenance (a) lacks sufficient property to provide for his or her reasonable minimum needs; or (b) is unable to support him or her self through employment because of an incapacitating physical or mental disability; or (c) is the custodian of a child which requires substantial care and supervision because of a physical or mental disability which makes it necessary that the spouse not be employed outside the home; or (d) clearly lacks earning ability in the labor market adequate to provide for the spouse's minimum reasonable needs. If the court determines that a spouse is eligible for maintenance, the following factors are then considered in the award: (1) the financial resources of the spouse seeking maintenance, including both separate and community property and liabilities; (2) the spouse's ability to meet his or her needs independently; (3) the education and employment skills of the spouses; (4) the time necessary for the supported spouse to acquire sufficient training or education to enable him or her to find employment; (5) the availability and feasibility of that training; (6) the duration of the marriage; (7) the age, employment history, earning ability, and physical and emotional condition of the spouse seeking maintenance; (8) the ability of the supporting spouse to meet their own needs and make any child support payments; (9) excessive or abnormal expenditures, concealment or destruction of any property by either spouse; (10) the comparative financial resources of the spouses, including medical, retirement, insurance or other benefits, and any separate property; (11) the contribution of one spouse to the education, training, or increased earning power of the other spouse; (12) the contribution of either spouse as homemaker; (13) any marital misconduct of the spouse seeking maintenance; (14) the efforts of the spouse seeking maintenance to seek employment; (15) the efforts of the spouse seeking maintenance to obtain self-support skills while the divorce is pending or during any separation; and (16) property brought to the marriage by either spouse. [Texas Codes Annotated; Family Code, Chapter 8.001—8.011].

SPOUSE'S NAME: Upon request, the name of either spouse may be changed. [Texas Codes Annotated; Family Code, Chapter 45.105, and 45.106].

CHILD CUSTODY: Joint or sole managing conservatorship (custody) is determined according to the best interests of the child. The sex of the parents is not a factor for consideration. The wishes of the child may be considered. The factors to be considered in determining the terms and conditions for possession of a child by the possessory conservator (parent with visitation) are as follows: (1) the age, circumstances, needs, and best interests of the child; (2) the circumstances of the parents; (3) evidence of any spouse or child abuse; and (4) any other relevant factor. The factors specified in the statute for consideration in decisions regarding joint managing conservatorship are: (1) whether the physical, psychological, or emotional needs and development of the child will benefit; (2) the ability of the parents to give first priority to the welfare of the child and reach shared decisions in the child's best interests; (3) whether each parent can encourage and accept a positive relationship between the child and the other parent; (4) whether both parents participated in child rearing before the filing of the suit; (5) the geographical proximity of the homes of the parents; (6) if the child is 14 years old or older, the preference of the child; and (7) any other relevant factor. The court may not award joint managing conservatorship is there is any credible evidence of spousal or child abuse or neglect. Parents may file a written agreement with the court regarding joint managing conservatorship. The court will award joint managing conservatorship based on an agreement between the parents if the agreement: (1) establishes the county of residence of the child; (2) states the rights and duties of each parent regarding the child's present and future care, support, and education; (3) includes provisions to minimize disruption of the child's schooling, daily routine and association with friends; (4) was entered into voluntarily and knowingly; and (5) is in the best interests of the child. In addition, there are standard terms for a court's order on a child's conservatorship set out in the statute that are presumed to be the minimum allowable time that the parent who is not awarded the primary physical residence of the child is to have the child. [Texas Codes Annotated; Family Code, Chapter 153.004 to 153.434].

CHILD SUPPORT: Either or both parents may be ordered to make periodic, lump-sum, or both type of child support payments. There are official child support guidelines set out in the statute and these are presumed to be reasonable and in the best interests of the child. The factors for consideration are: (1) the age and needs of the child; (2) the ability of the parents to contribute to the support of the child; (3) any financial resources available for the support of the child; (4) the amount of possession and access to the child; (5) the net resources of the parent to pay support, including the earning potential of the parent to pay support if the actual income of that parent is significantly less than what that parent could earn, if intentionally unemployed or underemployed; (6) any child care expenses necessary for the employment of either parent; (7) whether a parent has custody of another child and any child support expenses being paid or received for the care of another child; (8) the amount of alimony being currently paid or received; (9) provisions for health care; (10) any special educational or health care needs of the child; (11) any benefits a parent receives from an employer; (12) any debts or obligations of a parent; (13) any wage or salary deductions of the parents; (14) the cost of traveling to visit the child; (15) any positive or negative cash flow from any assets, including a business or investments; (16) any provisions for health care or insurance; (17) any special or extraordinary educational, health care, or other expenses of the parents or the child; and (18) any other relevant factor. The court may order health insurance coverage to be provided for the child. In addition, the court may order income withholding to secure the payment of child support. [Texas Codes Annotated; Family Code, Chapter 154.001-154.309].

PREMARITAL AGREEMENT: The agreement must be in writing and signed by both parties and is enforceable without consideration. The agreement is not enforceable if the party proves that (1) the agreement was not voluntarily signed; (2) the agreement was unconscionable when signed or before signing, the party was not provided a fair and reasonable disclosure of the property or financial obligations of the other party, did not voluntarily waive any right to the disclosure of this information, and did not have adequate knowledge of these obligations. If the marriage is determined to be void, the agreement is enforceable only to the extent necessary to avoid an inequitable result. [Texas Codes Annotated; Family Code, Chapters 4.002, 4.006, and 4.007].

UTAH

RESIDENCY REQUIREMENTS AND WHERE TO FILE: Either spouse must have been resident of Utah (or a member of the Armed Forces stationed in Utah) and a resident of the county where the divorce is filed for more than 3 months immediately prior to filing. In addition, there is a 90-day waiting period after filing before a divorce will be granted. [Utah Code Annotated; Sections 30-3-1 and 30-3-18].

LEGAL GROUNDS FOR DIVORCE: No-Fault: (1) irreconcilable differences of the marriage; or (2) living separate and apart without cohabitation for 3 years under a judicial decree of separation. [Utah Code Annotated; Section 30-3-1].

General: (1) impotence; (2) adultery; (3) conviction of a felony; (4) willful desertion for 1 year; (5) cruel and inhuman treatment; (6) willful neglect; (7) incurable insanity; and (8) habitual intemperance (drunkenness). [Utah Code Annotated; Section 30-3-1].

NAME OF COURT IN WHICH TO FILE FOR DIVORCE: District Court (may be Family Court Division of District Court). "In the District Court of the _____ Judicial District, In and for _____ County, State of Utah."

DOCUMENT CAPTION INFORMATION: Complaint for Divorce. "In Re: the Marriage of: _____, Petitioner and _____, Respondent." Final document title: Decree of Divorce.

LEGAL SEPARATION: The grounds for legal separation are: (1) willful desertion; (2) living separate and apart without cohabitation; and (3) gross neglect. The deserting spouse must be a resident of Utah, or own property in the state which the deserted spouse lives in. [Utah Code Annotated; Section 30-4-1].

SIMPLIFIED OR SPECIAL DIVORCE PROCEDURES: Uncontested divorce hearings may be held before a court commissioner. However, a divorce can not be granted upon default, and legal evidence and testimony must be taken in every divorce case. However, in a default case, the evidence may be contained in an affidavit of the petitioner. In addition, a sample Petition for Divorce is contained in Utah Rules of Civil Procedure, Appendix of Forms, Form

#18. Finally, a financial verification form is also required in child support cases. [Utah Code Annotated; Sections 30-3-4, 30-3-4.2, 78-3-3.1, and 78-45-7.5(5), Utah Rules of Civil Procedure, Appendix of Forms, and the Utah Rules of the Judicial Council].

MEDIATION OR COUNSELING REQUIREMENTS: There is a 90-day waiting period after filing for divorce before any hearing may be held. Upon the request of either or both of the spouses (shown by filing a Petition for Conciliation with the court), the court may refer both of the spouses to a domestic relations counselor. If child custody is involved, both parents must attend a course in the effects of divorce on children. This requirement may be waived if the court determines that it is unnecessary. [Utah Code Annotated; Sections 30-3-4, 30-3-15.2, 30-3-16.2, and 30-3-18].

PROPERTY DISTRIBUTION: Utah is an "equitable distribution" state. All of the spouse's property, including gifts, inheritances, and any property acquired prior to or during the marriage, will be divided equitably by the court. There are no factors for consideration specified in the statute. [Utah Code Annotated; Sections 30-3-5 and 30-3-12].

ALIMONY/MAINTENANCE/SPOUSAL SUPPORT: Either spouse may be ordered to pay an equitable amount of alimony to the other. The following factors are to be considered: (1) the financial condition and needs of the recipient spouse; (2) the recipient's earning capacity and ability to produce income; (3) the ability of the paying spouse to provide support; (4) the length of the marriage; (5) the standard of living at the time of separation; (6) any marital fault of the spouses; (7) if the marriage has been of long duration and the marriage dissolves on the threshold of a major change in the income of one of the spouses; (8) if one spouse's earning capacity has been greatly enhanced by the other's efforts; and (9) any other relevant factors. In general, the court will not award alimony for a period longer than the marriage existed. Alimony terminates upon remarriage or cohabitation with another person. [Utah Code Annotated; Sections 30-3-3 and 30-3-5].

SPOUSE'S NAME: There is no statutory provision in Utah for restoration of a wife's maiden name upon divorce. However, there is a general statutory provision for changing a name upon petition to the court. [Utah Code Annotated; Sections 42-1-1].

CHILD CUSTODY: Joint or sole child custody is determined according to the best interests of the child, and after a consideration of the following factors: (1) the past conduct and moral standards of the parents; (2) the welfare of the child; (3) the child's preference if the child is at least 12 years of age; (4) which parent is likely to act in the best interests of the child; and (5) which parent is likely to allow frequent and continuing contact with the other parent. There is a presumption that a spouse who has been abandoned by the other spouse is entitled to custody of the children. If there is an allegation of child abuse by either spouse, the court must order an investigation by the Division of Family Services or the Utah Department of Human Services. Joint custody may be ordered if (1) it will be in the best interests of the child; and (2) both parents agree to joint custody; or (3) both parents appear capable of implementing joint custody; and (4) based upon a consideration of the following factors: (1) whether the physical, psychological, or emotional needs and development of the child will benefit; (2) the ability of the parents to give first priority to the welfare of the child and reach shared decisions in the child's best interests; (3) whether each parent can encourage and accept a positive relationship between the child and the other parent; (4) whether both parents participated in child rearing before the filing of the divorce; (5) the geographical proximity of the homes of the parents; (6) if the child is of sufficient age and maturity, the preference of the child; (7) the maturity of the parents and their willingness and ability to protect the child from conflict that may arise between the parents; and (8) any other factor that the court finds relevant. The court may not discriminate against a parent with a disability when considering custody issues. The court may order that dispute resolution be attempted prior to any enforcement or modification of custody terms. There are also advisory visitation guidelines in the statutes. [Utah Code Annotated; Sections 30-2-10, 30-3-5, 30-3-5.2, 30-3-10, 30-3-10.1, 30-3-10.2, 30-3-10.3, 30-3-10.6 and 30-3-33].

CHILD SUPPORT: Either or both parents may be ordered to provide child support, including medical and dental expenses and health insurance. The court may also order the non-custodial parent to provide day care and child care expenses while the custodial parent is at work or undergoing training. Income withholding may be ordered by a court to guarantee any child support payments. There are official Child Support Guidelines. These Guidelines are presumed to be correct unless there is a showing that the amount would be unjust or inappropriate under the particular circumstances in a case. Factors for consideration in awarding support amounts outside the guidelines are: (1) the standard of living and situation of the parties; (2) the relative wealth and income of the parties; (3) the earning abilities of the parents; (4) the needs of the parents and the child: (5) the ages of the parents and the child: (6) the responsibilities of the parents for the support of others. A child support worksheet is contained in the statute. In addition, a financial verification form is also required. [Utah Code Annotated; Sections 30-3-5, 30-3-5.1, 78-45-7 to 78-45-7.5].

PREMARITAL AGREEMENT: The agreement must be in writing and signed by both parties and is enforceable without consideration. The agreement is not enforceable if it is proven that (1) the agreement was not executed voluntarily; (2) the agreement was fraudulent and that before the execution the party was not provided a reasonable disclosure of the property or financial obligations, did not voluntarily waive the right to the disclosure of this information, and did not have adequate knowledge of these obligations. If a provision of the agreement modifies or eliminates spousal support and that causes one party to be eligible for public assistance at the time of separation or dissolution, a court may require that the other party provide support so as to avoid the eligibility. If a marriage is determined to be void, the agreement is enforceable only to the extent necessary to avoid an inequitable result. [Utah Code Annotated; Sections 30-8-3, 30-8-6, and 30-8-7].

VERMONT

RESIDENCY REQUIREMENTS AND WHERE TO FILE: Either spouse must have been a resident of Vermont for at least 6 months before the divorce is filed and for 1 year before the divorce is made final. In cases involving child custody, there is a 6 month waiting period after the defendant has been served with the divorce papers before a hearing will be held. The divorce may be filed for in any county where either or both of the spouses reside. [Vermont Statutes Annotated; Title 15, Sections 592 and 593; Vermont Rules for Family Proceedings, Rule 4].

LEGAL GROUNDS FOR DIVORCE: No-Fault: Living separate and apart without cohabitation for 6 consecutive months and the resumption of marital relations is not reasonably probable. [Vermont Statutes Annotated; Title 15, Section 551].

General: (1) adultery; (2) imprisonment for 3 years or more or for life; (3) willful desertion for 7 years; (4) cruel and inhuman treatment of intolerable severity; (5) incurable mental illness; and (6) gross neglect. [Vermont Statutes Annotated; Title 15, Section 551].

NAME OF COURT IN WHICH TO FILE FOR DIVORCE: Family Court. "State of Vermont, Family Court, _____ County."

DOCUMENT CAPTION INFORMATION: Complaint for Divorce. "In Re: the Marriage of: _____. Plaintiff and _____, Defendant." Final document title: Decree of Divorce.

LEGAL SEPARATION: The grounds for legal separation (divorce from bed and board) are: (1) living separate and apart without cohabitation for 6 months; (2) adultery; (3) imprisonment for 3 years or more or for life; (4) willful desertion for 7 years; (5) cruel and inhuman treatment of intolerable severity; (6) incurable mental illness; and (7) gross neglect. Either spouse must be a resident of Vermont for 6 months before filing for legal separation. [Vermont Statutes Annotated; Title 15, Sections 551, 555, and 592].

SIMPLIFIED OR SPECIAL DIVORCE PROCEDURES: Standard forms are available. There are no simplified divorce procedures in Vermont. An official statistical data sheet and a statement of income and assets must also be filed with the Complaint. [Vermont Statutes Annotated; Title 15, Section 662 and Vermont Rules for Family Proceedings; Rule 4].

MEDIATION OR COUNSELING REQUIREMENTS: If one of the spouses denies under oath that they have lived apart for the required period, the court may delay the proceedings for 30 to 60 days and suggest that the spouses seek counseling. [Vermont Statutes Annotated; Title 15, Section 552].

PROPERTY DISTRIBUTION: Vermont is an "equitable distribution" state. All property is subject to being divided on an equitable basis, regardless of when it was acquired or how the title is held, including any gifts and inheritances. The factors to be considered are: (1) contribution of each spouse to the acquisition of the property, including as homemaker; (2) value of each spouse's property; (3) length of the marriage; (4) age and health of the spouses; (5) occupations of the spouses; (6) amount and sources of income of the spouses; (7) vocational skills of the spouses; (8) employability of the spouses; (9) liabilities and needs of each spouse and the opportunity of each for further acquisition of capital assets and income; (10) whether the property award is instead of or in addition to maintenance; (11) how and by whom the property was acquired; (12) merits of each spouse; (13) any custodial provisions for the children, including the desirability of awarding the family home to the parent with custody; and (14) contribution by one spouse to the education, training, or increased earning power of the other. [Vermont Statutes Annotated; Title 15, Section 751].

ALIMONY/MAINTENANCE/SPOUSAL SUPPORT: Either spouse may be ordered to pay maintenance to the other, without regard to marital fault. The maintenance may be rehabilitative (temporary) or permanent and will be awarded if the spouse seeking maintenance: (1) lacks sufficient income or property to provide for his or her reasonable needs; and (2) is unable to support him or herself through appropriate employment at the standard of living established during the marriage or is the custodian of any children. The factors to be considered are: (1) time necessary to acquire sufficient education and training to enable the spouse to find appropriate employment, and that spouse's future earning capacity; (2) standard of living established during the marriage; (3) duration of the marriage; (4) ability of the spouse from whom support is sought to meet his or her needs while meeting those of the other spouse; (5) the financial resources of the spouse seeking maintenance, including property and such spouse's ability to meet his or her needs independently; (6) age of the spouses; (7) physical and emotional conditions of the spouses; and (8) effects of inflation on the cost of living. The court may require security for any maintenance payments. [Vermont Statutes Annotated; Title 15, Sections 752 and 757].

SPOUSE'S NAME: A wife may resume the use of her former or maiden name upon divorce, unless a good cause is shown why she should not. [Vermont Statutes Annotated; Title 15, Section 558].

CHILD CUSTODY: Joint or sole child custody may be awarded based on the best interests of the child, and the following: (1) wishes of the parents; (2) child's adjustment to his or her home, school, and community; (3) relationship of the child with parents, siblings, and other significant family members; (4) ability and disposition of each parent to provide love, affection, and guidance; (5) ability of each parent to provide food, clothing, medical care, other material needs, and a safe environment; (6) ability of each parent to meet the child's present and future developmental needs; (7) ability and disposition of each parent to foster a positive relationship and frequent and continuing contact with the other parent, including physical contact unless it will result in harm to the child or parent; (8) quality of the child's relationship with the primary care provider, given the child's age and development; and (9) ability and disposition of the parents to communicate, cooperate with each other, and make joint decisions concerning the children where parental rights and responsibilities are to be shared. Neither parent is assumed to have a superior right to have custody. No preference to be given because of parent's sex. [Vermont Statutes Annotated; Title 15, Section 665].

CHILD SUPPORT: Either or both of the parents may be required to pay child support, based on a consideration of the following factors: (1) financial resources of the child; (2) standard of living the child would have enjoyed if the marriage had not been dissolved; (3) physical and emotional conditions and educational needs of the child; (4) financial resources, needs, and obligations of both parents; (5) inflation with relation to the cost of living; (6) costs of any educational needs of either parent (7) travel expenses related to parent-child contact; and (8) other relevant factors. Health insurance coverage for the child may be ordered to be provided. The court may require security or wage withholding. Every order of child support must be made subject to a wage assignment in the event of delinquency and require the payments to be made to the registry in the Office of Child Support, unless the situation falls under an exception to the rules shown in Vermont Statutes Annotated; Title 33, Section 4103. There are official child support guidelines available from the Vermont Department of Human Services which are presumed to be correct, unless they are shown to be unfair under the circumstances. There is an official child support computation worksheet available. [Vermont Statutes Annotated; Title 15, Sections 653-669, 757, and 781-783, Title 33, Section 4103; and Vermont Rules for Family Proceedings, Rule 4].

PREMARITAL AGREEMENT: Vermont has no specific statutes pertaining to premarital agreements.

VIRGINIA

RESIDENCY REQUIREMENTS AND WHERE TO FILE: One of the spouses must have been a resident of Virginia for at least 6 months prior to filing for divorce. The divorce may be filed for in: (1) the county or city in which the spouses last lived together; or at the option of the plaintiff: (2) the county or city where the defendant resides, if the defendant is a resident of Virginia; or (3) if the defendant is a non-resident of Virginia, the county or city where the plaintiff resides. [Code of Virginia; Title 8, Section 8.01-261; and Title 20, Sections 20-96 and 20-97].

LEGAL GROUNDS FOR DIVORCE: No-Fault: (1) living separate and apart without cohabitation for 1 year; or (2) living separate and apart without cohabitation for 6 months if there are no minor children and the spouses have entered into a separation agreement. [Code of Virginia; Title 20, Section 20-91].

General: (1) adultery (including homosexual acts); (2) abandonment; (3) conviction of a felony and imprisonment for 1 year; (4) cruelty; and (5) willful desertion. [Code of Virginia; Title 20, Section 20-91].

NAME OF COURT IN WHICH TO FILE FOR DIVORCE: Circuit Court; or Juvenile and Domestic Relations Court; or Experimental Family Court. "Virginia: In the _____ Court of _____." [Code of Virginia; Title 20, Section 20-96.1].

DOCUMENT CAPTION INFORMATION: Complaint for Divorce. "In Re: the Marriage of: _____, Plaintiff and _____, Defendant." Final document title: Decree of Divorce.

LEGAL SEPARATION: The grounds for legal separation are: (1) cruelty; (2) willful desertion; (3) abandonment; and (4) reasonable apprehension of bodily injury. One of the spouses must have been a resident of Virginia for at least 6 months prior to filing for legal separation. [Code of Virginia; Title 20, Sections 20-95 and 20-97].

SIMPLIFIED OR SPECIAL DIVORCE PROCEDURES: Separation agreements are specifically authorized by statute and will reduce the time required for living apart by 6 months. In addition, a spouse may waive service of process, but the waiver of service of process form must be signed in front of the clerk of the court. The testimony of either spouse must also, generally, be corroborated by a witness. [Code of Virginia; Title 20, Sections 20-99, 20-99.1:1, 20-107.3, and 20-109.1].

MEDIATION OR COUNSELING REQUIREMENTS: There are no legal provisions in Virginia for divorce mediation.

PROPERTY DISTRIBUTION: Virginia is an "equitable distribution" state. The separate property of each spouse, consisting of property (1) acquired prior to the marriage; (2) any gifts and inheritances; (3) any increase in the value of separate property, unless marital property or significant personal efforts contributed to such increases; and (4) any property acquired in exchange for separate property, will be retained by the spouse who owns it. The marital property, consisting of (1) all property acquired during the marriage that is not separate property; (2) all property titled in the names of both spouses, whether as joint tenants or tenants-by-the entireties; (3) income from or increase in value of separate property during the marriage if the income or increase arose from significant personal efforts; (4) any separate property which is commingled with marital property and can not be clearly traced, will be divided equitably by the court. The court may also order a payment from one spouse's retirement benefits, profit-sharing benefits, personal injury award, or worker's compensation award, to the other spouse. The factors for consideration are: (1) the contribution of each spouse to the acquisition, care, and maintenance of the marital property; (2) the liquid or non-liquid character of the property; (3) the length of the marriage; (4) the age and health of the spouses; (5) the tax consequences; (6) any debts and liabilities of the spouses, the basis for such debts and liabilities, and the property which serves as security for such debts and liabilities; (7) how and by whom the property was acquired; (8) the circumstances that contributed to the divorce; (9) the contributions, monetary and non-monetary of each spouse to the well-being of the family; (10) the contribution of each spouse to the well-being of the family; and (11) any other factor necessary to do equity and justice between the spouses. [Code of Virginia; Title 20, Section 20-107.3].

ALIMONY/MAINTENANCE/SPOUSAL SUPPORT: Either spouse may be awarded maintenance, to be paid in either a lump sum, periodic payments, or both. The factors for consideration are: (1) the ability and time necessary to acquire sufficient education and training to enable the spouse to find appropriate employment, and that spouse's future earning capacity; (2) the standard of living established during the marriage; (3) the duration of the marriage; (4) the financial resources of the spouse seeking maintenance, including marital property apportioned to such spouse and such spouse's ability to meet his or her needs independently; (5) the contribution of each spouse to the marriage, including services rendered in homemaking, child care, education, and career building of the other spouse; (6) the tax consequences to each spouse; (7) the age of the spouses; (8) the physical and emotional conditions of the spouses; (9) the educational level of each spouse at the time of the marriage and at the time the action for support is commenced; (10) the property of the spouses; (11) the circumstances which contributed to the divorce; and (12) any other factor the court deems just and equitable. However, permanent maintenance will not be awarded to a spouse who was at fault in a divorce granted on the grounds of adultery, unless such a denial of support would be unjust. [Code of Virginia; Title 20, Sections 20-95, 20-107.1 and 20-108.1].

SPOUSE'S NAME: Upon request, a spouse may have his or her former name restored. [Code of Virginia; Title 20, Section 20-121.4].

CHILD CUSTODY: Joint or sole child custody will be awarded based on the welfare of the child, and upon a consideration of the following factors: (1) the age of the child; (2) the child's preference; (3) the needs of the child; (4) the love and affection existing between the child and each parent; (5) the mental and physical health of all individuals involved; (6) the material needs of the child; (7) the role each parent has played in the care of the child; (8) any history of family abuse; and (9) any other factors necessary for the best interests of the child. No preference is to be given to either parent. [Code of Virginia; Title 20, Sections 20-124.2 and 20-124.3].

CHILD SUPPORT: Child support may be ordered to be paid by either parent, and is based on a consideration of the following factors: (1) the financial resources of the child; (2) the standard of living the child would have enjoyed if the marriage had not been dissolved; (3) the physical and emotional conditions and educational needs of the child; (4) the earning capacity of each parent; (5) the age and health of the child; (6) the division of marital property; (7) the monetary or non-monetary contributions of the parents to the family's well-being; (8) the education of the parents; (9) the ability of the parents to secure education and training; (10) the income tax consequences of child support; (11) any special medical, dental, or child care expenses; (12) the obligations, needs, and financial resources of the parents; and (13) any other relevant factors. Official child support guidelines are provided in the statute, which are presumed to be correct unless there is a showing that the amount would be unjust or inappropriate under the particular circumstances of the case based on the factors above (1-13) and the following additional factors: (1) support provided for other children or family members; (2) custody arrangements; (3) voluntary unemployment or under-employment, unless it is the custodial parent and the child is not in school and child care services are not available and the cost of child care services are not included in the computations for child support; (4) debts incurred during the marriage for the benefit of the child; (5) debts incurred for the purpose of producing income; (6) direct court-ordered payments for health insurance or educational expenses of the child; and (7) any extraordinary capital gains, such as gains from the sale of the marital home. [Code of Virginia; Title 20, Sections 20-107.2, 20-108.1, and 20-108.2].

PREMARITAL AGREEMENT: The agreement shall be in writing and signed by both parties and is enforceable without consideration. The agreement is not enforceable if it is proven that (1) the agreement was not executed voluntarily; (2) the agreement was unconscionable when executed and before execution the party was not provided a fair and reasonable disclosure of the property or financial obligations of the other party and did not waive the right to the disclosure of this information. If the marriage is determined to be void, the agreement is enforceable only to the extent necessary to avoid an inequitable result. [Code of Virginia; Title 20, Sections 20-149 and 20-151].

WASHINGTON

RESIDENCY REQUIREMENTS AND WHERE TO FILE: The spouse filing for dissolution of marriage must be a resident of Washington or a member of the Armed Forces stationed in Washington. The dissolution of marriage may be filed for in any county where either the petitioner or respondent resides. In addition, the court will not act on the petition until 90 days has elapsed from the filing and the service of summons on the respondent. [Revised Code of Washington Annotated; Title 26, Chapters 26.09.010 and 26.09.030].

LEGAL GROUNDS FOR DISSOLUTION OF MARRIAGE: No-Fault: Irretrievable breakdown of the marriage. [Revised Code of Washington Annotated; Title 26, Chapter 26.09.030].

General: Irretrievable breakdown of the marriage is the only grounds for dissolution of marriage in Washington. [Revised Code of Washington Annotated; Title 26, Chapter 26.09.030].

NAME OF COURT IN WHICH TO FILE FOR DISSOLUTION OF MARRIAGE: Superior Court; or Family Court (on request). "In the _____ Court of the State of Washington, In and For the County of _____."

DOCUMENT CAPTION INFORMATION: Petition for Dissolution of Marriage. "In Re: the Marriage of: _____, Petitioner and _____, Respondent." Final document title: Decree of Dissolution of Marriage.

LEGAL SEPARATION: The only grounds for legal separation in Washington is the irretrievable breakdown of the marriage. The spouse filing for legal separation must be a resident of Washington or a member of the Armed Forces stationed in Washington. The court will not act on the petition until 90 days has elapsed from the filing and the service of summons on the respondent. [Revised Code of Washington Annotated; Title 26, Chapter 26.09.030].

SIMPLIFIED OR SPECIAL DISSOLUTION OF MARRIAGE PROCEDURES: All divorce cases must be filed on official Washington forms. The forms are available in either printed version or on computer diskette from the Washington Office of the Administrator for the Courts (Forms Order Line: (360) 357-2128. Separation agreements are specifically authorized by law and, if fair, all portions of the agreements are binding on the court. [Revised Code of Washington Annotated; Title 26, Chapters 26.09.020, 26.09.070, and 26.09.080].

MEDIATION OR COUNSELING REQUIREMENTS: Upon the request of either of the spouses, or on the court's own initiative, the spouses may be referred to a counseling service of their choice. A report must be requested from the counseling service within 60 days of the referral. Contested issues relating to custody or visitation will be referred to mediation. There may also be mandatory settlement conferences if there are contested issues. [Revised Code of Washington Annotated; Title 26, Chapters 26.09.015, 26.09.030, and 26.09.181].

PROPERTY DISTRIBUTION: Washington is a "community property" state. Each spouse retains his or her separate property, consisting of: (1) all property acquired prior to marriage; (2) any gifts or inheritances; and (3) any increase in value of the separate property. "Quasi-community" property is property that is acquired while a spouse resides outside of Washington, but that would have been considered community property if acquired while they were living in Washington. "Quasi-community" property is divided as if it were community property. The court will divide the community property of the spouses, consisting of all other property acquired during the marriage, equally or equitably, after a consideration of the following: (1) the nature and extent of each spouse's separate property; (2) the economic circumstances of each spouse at the time the division of property is to become effective; (3) the length of the marriage; (4) the nature and extent of community property; and (5) the desirability of awarding the family home and the right of occupancy for reasonable periods to the custodial parent if there are minor children. Marital misconduct is not to be considered. [Revised Code of Washington Annotated; Title 26, Chapters 26.09.080, 26.16.010, 26.16.020, 26.16.030, and 26.16.220].

ALIMONY/MAINTENANCE/SPOUSAL SUPPORT: Either spouse may be ordered to pay maintenance to the other spouse. Marital misconduct is not to be considered. The factors for consideration are: (1) the time necessary to acquire sufficient education and training to enable the spouse to find appropriate employment, and that spouse's future earning capacity; (2) the standard of living established during the marriage; (3) the duration of the marriage; (4) the ability of the spouse from whom support is sought to meet his or her needs while meeting those of the spouse seeking support; (5) the financial resources of the spouse seeking maintenance, including separate or community property apportioned to such spouse and such spouse's ability to meet his or her needs independently; (6) the needs and obligations of each spouse; (7) the age of the spouses; (8) the physical and emotional conditions of the spouses; and (9) any child support responsibilities for a child living with the parent. Maintenance payments may be required to be paid through the clerk of the court, or through the Washington State Support Registry if there are also child support payments being made. [Revised Code of Washington Annotated; Title 26, Chapters 26.09.050, 26.09.090, and 26.09.120].

SPOUSE'S NAME: Upon request and for a just and reasonable cause, the wife's former or maiden name may be restored. [Revised Code of Washington Annotated; Title 26, Chapters 26.09.050 and 26.09.150].

CHILD CUSTODY: Joint or sole child custody will be determined according to the best interests of the child. Every petition for dissolution of marriage in which a minor child is involved must include a proposed parenting plan. The parents may make an agreement regarding a parenting plan.

The objectives of the parenting plan are to: (1) provide for the child's physical care; (2) maintain the child's emotional stability; (3) provide for the child's changing needs, as the child grows and matures, in a way that minimizes the need for future modifications; (4) set out the authority and responsibility of each parent; (5) minimize the child's exposure to harmful parental conflict; (6) encourage the parents to reach agreements rather than go to court; and (7) otherwise protect the best interests of the child.

The parenting plan should contain provisions for (1) dispute resolution; (2) a residential schedule for the child; (3) allocation of decision-making authority relating to the child.

The factors which are considered in determining decision-making authority are: (1) if both parents agree to mutual decision-making; (2) the existence of any physical or sexual child or spouse abuse, neglect or abandonment; (3) the history of participation of each parent in the decision-making process; (4) whether the parents have demonstrated an ability and desire to cooperate in the decision-making process; (5) the parents geographical proximity to each other, to the extent that it would affect their ability to make timely mutual decisions.

The factors which are considered in determining residential provisions for the child are: (1) the strength, nature, and stability of the child's relationship with each parent, including the parent's performance of daily parental functions; (2) any spouse or child abuse or neglect or substance abuse; (3) the history of participation of each parent in child-rearing; (4) the wishes of the parents; (5) the wishes of the child, if of sufficient age and maturity to express an opinion; (6) the child's relationship with siblings and other significant family members; (7) any agreement between the parties; and (8) each parent's employment schedule. Factor (1) is to be given the most weight. A mandatory settlement conference may be required.

Equal-time alternating residential provisions will only be ordered if: (1) there is no child or spouse abuse, neglect, or abandonment, or substance abuse; (2) the parents have agreed to such provisions; (3) there is a history of shared parenting and cooperation; (4) the parents are available to each other, especially in terms of geographic location; and (5) the provisions are in the best interests of the child. The court may order an investigation concerning

179

parenting arrangements for the child. [Revised Code of Washington Annotated; Title 26, Chapters 26.09.181—26.09.220].

CHILD SUPPORT: Either parent may be ordered to pay child support. Marital misconduct is not a factor to be considered. All relevant factors may be considered. Official child support guidelines and worksheets are available from the Washington Department of Social and Health Services and from the clerk of the court. The official guidelines are presumed to be correct, unless there is a showing that the amount is unjust or inappropriate under the particular circumstances of a case. Mandatory wage assignments may be required if the child support payments are over 15 days past due. Child support payments may be required to be paid through the Washington State Support Registry or directly to the parent, if an approved payment plan is accepted by the court. The court may require either parent to provide health insurance coverage for the child. [Revised Code of Washington Annotated; Title 26, Chapters 26.09.040, 26.09.050, 26.09.100, 26.09.120, 26.18.070, 26.09.105 and 26-19 Appendix].

PREMARITAL AGREEMENT: Washington has no specific statutes pertaining to premarital agreements.

WEST VIRGINIA

RESIDENCY REQUIREMENTS AND WHERE TO FILE: One of the spouses must have been a resident of West Virginia for at least 1 year immediately prior to filing. However, if the marriage was performed in West Virginia and one spouse is a resident when filing, there is no durational time limit. The divorce should be filed for in: (1) county in which the spouses last lived together; or (2) the county where the defendant lives if a resident; or (3) the county where the plaintiff lives, if the defendant is a non-resident. [West Virginia Code; Sections 48-2-5 to 48-2-8].

LEGAL GROUNDS FOR DIVORCE: No-Fault: (1) irreconcilable differences have arisen between the spouses; or (2) living separate and apart without cohabitation and without interruption for 1 year. [West Virginia Code; Section 48-2-4].

General: (1) adultery; (2) abandonment for 6 months; (3) alcoholism and/or drug addiction; (4) confinement for incurable insanity for 3 years; (5) physical abuse or reasonable apprehension of physical abuse of a spouse or of a child; (6) conviction of a felony; (7) cruel and inhuman treatment, including false accusations of adultery or homosexuality; (8) willful neglect of a spouse or a child; and (9) habitual intemperance (drunkenness). [West Virginia Code; Section 48-2-4].

NAME OF COURT IN WHICH TO FILE FOR DIVORCE: Circuit Court. "Circuit Court of _____ County, West Virginia."

DOCUMENT CAPTION INFORMATION: Complaint for Divorce. "In Re: the Marriage of: _____, Plaintiff and _____, Defendant." Final document title: Decree of Divorce.

LEGAL SEPARATION: The grounds for legal separation (separate maintenance) are the same as for divorce. One of the spouses must have been a resident of West Virginia for at least 1 year prior to filing for legal separation. [West Virginia Code; Sections 48-2-7 and 48-2-8].

SIMPLIFIED OR SPECIAL DIVORCE PROCEDURES: If one spouse files a verified complaint for divorce on the grounds of "irreconcilable differences", the other spouse may file a verified "answer" admitting the "irreconcilable differences" and a divorce will be granted. Circuit clerks are required to have supplies of an official "answer" form on hand, free of charge. No witnesses will be necessary for any proof for a divorce on the grounds of "irreconcilable differences." In other cases, witnesses will be required. The court may approve or reject a marital settlement agreement of the spouses. Standard financial disclosure forms may be required to be filed. [West Virginia Code; Sections 48-2-4, 48-2-16, and 48-2-33; and West Virginia Rules of Civil Procedure-Rule 80].

MEDIATION OR COUNSELING REQUIREMENTS: There are no legal provisions in West Virginia for divorce mediation or counseling.

PROPERTY DISTRIBUTION: West Virginia is an "equitable distribution" state. Marital property is to be divided equally and without regard to any marital misconduct. However, this equal division may be altered based on a consideration of the following factors: (1) contribution of each spouse to the acquisition of the marital property, including the contribution as homemaker and in child-care; (2) value of each spouse's separate property; (3) amount and sources of income of the spouses; (4) conduct of the spouses during the marriage only as it relates to the disposition of their property; (5) value of the labor performed in a family business or in the maintenance or improvement of tangible marital property; (6) contribution of one spouse toward the education or training of the other which has increased the income-earning ability of the other spouse; (7) the foregoing by either spouse of employment or other income-earning activity through an understanding of the spouses or at the insistence of the other spouse; and (8) any other factor necessary to do equity and justice between the spouses. [West Virginia Code; Sections 48-2-21 and 48-2-32].

ALIMONY/MAINTENANCE/SPOUSAL SUPPORT: Either spouse may be ordered to provide the other spouse with alimony. The factors to be considered are: (1) whether the spouse seeking alimony is the custodian of a child whose condition or circumstances make it appropriate for that spouse not to seek outside employment; (2) time and expense necessary to acquire sufficient education and training to enable the spouse to find appropriate employment, and that spouse's future earning capacity; (3) duration of the marriage; (4) comparative financial resources of the spouses, including their comparative earning abilities in the labor market; (5) amount of time the spouses actually lived together as wife and husband; (6) tax consequences to each spouse; (7) age of the spouses; (8) physical and emotional conditions of the spouses; (9) vocational skills and employability of the spouse seeking alimony; (10) any custodial and child support responsibilities; (11) educational level of each spouse at the time of the marriage and at the time the action for divorce is commenced; (12) cost of education of minor children and of health care for each spouse and the minor children; (13) distribution of marital property; (14)

legal obligations of the spouses to support themselves or others; (15) present employment or other income of each spouse; and (16) any other factor the court deems just and equitable. The marital misconduct of the spouses will be considered and compared. Alimony will not be awarded to any spouse who: (1) was adulterous; (2) has been convicted of a felony during the marriage; or (3) deserted or abandoned his or her spouse for 6 months. The court may require health and/or hospitalization insurance coverage as alimony. [West Virginia Code; Sections 48-2-13, 48-2-15, and 48-2-16; and West Virginia Case Law].

SPOUSE'S NAME: Upon request, either spouse may resume the use of his or her former name. [West Virginia Code; Section 48-2-23].

CHILD CUSTODY: Either parent may be awarded custody. There is a presumption in favor of the parent who has been the primary caretaker of the child. There are no other factors for consideration specified in the statute. There is no specific statutory provision in West Virginia for joint custody. [West Virginia Code; Section 48-2-15].

CHILD SUPPORT: Either parent may be required to provide periodic child support payments, including health insurance coverage. The factors for consideration specified in the statute are: (1) whether the spouse seeking support is the custodian of a child whose condition or circumstances make it appropriate for that spouse not to seek outside employment; (2) time and expense necessary to acquire sufficient education and training to enable the spouse to find appropriate employment, and that spouse's future earning capacity; (3) duration of the marriage and the actual period of cohabitation as husband and wife; (4) comparative financial resources of the spouses, including their comparative earning abilities in the labor market; (5) needs and obligations of each spouse; (6) tax consequences to each spouse; (7) age of the spouses; (8) physical and emotional conditions of the spouses; (9) vocational skills and employability of the spouse seeking support and maintenance; (10) any custodial responsibilities; (11) educational level of each spouse at the time of the marriage and at the time the action for divorce is commenced; (12) cost of education of minor children and of health care for each spouse and the minor children; (13) distribution of marital property; (14) any legal obligations of the spouses to support themselves or others; and (15) any other factor the court deems just and equitable. One of the parents may also be granted exclusive use of the family home, and all of the goods and furniture necessary to help in the rearing of the children. The court may require health and hospitalization insurance coverage as child support. Provisions for income withholding shall be included in every divorce decree to guarantee the support payments. Child support guidelines are available from the West Virginia Child Advocate Office. These guidelines are presumed to be correct, unless it is shown that the amount is unjust or inappropriate under the particular circumstances of a case. [West Virginia Code; Sections 48-2-13, 48-2-15, 48-2-15a and 48-2-16].

PREMARITAL AGREEMENT: West Virginia allows the husband and wife to make contracts with each other and to be held liable for these contracts. The contract must be in writing and signed by the parties to be enforceable. [West Virginia Code; Sections 48-3-8 and 48-3-9].

WISCONSIN

RESIDENCY REQUIREMENTS AND WHERE TO FILE: One of the spouses must have been a resident of Wisconsin for 6 months and of the county where the divorce is filed for 30 days immediately prior to filing. No hearing on the divorce will be scheduled until 120 days after the defendant is served the summons or after the filing of a joint petition. [Wisconsin Statutes Annotated; Sections 767.05 and 767.083].

LEGAL GROUNDS FOR DIVORCE: No-Fault: Irretrievable breakdown of the marriage. The irretrievable breakdown of the marriage may be shown by : (1) a joint petition by both spouse's requesting a divorce on these grounds; or (2) living separate and apart for 12 months immediately prior to filing; or (3) if the court finds an irretrievable breakdown of the marriage with no possible chance at reconciliation. [Wisconsin Statutes Annotated; Sections 767.07 and 767.12].

General: Irretrievable breakdown of the marriage is the only grounds for divorce in Wisconsin. [Wisconsin Statutes Annotated; Section 767.07].

NAME OF COURT IN WHICH TO FILE FOR DIVORCE: Circuit Court/Family Court. "State of Wisconsin: Circuit Court, _____ County."

DOCUMENT CAPTION INFORMATION: Petition for Divorce. "In Re: the Marriage of: _____, Petitioner [or Co-Petitioner if the petition is filed jointly] and _____, Respondent [or Co-Petitioner if the petition is filed jointly]." [See below under Simplified Or Special Divorce Procedures]. Final document title: Decree of Divorce.

LEGAL SEPARATION: Irretrievable breakdown of the marriage is the only grounds for legal separation in Wisconsin. The residency requirements are the same as for divorce. [Wisconsin Statutes Annotated; Sections 767.05 and 767.07].

SIMPLIFIED OR SPECIAL DIVORCE PROCEDURES: The spouses may file a joint petition for divorce in which they both consent to personal jurisdiction of the court and waive service of process. A copy of a guide to Wisconsin Court procedures for obtaining a divorce is to be provided to the spouses upon filing for divorce. Also, if children are involved an official child support form (which is available from the court clerk) and a financial disclosure form must be filed with the petition. In addition, separation agreements are specifically authorized by law. Finally, in cases in which both spouses agree that the marriage is broken and have agreed on all material issues, the case may be held before a family court commissioner. [Wisconsin Statutes Annotated; Sections 766.58, 767.081, 767.085, 767.10, and 767.27].

MEDIATION OR COUNSELING REQUIREMENTS: The court must inform the spouses of the availability of counseling services. Upon request or on the court's own initiative, the court may order counseling and delay the divorce proceedings for up to 90 days. If custody of a child is a contested issue, mediation is required. If joint custody is requested, mediation may be required. In addition, the court may order parents in any child custody situation to attend a educational program on the effects of divorce on children. [Wisconsin Statutes Annotated; Sections 767.082, 767.083, 767.11 and 767.115].

PROPERTY DISTRIBUTION: Wisconsin is now a "community property" state. There is a presumption that all marital property should be divided equally. Marital property is all of the spouse's property except separate property consisting of: (1) property inherited by either spouse; (2) property received as a gift by either spouse; or (3) property paid for by funds acquired by inheritance or gift. The equal distribution may be altered by the court, without regard to marital misconduct, based on the following factors: (1) the contribution of each spouse to the acquisition of the marital property, including the contribution of each spouse as homemaker; (2) the value of each spouse's separate property; (3) the length of the marriage; (4) the age and health of the spouses; (5) the occupation of the spouses; (6) the amount and sources of income of the spouses; (7) the vocational skills of the spouses; (8) the employability and earning capacity of the spouses; (9) the federal income tax consequences of the court's division of the property; (10) the standard of living established during the marriage; (11) the time necessary for a spouse to acquire sufficient education to enable the spouse to find appropriate employment; (12) any premarital or marital settlement agreements; (13) any retirement benefits; (14) whether the property award is instead of or in addition to maintenance; (15) any custodial provisions for the children; and (16) any other relevant factor. The court may also divide any of the spouse's separate property in order to prevent a hardship on a spouse or on the children of the marriage. [Wisconsin Statutes Annotated; Sections 766.01 to 766.97 and 767.255].

ALIMONY/MAINTENANCE/SPOUSAL SUPPORT: Either spouse may be ordered to pay maintenance to the other spouse, without regard to marital misconduct. The factors for consideration are as follows: (1) the time necessary to acquire sufficient education and training to enable the spouse to find appropriate employment, and that spouse's future earning capacity; (2) the duration of the marriage; (3) the financial resources of the spouse seeking maintenance, including marital property apportioned to such spouse and such spouse's ability to meet his or her needs independently; (4) the comparative financial resources of the spouses, including their comparative earning abilities; (5) the contribution of each spouse to the marriage, including services rendered in homemaking, child care, education, and career building of the other spouse; (6) the tax consequences to each spouse; (7) the age of the spouses; (8) the physical and emotional conditions of the spouses; (9) the vocational skills and employability of the spouse seeking maintenance; (10) the length of absence from the job market; (11) the probable duration of the need of the spouse seeking maintenance; (12) any custodial and child support responsibilities; (13) the educational level of each spouse at the time of the marriage and at the time the divorce is filed for; (14) any mutual agreement between the spouses; and (15) any other relevant factor. The court may combine maintenance and child support payments into a single "family support" payment. The maintenance payments may be required to be paid through the clerk of the court. [Wisconsin Statutes Annotated; Sections 767.26, 767.261, and 767.29].

SPOUSE'S NAME: Upon request, either spouse's former name may be restored. [Wisconsin Statutes Annotated; Section 767.20].

CHILD CUSTODY: Joint or sole child custody ("legal custody and physical placement") may be awarded based on the best interests of the child, and the following: (1) preference of the child; (2) the wishes of the parents; (3) the child's adjustment to his or her home, school, and community; (4) the mental and physical health of all individuals involved; (5) the relationship of the child with parents, siblings, and other significant family members; (6) any findings or recommendations of a neutral mediator; (7) the availability of child care; (8) any spouse or child abuse; (9) any significant drug or alcohol abuse; (10) whether one parent is likely to unreasonably interfere with the child's relationship with the other parent; and (11) any other factors (except the sex and race of the parent). [Wisconsin Statutes Annotated; Section 767.24].

CHILD SUPPORT: Either or both parents may be ordered to pay child support and health care expenses. The factors to be considered are: (1) the financial resources of the child; (2) the standard of living the child would have enjoyed if the marriage had not been dissolved; (3) the physical and emotional conditions and educational needs of the child; (4) the financial resources, earning capacity, needs, and obligations of the parents; (5) the age and health of the child; (6) the desirability of the parent having custody remaining in the home as a full-time parent; (7) the cost of day care to the parent having custody if that parent works outside the home, or the value of the child care services performed by that parent; (8) the tax consequences to each parent; (9) the award of substantial periods of physical placement to both parents (joint custody); (10) any extraordinary travel expenses incurred in exercising the right to periods of physical placement; (11) the best interests of the child and (12)

any other relevant factors. There are official guidelines and percentage standards for child support are available from the Wisconsin Department of Health
and Social Services. The court may require that child support payments be
guaranteed by an assignment of income, that the payments be made through
the clerk of the court, or that health insurance be provided for the children.
The court may also order a parent to seek employment. The court may order
spousal maintenance and child support payments be combined into a "family
support" payment. [Wisconsin Statutes Annotated; Sections 767.10, 767.25,
767.261, 767.265, 767.27, and 767.29].

PREMARITAL AGREEMENT: Wisconsin has no specific statutes pertaining to
premarital agreements.

WYOMING

RESIDENCY REQUIREMENTS AND WHERE TO FILE: (1) the spouse filing for divorce must have been a resident of Wyoming for 60 days immediately prior to filing; or (2) the marriage must have been performed in Wyoming and the spouse filing must have resided in Wyoming from the time of the marriage until the time of the filing. The divorce may be filed for in the county where either spouse lives. There is a waiting period of 20 days after filing before a divorce will be granted. [Wyoming Statutes Annotated; Title 20, Chapters 20-2-104, 20-2-107, and 20-2-108].

LEGAL GROUNDS FOR DIVORCE: No-Fault: Irreconcilable differences. [Wyoming Statutes Annotated; Title 20, Chapter 20-2-104].

General: Confinement for incurable insanity for 2 years. [Wyoming Statutes Annotated; Title 20, Chapter 20-2-105].

NAME OF COURT IN WHICH TO FILE FOR DIVORCE: District Court. "In the District Court In and For _____ County, Wyoming."

DOCUMENT CAPTION INFORMATION: Complaint for Divorce. "In Re: the Marriage of: _____, Plaintiff and _____, Defendant." Final document title: Decree of Divorce.

LEGAL SEPARATION: The grounds for legal separation are irreconcilable differences. The spouse filing for legal separation must have been a resident of Wyoming for 60 days immediately prior to filing or the marriage must have been performed in Wyoming and the spouse filing must have resided in Wyoming from the time of the marriage until the time of the filing. The legal separation may be filed for in the county where either spouse lives. [Wyoming Statutes Annotated; Title 20, Chapters 20-2-102, 20-2-104, 20-2-106, and 20-2-107].

SIMPLIFIED OR SPECIAL DIVORCE PROCEDURES: A sample Complaint for Divorce form is contained in Wyoming Rules of Civil Procedure, Appendix of Forms, Form #15.

MEDIATION OR COUNSELING REQUIREMENTS: In cases involving child custody, the court may order the parents to attend appropriate classes regarding the impact of divorce on children. [Wyoming Statutes Annotated; Title 20, Chapters 20-2-113].

PROPERTY DISTRIBUTION: Wyoming is an "equitable distribution" state. All of the spouse's property will be divided in an equitable manner, including property acquired prior to the marriage, and gifts and inheritances, based on a consideration of the following factors: (1) the economic circumstances of each spouse at the time the division of property is to become effective; (2) how and by whom the property was acquired; (3) the merits of each spouse; (4) the burdens imposed upon either spouse for the benefit of the children; (5) the conduct of the spouses; (6) any liabilities imposed upon the property; and (7) any other factor necessary to do equity and justice between the spouses. [Wyoming Statutes Annotated; Title 20, Chapter 20-2-114].

ALIMONY/MAINTENANCE/SPOUSAL SUPPORT: Either spouse may be awarded alimony in the form of a specific sum or property after consideration of the other's ability to pay. Real estate or profits from real estate may be ordered transferred to the other spouse for alimony for life. Marital fault is not a factor. No other factors are specified in the statute. [Wyoming Statutes Annotated; Title 20, Chapter 20-2-114].

SPOUSE'S NAME: There is no statutory provision in Wyoming for the restoration of a wife's name upon divorce. However, there is a general statutory provision for name change upon petitioning the court. [Wyoming Statutes Annotated; Title 1, Chapter 1-25-101].

CHILD CUSTODY: Child custody may include joint, sole, or shared custody, as long as it is in the best interests of the child. Child custody will be awarded according to what appears to be most expedient and beneficial for the well-being of the child. The sex of the parent is not to be considered. Other factors to be considered are: (1) the child's wishes; (2) the relative competency of both parents; (3) any evidence of spousal or child abuse or violence. If both parents are considered fit, the court may order any custody arrangement that encourages the parents to share in the rights and responsibilities of child rearing. [Wyoming Statutes Annotated; Title 20, Chapters 20-2-112 and 20-2-113].

CHILD SUPPORT: Either parent may be ordered to pay child support. A trustee may be appointed to invest the support payments and apply the income to the support of the children. Child support payments shall be ordered to be paid through the clerk of the district court. A court may order income withholding to guarantee any child support payments. There are official Child Support Guidelines. These Guidelines are presumed to be correct unless there is a showing that the amount would be unjust or inappropriate under the particu-lar circumstances in a case. Deviation from the guidelines will be allowed after a consideration of the following factors: (1) the age of the child; (2) the cost of necessary child care; (3) any special health care or educational needs of the child; (4) the responsibility of either parent for the support of others; (5) the value of services contributed by either parent; (6) any pregnancy expenses; (7) visitation transportation costs; (8) the ability of parents to provide health insurance through employment benefits; (9) the amount of time the child spends with each parent; (10) other necessary expenses for the child's benefit; (11) the relative net income and financial condition of each parent; (12) whether a parent has violated any terms of the divorce decree; (13) whether either parent is voluntarily unemployed or underemployed; and (14) any other rel-evant factors. [Wyoming Statutes Annotated; Title 20, Chapters 20-2-112, 20-2-113, 20-6-221, 20-6-302, and 20-6-304].

PREMARITAL AGREEMENT: Wyoming has no specific statutes pertaining to premarital agreements.

Nova Publishing Company

Small Business and Consumer Legal Books and Software

Quick Reference Law Series:

Laws of the United States: Corporations	$16.95
Laws of the United States: Divorce	$16.95
Laws of the United States: Partnerships (available 7/99)	$16.95
Laws of the United States: Limited Liability Companies (available 7/99)	$16.95
Laws of the United States: Wills and Trusts (available 7/99)	$16.95

The Small Business Library:

Simplified Small Business Accounting (2nd Edition)	$19.95
The Complete Book of Small Business Legal Forms (2nd Edition)	$19.95
w/Forms-on-Disk (3.5" IBM)	$29.95
Incorporate Your Business: The National Corporation Kit (2nd Edition)	$19.95
w/Forms-on-Disk (3.5" IBM)	$29.95
The Small Business Start-up Kit: Partnerships (available 12/99) w/CD	$24.95
The Small Business Start-up Kit: C-Corporations (available 12/99) w/CD	$24.95
The Small Business Start-up Kit: S-Corporations (available 12/99) w/CD	$24.95
The Small Business Start-up Kit: Limited Liability Company (12/99) w/CD	$24.95
The Small Business Start-up Kit: Sole Proprietorship (avail 12/99) w/CD	$24.95

Legal Self-Help Series:

Debt Free: The National Bankruptcy Kit (2nd Edition)	$19.95
The Complete Book of Personal Legal Forms (2nd Edition)	$19.95
w/Forms-on-Disk (3.5" IBM)	$29.95
Divorce Yourself: The National No-Fault Divorce Kit (4th Edition)	$24.95
w/Forms-on-Disk (3.5" IBM)	$34.95
Prepare Your Own Will: The National Will Kit (4th Edition)	$15.95
w/Forms-on-Disk (3.5" IBM)	$27.95

ORDERING INFORMATION:

Visa/MasterCard. $3.50 shipping for first title and $.75 for each additional title.
Mail: National Book Network, 4720 Boston Way, Lanham MD 20706
Phone: 800-462-6420   FAX: 800-338-4550
Internet: www.novapublishing.com in association with Amazon.com